PRISMS OF THE PEOPLE

Chicago Studies in American Politics

A series edited by Benjamin I. Page, Susan Herbst,
Lawrence R. Jacobs, Adam J. Berinsky, and Frances Lee

Also in the series:

Prisms of the People

POWER AND ORGANIZING IN
TWENTY-FIRST-CENTURY AMERICA

+ + + + + + + + + + + + + + + +

HAHRIE HAN
ELIZABETH MCKENNA
MICHELLE OYAKAWA

THE UNIVERSITY OF CHICAGO PRESS
CHICAGO AND LONDON

The University of Chicago Press, Chicago 60637
The University of Chicago Press, Ltd., London
© 2021 by Hahrie Han, Elizabeth McKenna,
and Michelle Oyakawa
Published 2021
Printed in the United States of America

30 29 28 27 26 25 24 23 22 21   1 2 3 4 5

ISBN-13: 978-0-226-74387-5 (cloth)
ISBN-13: 978-0-226-74390-5 (paper)
ISBN-13: 978-0-226-74406-3 (e-book)

DOI: https://doi.org/10.7208
/chicago/9780226744063.001.0001

Library of Congress Cataloging-in-Publication Data

Names: Han, Hahrie, author. | McKenna, Elizabeth, author. |
    Oyakawa, Michelle, author.
Title: Prisms of the people : power and organizing in twenty-
    first-century America / Hahrie Han, Elizabeth McKenna,
    Michelle Oyakawa.
Other titles: Power and organizing in twenty-first-century
    America | Chicago studies in American politics.
Description: Chicago ; London : The University of Chicago
    Press, 2021. | Series: Chicago studies in American politics |
    Includes bibliographical references and index.
Identifiers: LCCN 2020027440 | ISBN 9780226743875 (cloth) |
    ISBN 9780226743905 (paperback) | ISBN 9780226744063
    (ebook)
Subjects: LCSH: Social movements—United States. | Social
    movements—United States—Case studies. | Political
    science—Decision making. | Political leadership—
    United States. | Power (Social sciences)—United States. |
    Organizational sociology.
Classification: LCC HM881 .H358 2021 | DDC 303.48/4—dc23
LC record available at https://lccn.loc.gov/2020027440

♾ This paper meets the requirements of ANSI/NISO
Z39.48-1992 (Permanence of Paper).

Contents

1 *Introduction*

It was April 13, 2010. Jeff was at the airport heading home to Arizona when he heard the news.[1] Senate Bill (SB) 1070 had passed the Arizona statehouse by a vote of thirty-five to twenty-one and was on its way to Governor Jan Brewer's desk, where she was expected to sign it. Authored by state senate president Russell Pearce—with the backing of the conservative American Legislative Exchange Council (ALEC)—SB 1070 was an omnibus bill that became known as the "show-me-your-papers" law, because it deputized local police to determine people's immigration status. "It's beyond the pale," Chris Newman of NDLON (National Day Laborer Organizing Network) told the *Los Angeles Times* when asked about the bill (Riccardi 2010). Brewer had five days to decide whether she would sign it.

"Oh my god," Jeff thought. "This is really happening." Even though immigration had been the focus of fierce political conflict in recent years, SB 1070 represented an unexpectedly harsh attack on immigrant communities across the state. The child of an undocumented single mother, Jeff knew he wanted to take action but did not know what to do. He called Michele, a community organizer who had just led a nonviolent direct-action training he had attended in Nevada. Michele had been involved in the DREAMer movement since its founding and spent the two years prior to SB 1070's passage traveling around the country training young people like Jeff in movement building.[2] Although she was bearing witness to the repeated battering of immigrant rights from her vantage point in the national movement for immigration reform, Michele was shocked that a bill as extreme as SB 1070 could be politically viable. Jeff agreed.

"We just trained for this," he said on that phone call. "What do we do?"[3]

This book is about the strategic choices that leaders like Jeff make in response to uncertain moments that evoke the question "What do we do?" For the purposes of exposition, we name particular leaders making particular choices in this book, but the reality is that these leaders are all rooted in contemporarily broad and historically deep networks of other leaders engaged in similar kinds of strategic choice-making. Every day, across America, thousands of leaders of collective action are making choices about how best to identify, recruit, and develop people to engage in public life, and how to translate that participation into political power over the outcomes they care about. Some leaders are working on local issues in their communities, while others are part of dispersed national networks. Some are working within historic community-organizing traditions, while others are innovating at the edge of new digital technologies. Some are very isolated, while others (like the ones in our study) are embedded in ongoing practitioner conversations about strategies for collective action. Some represent scrappy organizations with minimal budgets, while others are part of formalized nonprofits with extensive resources to match. What unifies all of these leaders and organizations is the fact that at some point they all face a moment in which they ask, "What do we do?"

Our book describes the way leaders of collective action working in different states and on different campaigns answered that question. These are not just any leaders or examples of collective action, however. The leaders and organizations in our case studies successfully met the challenge of building a constituency and turning the actions of that constituency into power—which is no small feat in twenty-first-century America, particularly for the low-income constituencies of color in which many of these leaders organized. In this historic moment, for people across America, the link between participation and power seems broken. The very core of democracy—*demos kratia* in Greek, translated as "people rule"—feels impotent. By bucking these trends and showing how people can become power, the leaders and organizations in our study illustrated a distinct vision of how to make democracy possible.

The story that we tell in this book is an outlier in other ways as well. Our story is one of people beholden to people—of leaders and constituents embedded in organizations, and the strategic constraints and possibilities that those organizational relationships create for exercising power in politics. Given this, we deviate from trends in the study and practice of collective action in two key ways.

First, we focus on strategy in dynamic political environments. Coaches, generals, and CEOs recognize the importance of strategy for navigating competitive, dynamic terrain in sports, war, and business. Politics is similarly competitive and dynamic. The study and practice of collective action, however, often underestimates the way political uncertainty conditions the strategic choices leaders make. Many familiar models of collective action are based on unitary approaches to strategy that focus on stockpiling resources like people, actions, or money. Whether the goal is achieving symbolic, disruptive, or other kinds of power, these models assess the effectiveness of collective action by the scale of resources (from money to activism to public opinion) amassed. In contrast, our cases showed alternative strategic logics that focused on preparing for inevitable political uncertainty by cultivating constituency bases with certain kinds of characteristics.

Second, we focus on the *collective* side of collective action. Copious research on and practical studies of collective action examine action: how do we generate the actions we need? Research identifies messages, tools, tactics, and technological innovations that are more likely to get people involved. But what makes collective action collective? We argue that collective action is more than the additive sum of individual actions. Instead, the leaders and organizations we studied were able to exert power in large part because they were grounded in constituencies that had committed to standing together, to becoming something new together that they could not be alone. In choosing to stand with each other, these constituencies became cognizant of not only their rights to express their interests in the political process and the organizations of which they were a part, but also the responsibilities they needed to accept to make that possible. These constituencies, nurtured in organizations, were thus able to hold tensions that often seem to contradict each other—commitment and flexibility, ideology and pragmatism—making possible a different kind of politics.

Putting these strands together, our book elucidates a political logic, visible in all of our cases, that we encapsulate with the metaphor of a prism. We use the term *prism* throughout the book to reinforce the notion that what happens inside these cases of collective action (the design at the heart of the prism) determines what kind of power (or light) is refracted outside. Just as not all prisms are the same in terms of how they refract light, not all organizations are the same in terms of how they refract power. Each organization has, at its core, a set of strategic design choices about how to build constituency within the organization. Those choices shape its ability to exert power in the public domain.

Why use the metaphor of prisms? White light enters a prism and, based on the design at the center of the prism, becomes transformed into colorful vectors of light. In our metaphor, the organization (a term we use to refer generally to vehicles of collective action) is the prism that refracts the actions of a constituency into political power. The shape and extent of the vector of power the prism can project depend on design choices internal to the prism.

Why do those choices about internal practice shape the vectors of power projected into the world? There are four key steps to this argument. First, the organizations we are studying are contesting for power in inherently uncertain environments. Second, organizations cannot predict or control the challenges they are likely to face, but they can control the way they prepare for contingency. The best way to prepare is to develop a set of resources they can wield with flexibility and independence when contingency arises. Third, for people-powered organizations, the most important resource they have is people. They need constituencies that are independent (meaning the constituency can spring into action without a donor or anyone else giving the organization resources to activate it), committed (meaning the constituency is loyal to the organization and to each other), and flexible (meaning the constituency will shift with the organization even as the political choices and terrain shift). Fourth, whether a constituency is independent, committed, and flexible depends on the design at the center of the metaphorical prism. In all of our cases, the key patterned choice leaders made was investing in organizational designs that enabled them to build independent, flexible, and committed constituency bases.

We argue that those design choices at the center of the prism shaped the ability of the leaders and organizations in our cases to project vectors of political power outside—not because of the sheer volume of resources they amassed but because of the way they expanded leaders' strategic choice set. Our argument pivots, thus, to contend that power is not a function of organizational resources alone; it is a function of the breadth of strategic choices an organization has to navigate political uncertainty.

Although metaphors are never perfect, in this case, the metaphor of a prism is useful for three additional reasons. First, it underscores the transformative power of the organizations in our study to act not as neutral repositories of activism but as vehicles that transform people's activity and engagement into political power. Second, just as tiny prisms can refract light as far as it will travel, the leaders in our study could exert power at a much larger scale than their numbers might suggest, because of their internal organizational designs. Third, prisms emit both visible and invisible light. While we assert that some forms of power are measurable in new and interesting ways, we also acknowledge that power operates in complex ways and is therefore often difficult to measure using the traditional methods of social science. In sum, we argue that the organizations in our case studies exhibit a mutually reinforcing relationship between, on the one hand, constituencies equipped to exercise rights and responsibilities within a collective and, on the other hand, the capacity of their leaders to exert power strategically in the public domain.

Throughout our book, we describe what prisms of the people are and how they work. But first, we must finish our story about Jeff and Michele. What did they do?

The Pushback against SB 1070

The phone conversation Jeff and Michele had could have gone in many different directions. The two were not nationally known leaders in the immigration reform movement. If reporters from the *New York Times* were looking for someone to help them understand how advocates would respond in Arizona, they would not have called Jeff or Michele. If philanthropists or wealthy donors wanted to give money to someone to fight back against SB 1070, they would not have called Jeff or Michele. While Michele had an affiliation with the Reform Immigration for America campaign, a national multimillion-dollar effort to pass comprehensive immigration reform under the Obama administration, she was a trainer, not a nationally known spokesperson.

Jeff and Michele could have easily said, "Let's wait and see what the leaders in DC say," or "Let's wait until we can raise the money to fight." They could have fallen back on tried-and-true strategies for grassroots political action, such as petitions and phone banking. They could have said, "Let's start a petition, and get everyone we know to call Governor Brewer to stop her from signing the bill." These familiar, broadly accepted techniques likely would have drawn widespread support from inside and outside Arizona. Given their existing networks and national attention on SB 1070, they likely would have generated large numbers to demonstrate the breadth of support for their position.[4]

Alternatively, they could have chosen despair: "What's the point?" Jeff and Michele were, at best, midlevel organizers in a complex national fight about one of the most polarizing issues of the day. They had marched in the 2006 immigration protests. Despite being the largest mass mobilizations in the United States at the time since the anti-war demonstrations of the early 1970s, the 2006 marches did little to quell the bitter fight around immigration (Andrews, Caren, and Browne 2018). In 2008, with the election of Barack Obama as president and Democratic control of both houses of Congress, professional immigration-reform advocates hoped their moment had come. Yet by 2010 Jeff, Michele, and others were experiencing the flailing decline of comprehensive immigration reform—despite what scholars would have identified as a favorable political opportunity structure for it.

In Arizona, the immigrant community had not only good reason for despair but also good reason for fear. The passage of SB 1070 buoyed anti-immigrant hard-liners in the legislature. Self-appointed minutemen patrolled the borders with assault weapons. US Immigrations and Customs Enforcement (ICE) officers raided workplaces, day laborer centers, and other gathering sites. One interviewee told us that the national news media accounts "actually sort of soft-sell the story. . . . They looked like death squads, the Phoenix police. They would literally patrol when we'd do marches . . . alongside of us with squad cars, with people wearing black ski masks . . . [and] there were demonstrations of white nationalists on the lawn of the Arizona capital with actual M16s." Arizona's immigrant community had good reason to fear for their physical and material well-being. Passivity in the face of threat would have been understandable.

Jeff and Michele chose none of these options. Their conversation went in a different direction.

"I remember saying, well . . . what do the people need?" Michele said.

"I want them to see our faces," Jeff replied.

SB 1070 directly challenged everything Jeff, Michele, and other immigrant rights advocates in Arizona had been working toward. Faced with a decision about how to respond, they chose not only collective action but also a specific kind of collective action that bucked conventional wisdom. After their phone conversation, Michele coached Jeff as he worked with a team of leaders to organize a vigil on the lawn outside the Arizona State Capitol. The vigil started with seven people. "By lunch [on Sunday, April 18], we were 30; by night 100. On Monday, 200; Tuesday, 300," Jeff remembered (Garcia 2010). On April 22, the numbers swelled as local students staged mass walkouts to support the protest. Michele said, "[We knew that] if the vigil [was] not growing every twenty-four hours, it [was] dying. [So we had] to get [people] there. A whole team of people was reaching out in the schools, in Latino businesses, and phone banking. . . . And people were scared . . . people didn't want to come to the vigil at that time, because in those moments, it was very scary."

The vigil continued for 104 days without interruption, persisting even after Brewer signed the bill. An interviewee who is sometimes called the "father" of the Arizona Tea Party told us that immigration is "the number one issue for a lot of the Tea Party type people," but "I almost feel like the intensity is stronger on [the other] side . . . during the 1070 fight, . . . in the [Arizona] Capitol demonstration, there [were] more people on the pro-immigration side."

In this uncertain moment, Jeff and his allies made an unconventional choice. Prevailing wisdom would dictate that they should wait for the big money, get more powerful spokespeople to speak on behalf of their constituents, test different messages with moderate voters, or instigate actions that could spread virally. At the moment when their constituents were at their most vulnerable, however, these leaders chose to call the people who would be most affected by the law out into the open on the Arizona Capitol lawn. Once the vigil began, they realized they could use it as a leadership training ground to build an immigrant rights movement in the state. They learned to ask more of the people who attended, instead of having them be just another body for a head count or media headline, as is often the case at protests. Through 114-degree heat, using ice cubes to cool their faces, young people and a group of undocumented women became the core of the vigil. Jeff reflected on the shared leadership that these "terrible moments" demand: "There isn't one person that launche[s] a movement; it's a collective effort where people step in and out of leadership. It's a collective moment that is fueled by multiple actors, seemingly unrelated but all sharing a vision, a struggle, a hope."

At first, this shared vision, struggle, and hope seemed in vain. On April 23, 2010, Brewer signed Senate Bill 1070 into law. But many newly engaged protesters refused to go home, pledging to stay put until the law was struck down. "Oh shit," the organizers thought. By creating a collective context in which women, high school students, and other young undocumented leaders became committed to each other rather than to a fleeting legislative battle, the vigil had more downstream consequences than they initially imagined.[5] Now, the organizers could not leave the people to protest alone. They realized that they had to build the organizational infrastructure that would translate the rawness of the moment into longer-term political power. At one point, the notoriously anti-immigrant Sheriff Joe Arpaio came and threatened a group of women who were in a prayer circle. "And an undocumented woman walked up to him and put her hand up [to his face], and she was like, 'Respect. We're praying right now,'" an interviewee remembered. The three-month-long action became a crucible for learning, leadership development, organization building, and strategizing that laid the foundation for a broader immigrant rights movement in the state.

How can we make sense of the choices that Jeff, Michele, and other leaders in Arizona made? Because Brewer signed the bill into law, the vigil may seem, at first, like a defeat. We take a broader view, however, that centers the question of power, instead of any one policy fight or election. After SB 1070, a wide network of leaders and organizations emerged throughout Arizona to harness and develop the leadership and capacity that had been seeded during the fight. Over time, this ecosystem of leaders and organizations matured into an interconnected movement able to contest for political power. As one national leader told us, "I get to work with immigrant rights organizations all around the country. There's nothing like it. There's nothing like the leadership development that has occurred in Arizona in the last ten years." Organizations like Promise Arizona, LUCHA (Living United for Change in Arizona), One Arizona, Poder in Action (formerly Center for Neighborhood Leadership), Puente, and many others developed, creating a cohort of immigrant leaders in the state whose understanding of how collective action could build power stemmed from the leaders' strategic response to a sudden attack on their community.

Even if the vigil did not stop Brewer from signing the bill, it became a crucible for developing the collective capacities that made prisms of people power able to participate in the ongoing contestation for power in Arizona. This book unpacks how and why investing in the collective capacities at the heart of the prism is strategic by examining six case studies. We have intentionally selected outlying cases that represent instances in which ordinary people helped build the power they needed to influence the outcomes they cared about—an all-too-rare occurrence in twenty-first-century American democracy.

Our Question

How do vehicles of collective action build and exercise political power, given the improbability of their success? The organizations, movements, networks, and associations that build and sustain collective action—which we will generally refer to as organizations, broadly defined—play a unique role in American democracy. These organizations reach simultaneously inward to develop the capacities ordinary people need to act as agents of change in society, and outward to pressure decision makers to heed the concerns of these constituents (Andrews and Edwards 2004; Fung 2003; Skocpol and Fiorina 1999). Whether these vehicles take the form of formal bureaucratic organizations or more dispersed movement networks, all of them operate as intermediary institutions between the mass public and governmental institutions. Yet, given the strong status-quo bias in American politics, in most cases, collective action fails. Nonetheless, the centrality of these types of organizations to the democratic project calls for more research unpacking the core logic that makes it possible for them to translate the actions of their constituency into political influence.

Most existing research focuses more on *what* vehicles of collective action need rather than on *how* they turn what they have into what they need. One stream of research, for instance, has focused on the free-rider problem. In 1965 Mancur Olson's canonical book *The Logic of Collective Action* positioned the free-rider problem as the central problem to be solved in collective action.

Namely, given the availability of public goods like clean water or neighborhood policing to all people in a given jurisdiction, how can individual temptations to free ride be overcome? As Olson argued, most people can enjoy the benefits of clean water without doing the work of obtaining it, thus free riding off the work of others. This framing of the collective action problem focused considerable subsequent research on the question of how organizations generate collective action at scale: How can selective incentives (benefits available to only those who help earn them), notions of civic duty, culture, relational ties, mobilizing structures, and other factors ameliorate the temptation to free ride (Olson 1965; for syntheses, see, e.g., Walker 1991; Baumgartner and Leech 1998; Buechler 2000)?

A parallel stream of research focusing on social movements has examined the conditions and resources that vehicles of collective action need to effect change. This work has outlined a broad set of material and human resources (e.g., McCarthy and Zald 1977, 2001; Cress and Snow 2000); contextual conditions, such as state capacity, opportunity structures, inequality, or levels of cognitive liberation within a constituency (e.g., McAdam 1982; Tilly 2000; Meyer 2004); and cultural factors (Jasper 1997) needed to make collective action politically influential (for syntheses, see Amenta et al. 2010; Andrews and Edwards 2004; Baumgartner et al. 2009; McAdam, Tarrow, and Tilly 2001). Some research on organizations building civic capacity has started to examine the development of particular human resources, such as the organizing practices used to build constituencies' capacity for action and develop leaders (Warren 2001; Wood 2002; Oyakawa 2015; Delehanty and Oyakawa 2018; Flores and Cossyleon 2016; Cossyleon 2018). All of these factors create important constraints and opportunities but focus more on the resources needed than the strategic choices leaders can make to turn resources into power (see, e.g., Ganz 2000; Tarrow 1998; and Morris and Staggenborg 2004 for articulations of this critique).

As a result, a funny puzzle about collective action remains. Without more research on how resources are combined to achieve power, it is as if we are giving a cook a list of ingredients without a recipe for how and when those ingredients should be sourced and combined. Scholars have conceptualized the explanatory problem as a question of what the right ingredients are instead of as a question of where they come from and how to combine them. Yet, organizations and leaders who make strategic choices that translate resources into power need better theory to guide those choices—the answer to the question "What do we do?" (Ahlquist and Levi 2014; Ganz 2009; Clemens 1997; Hansen 1991). There is still more to learn about the range of strategies that enable organizations and leaders to translate collective resources into actual power to achieve the change that they seek.

This is the puzzle our book intends to address. The cooking analogy only goes so far; collective action will never be as formulaic as a recipe. For instance, the book describes the work of leaders and organizations that have emerged through well-established schools of community organizing and are embedded in the legacies of struggle and leadership of generations of organizers who have all developed theories of how to build collective action and power. Our argument is not that any one of these methods is superior to the others.[6] Nor do we offer a stepwise formula for making collective action work. Instead, we uncover core principles that bring coherence to alternative logics of collective action. We show why choices like the ones Jeff, Michele, and other leaders made make sense if we take seriously the effort to build political power.

The question is not merely an academic exercise. The practice of collective action in twenty-first-century America often emphasizes an accrual of resources over questions of how those resources are used, and this has real-life consequences for organizational leaders. Grassroots organizations are under enormous pressure to demonstrate the breadth of their public support, the number of dollars they have raised, or the number of votes they can turn out. Is that, however, the only way to make collective action powerful?

Our Analytic Approach: Studying What Is Possible

This book is devoted to examining how people can, with intention, build and strengthen organizations that make the democratic promise more plausible. To understand the strategic logic of powerful collective action, we examine outliers. Specifically, we bring an analytic lens to six case studies of improbable collective action, including the story in Arizona. Our analysis focuses on grassroots organizations in four states—Arizona, Minnesota, Ohio, and Virginia—that have been able to (1) build capacity by engaging constituents in the everyday work of democracy and (2) translate those actions into effective political influence. We also examine two additional cases in Kentucky and Nevada that provide insight on the internal organizational practices that make such work possible. We deliberately chose organizations that were working on different issues, in different political climates, with different constituencies—thus allowing us to vary the factors commonly known to affect the outcome of collective action. Despite working in such varied environments, each of these cases demonstrates success. We asked, Are there shared principles or practices that characterize their work? What can we learn from examining cross-case commonalities?

AN OUTLIER: LUCHA'S IMPROBABLE 2016 FIGHT
FOR MINIMUM WAGE IN ARIZONA

The practices of building constituency and power that undergird our cases are grounded in diverse research traditions on social movements, interest groups, management of common-pool resources, labor studies, faith-based organizing, and so on (Skocpol, Ganz, and Munson 2000; Skocpol 2003; Wilson 1973; Lipset 1956; Ahlquist and Levi 2014; Andrews et al. 2010; Ostrom 1990). Similarly, the leaders we describe were all cognizant of the way they borrowed practice and insight from contemporary and historical networks of other organizing leaders from whom they had learned and who had waged similar struggles in the past. Despite these roots in traditions of scholarship and practice, our cases still stand out against dominant models of politics in the twenty-first century.

Consider, for instance, ongoing work in Arizona. Since 2010, the organizations and leaders that emerged from the pushback against SB 1070 have been central to a series of battles around policies affecting Arizona's immigrant community, battles that highlight some core strategic disputes. These organizations and leaders ran various kinds of campaigns, including ousting Russell Pearce—the architect of SB 1070 and the first statewide leader to be recalled in Arizona history—in 2011, electing allied officials to a majority of seats on the Phoenix City Council, passing minimum wage legislation, and ultimately voting Sheriff Joe Arpaio, the self-proclaimed "meanest sheriff in America," out of office after his twenty-four-year reign (Mydans 1995). Throughout all these campaigns, grassroots leaders' strategies put them in conflict with parts of the mainstream political establishment in Arizona and across the country.

Proposition 206, also known as the Fair Wages and Healthy Working Families Act, exemplifies some of these tensions. Proposition 206 was designed to gradually increase the minimum wage in Arizona from the federal minimum wage of $7.25 in 2016 to $12.00 by 2020, with cost-of-living increases thereafter. In addition, Proposition 206 proposed giving forty hours of annual paid time off to employees of businesses with fifteen or more employees, and twenty-four hours to those of businesses with fewer than fifteen employees. Employees could use this paid sick time for a wide range of reasons, including medical care, dependent care, and personal emergencies, such as incidents of domestic violence.

Initially, some progressive funders, party leaders, and unions were reluctant to put the minimum wage campaign on the Arizona ballot in 2016. The coexecutive directors of LUCHA and its 501(c)(3) counterpart ACE, Alejandra "Alex" Gomez and Tomás Robles—both of whom became career organizers in response to SB 1070—described to us the origins of the Proposition 206 campaign. In 2012, the Fight for Fifteen, a national campaign backed by the Service Employees International Union (SEIU), sought to raise the minimum wage by organizing fast-food workers. This bold move to "organize an unorganized private sector workforce numbering in the millions" (Gupta 2013) began with a one-day strike in New York City. By 2015, it had spread to 340 US cities. In April of that year, the Fight for Fifteen brought some sixty thousand people to the streets in what was reportedly the largest protest by low-wage workers in US history (Ashby 2017; Greenhouse and Kasperkevic 2015). After consulting with the members of their base, who told them that fair pay was one of their most urgent priorities, Tomás, Alex, and several of their allies within the state decided to bring the campaign to Arizona. Tomás and Alex noted that some philanthropists, national network representatives, and even union leaders told them that raising the minimum wage in a statewide ballot measure was neither possible nor strategic. "People would tell us, like, this is not an issue in Arizona. 'Why don't you do an immigration one? Why aren't you doing criminalization, or voting?' Nobody cares, and nobody thinks in Arizona you could pass an initiative for $15 an hour, or raising the minimum wage, or whatever," Tomás said.

LUCHA's constituents, however, made clear to Tomás and Alex that minimum wage was the cause they wanted to undertake, despite this skepticism from movement and party elites. "From our members and from those workers," Tomás said, "[We heard] 'Why don't we just raise the minimum wage ourselves?'" Even after LUCHA's team had laid the grassroots groundwork for a campaign, however, funders, some unions, and other political leaders continued to doubt they could win the campaign. "The number one thing that people would say to us is, 'You all are too young—Alex and I. You all do not have the experience or the strategy to be able to get such a monumental thing done. And if you go for this, you will fail. You will set progressive politics in Arizona back at least fifteen years [if you fail].'" Indeed, another statewide leader told us, "A lot of Dems didn't want [Prop. 206] because they didn't think they could win. They didn't want to spend their money on it. They wanted to spend money on other stuff and then maybe do [minimum wage] in 2018 where they could use it as a turnout driver."

The skepticism from funders and other mainstream political leaders was not unwarranted. In 2015, Republicans in Arizona had unified control of state government, holding the governorship, both houses of the state legislature, and the majority of seats to Congress. The Arizona Chamber of Commerce and the restaurant association pledged to fight a minimum wage increase. Over the course of the campaign, a business coalition against the minimum wage increase filed lawsuits challenging the signatures that got the initiative on the ballot and launched a public campaign called "Protect Arizona Jobs." Many of the low-wage workers who would benefit from the bill were under continued threat because of ongoing immigration battles, and those who were eligible were never considered reliable voters. A careful analysis of structural factors made investing in what would eventually become Proposition 206 seem risky, at best.

Nonetheless, LUCHA stubbornly persisted, fighting to obtain the resources they needed and to ensure that one of their own would formally lead the campaign. "[These] white organizations," Tomás told us, "some of them would be like, 'Well, we will fund you, but we want somebody else to run the campaign. We want somebody else to do it. We want basically an old white man or old white consultant from DC.'" These potential funders wanted to bring in establishment campaigners with "more experience." Initially, LUCHA wanted Alex to head the campaign for Proposition 206. "But it was just, like, a *woman, Latina*, absolutely not . . . [we] said, well, we're not gonna win that fight. . . . We have to organize all of our partners in the state to not let this moment slip from LUCHA's hands, and at least have Tomás be the campaign manager," Alex said. Alex and Tomás leveraged their relationships with other organizations in the state, including organizations the national funders knew they needed to have on board if they were to have any chance of winning the campaign. LUCHA's coexecutive directors thus built a coalition with these organizations to form a unified front, and then they pressured national leaders to name Tomás the Proposition 206 campaign manager.

Having won the battle to be in charge, Alex and Tomás were able to develop the strategy for the Proposition 206 campaign. Tomás knew winning the ballot initiative would be an uphill battle:

> I knew that the very first counterargument would be, "You're gonna screw over small businesses." So we felt, "Hey, what if we organize small business, and what if we bring them together?" . . . [In the public,] initially there was fear, right? "You're asking me to support something that will affect my bottom line for the greater good." And so it did take multiple conversations. [But] we ended up, with all the conversations we had, about 350 small businesses endorsed the campaign. . . . And so we really utilized one-to-one relational building, organizing in the campaign.

Alex and Tomás's ability to build and leverage this coalition both grew from and enhanced the work they had done to build their constituency base. Tomás further described the distinctions between the work they did and that of traditional campaigns:

> We did not want this to be a traditional campaign. Nowadays, tradition goes to hit heavy on social media and paid media, commercials, digital ads, mail pieces. And then, the last two or three months of the campaign, you give some funding for people who do door-to-door canvassing. And we were really against that. We saw this as an opportunity to build [the organization], and the only way to build is if you empower organizers to have meaningful conversations [with constituents] around the issues that resonate with them, that go deeper than just voting for an initiative. And so we fought to have organizers instead of canvassers.
>
> Now we did have canvassers, and they did come, and they knocked on doors. But the first iteration of the field campaign was grassroots organizers. . . . In addition to that, in places where we could, we assigned a LUCHA organizer. . . . And so these organizers [could build on the work of Prop. 206]. We would collect information for voters, but LUCHA organizers would follow up, we would talk to them not from Prop. 206, but from LUCHA. And as LUCHA, we talked about how we're leading this Prop. 206 campaign, but also, this is how we organize, these are the additional issues we organize. Would you be interested in becoming a LUCHA member?

After a grueling campaign, Proposition 206 won with 58 percent of the vote in November 2016 as the single highest vote-getter of anything on the ballot. It represented a significant victory for many immigrant and low-wage workers. The reaction of business interests after Proposition 206 passed in 2016 demonstrated the extent to which it was a meaningful loss for them. They immediately appealed to the Arizona Supreme Court to void the initiative (the appeal ultimately failed), and they turned to House Republicans to try to restrict future citizen-ballot initiatives like Proposition 206 altogether. As one interviewee told us, progressives in Arizona hadn't been a force in the state since the 1950s, when Barry Goldwater's election to the Phoenix City Council marked a hard rightward shift in the state's politics. In this historic context, the passage of Proposition 206 was an unqualified victory for the movement.

The battle between LUCHA's leaders and the philanthropists and other political leaders who supported them highlights the strategic dynamism that underlies any political fight, especially improbable ones like Proposition 206.

At every step of the campaign, Alex and Tomás were told that they should not work on minimum wage, that they could not win the campaign, and that they could not lead it. Alex and Tomás had to fight not only to run the campaign but also to do it on their terms, never certain about whether LUCHA would obtain the resources and support it needed in order for that to happen. Like Jeff, Michele, and the many other leaders who led the fight for immigration reform in Arizona, Alex and Tomás had to develop strategy while the odds were stacked against them, making risky choices that had unclear outcomes.

WHY STUDY OUTLIERS?

We specifically chose to study outliers like LUCHA because they stand out from an overwhelming narrative—namely that the democratic project has eroded in twenty-first-century America. The rhetoric of democracy promises government "of, by, and for" the people, but in practice the link between democratic participation and power seems broken, especially for those structurally disadvantaged by economic inequality, racism, or both. Most people find politics distasteful (e.g., Eliasoph 1998, 2011), are affectively turned off by people who hold different views (e.g., Mason 2018), and are increasingly segregated into homogenous communities that circumscribe the information they receive and the kinds of social interactions they have (e.g., Enos 2017). Even if people were more informed, deliberative, and engaged, however, the government would be unlikely to care (Gilens 2013; Bartels 2008; Achen and Bartels 2016). Elected officials are more polarized than ever before (e.g., Sides and Hopkins 2015; Lee 2016; Hacker and Pierson 2020), increasingly beholden to special interests (e.g., Drutman 2015), and gridlocked at every level.

Racism and nativism thread an ugly line through all of this data: trade books have popularized research showing we are predisposed to recoil from people who are different from us (e.g., Chua 2018); elected officials stoke the fires of parochialism to win elections (e.g., Haney Lopez 2013); and long-standing legacies of structural inequity make reform projects challenging at best. The prospects for changing people or institutions are equally bleak. Most evidence shows that persuasion of any kind is a hopeless task (e.g., Kalla and Broockman 2017), the algorithms and institutions that govern our public lives are beholden to incentives that drive people away from the public good (e.g., Tufekci 2015), and the civic associations that should be Tocquevillian "schools of democracy" are mostly incapable of engaging people in agentic action (e.g., Lee 2015; Skocpol 2003; Blee 2012). Copious, well-executed, and important research has taught us that humans are racist, petty, short-sighted, self-segregating beings who are impervious to change and more likely to build institutions that instantiate the privilege of certain groups instead of equalizing it.

Our argument does not refute these realities but instead posits that there is value in bringing the tools of social science to understand the alternatives—and that the democratic project desperately needs such insight. Social science is predisposed to uncover what Jewish theologian Maimonides called "the necessity of the probable" instead of the "plausibility of the possible." "Hope," he argued, "is the belief in the plausibility of the possible, as opposed to the necessity of the probable." For good reason, the intellectual architecture of mainstream social science focuses on what is likely to happen. If we only study probable outcomes, however, we cannot understand change—the status quo is always the most likely outcome.

In studying what is possible, we also bring civic and political organizations back into the conversation about the decline of democracy. These organizations used to be at the heart of the study of American politics in the early to mid-twentieth century (e.g., Dahl 2005; Truman 1951; Schattschneider 1960; Key 1956; etc.). The behavioral revolution, however, focused on more individualistic approaches to understanding the American political process (Downs 1957). This approach put more emphasis on voters, elected officials, and elections, and less on the role of intermediary organizations in shaping the relationship between the public and government (Hacker and Pierson 2010; Anzia 2019; Pierson and Schickler 2020). Our study reexamines these organizations to understand the possibilities they contain for shaping collective action in ways that take seriously the narrative that democracy is broken but also show a pathway through which the capacities of people-driven politics can be strengthened.

Our book thus brings an analytic lens to the audacity that sits at the heart of the democratic promise. In *The Federalist*, no. 51, James Madison states, "But what is government itself but the greatest of all reflections on human nature? If men were angels, no government would be necessary" (1788). Although the founding fathers enacted an elitist notion of democracy, they understood that the goal of democracy is to create a process that overcomes the undemocratic instincts people naturally harbor. Democracy itself, in other words, is not about accepting the "necessity of the probable" but about creating a process that enables the "plausibility of the possible." We contend that when people come together in prisms of people power, they can make the implausible possible and make democracy real.

Our Argument: The Strategic Logic of Prisms

What are prisms of people power? We use the term to refer to the two-way relationship between the ability of grassroots leaders and organizations to exercise power in dynamic political environments and the extent to which these leaders are accountable to an independent, committed, and flexible constituency. At the heart of the prism is a set of design choices organizational leaders make about whether and how to create accountability to an independent, committed, and flexible group of people. Those strategic design choices then shape the power these organizations can exert in the external world. The strategic logic at the heart of people's prisms, then, rests on recognizing the interconnectedness between the internal design choices and the way they prepare leaders to strategically negotiate power externally, even in changing, unpredictable political environments. Our book argues that the leaders and organizations across our cases exemplified the logic of such prisms. Scholars and practitioners alike have long recognized, but under-studied, the importance of both the strategic exercise of power and the work of building constituency internally. Our contribution is not in highlighting each on its own but in showing the way they operate in mutually reinforcing and transformative ways, like the light that enters and exits a prism.

The logic of our argument proceeds as follows:

- First, organizations seeking constituency-based political power are working toward political outcomes that are dynamic and fragile. The fragility is particularly heightened for low-income constituencies of color that have been historically marginalized. Their efforts to build political power are always uphill. Thus, achieving political power requires sustained work over a long period of time, and strategic creativity to overcome long-standing structural hurdles. Because political environments are inherently dynamic, we focus our analysis on leaders who make strategic choices about how to deploy the resources they accrue.
- Second, given the dynamism and fragility of their work, and their inability to anticipate all the challenges that will come their way, the most strategic choice that leaders seeking durable political power can make is to cultivate resources that will give them the most tools in their toolbox to respond to contingencies. In other words, we argue that even as leaders are buffeted by large structural patterns out of their control, one way they can exercise strategic agency is by expanding the choice set available to them in any given situation. Our argument thus shifts the

focus from asking what resources organizations have to asking what strategic choices are enabled by the resources they have.

- Third, for people-powered organizations, the resources that expand their strategic choice set are constituency bases that have three key characteristics: independence, commitment, and flexibility. *Independence* means they possess resources that are not beholden to another person or group's assessment of value. Organizations whose power comes from raising philanthropic dollars or elite access, for example, will always be dependent on philanthropy or elite access. *Commitment* means the members are loyal to the organization. *Flexibility* means that the constituency can adapt as political circumstances shift. When sitting at the proverbial negotiating table, the leaders in our case studies confronted questions like "How confident am I that I can deliver my base? Do I have the commitments and relationships I need to engage them in action?" The answers to those questions depended on prior choices leaders had made about not just whether to engage constituents in action but also how. Leaders who had cultivated constituencies with independence, commitment, and flexibility had a broader array of strategic choices they could deploy in negotiations over power.

- Fourth, prior choices leaders had made about how to design their prisms determined whether they had independent, committed, and flexible constituencies that were prepared for uncertain negotiations for power. These leaders recognized that in order to develop constituencies as an independent source of political power, they could not treat people's engagement like a spigot that could be turned on and off. Instead, these leaders had to be accountable to and in a durable relationship with that constituency. By staying rooted in and responsive to the needs of their constituency, the leaders in our cases were constrained by those needs but also confident they would have the kind of commitment they needed to exercise power over time. To maintain that kind of relationship, however, they had to build a set of relational ties, cultivate a set of bridging identities, and distribute the work of strategy in ways that would give their base ownership over and capacities for engaging in the work of collective action. Constituency-building practices thus constituted the defining characteristic of people's prisms.

What do these prisms look like in practice in the twenty-first century? Table 1.1 summarizes the differences between mainstream approaches to collective action and our argument about prisms, differences we detail throughout the book. To be clear, we are not arguing that one is better than the other. Instead, our position is that the dominant models of collective action have crowded out alternate pathways to realizing the promise of powerful collective action in the twenty-first century. Understanding how prisms of the people work is a necessary and urgent task, particularly for constituencies that are historically marginalized in America. Table 1.1 compares and contrasts the two models, demonstrating the variant assumptions each approach makes and the practices each engages in with regard to power, strategic leadership, and constituency building.

Although we cannot isolate the causal impact of any one strategic choice leaders like Tomás and Alex made, we can elucidate an underlying logic that we saw as a pattern across our cases. Like Tomás and Alex, all the leaders in our case studies faced, at some point, an unexpected challenge to their power. They all experienced many moments like the one Jeff described when it was not clear how to proceed and, indeed, times when they were on the losing side of a negotiation. Given the inherent improbability of success that characterizes their work, the leaders in our cases recognized the need to ready themselves for such challenges. The leaders could not always control when, where, and how these difficult moments appeared and unfolded, but they could control how they prepared for them and what options would be available to them if they lost.

That strategic logic of preparation is core to our argument. For leaders like Tomás and Alex, their method of prepping for contingency was to develop their constituency as a source of power that could be wielded in flexible ways over time. Cultivating collective capacities within a constituency became the strategic choice, because those practices generated the commitment, flexibility, and capabilities constituents needed to stay loyal to organizations like LUCHA through all the ups and downs of the fight for Proposition 206, or any battle for political power (Hirschman 1970). Alex and Tomás could not predict how the campaign for minimum wage would unfold. The gamble they made, however, was that they would be better able to weather whatever challenges came their way if they had an organization full of leaders and constituents with particular skills, capacities, and commitments to one another. Alex and Tomás made a strategic investment, then, in building LUCHA's constituency in a particular way. Their design choices about how to build a constituency in their prism were key to building power. People who have a say over the decisions that affect them are more likely to have the kinds of capacities and commitments that leaders like Alex and Tomás needed to build LUCHA's power over the long term.

Leaders like Tomás and Alex made certain choices about how to cultivate their constituents' voices because they recognized that the uncertainty of the

Table 1.1. A Comparison of Prisms of People Power to Dominant Models of Collective Action

	Dominant Models of Research on and Practice of Collective Action	Logic and Practices of Prisms of People Power
Power		
Assumptions about political context	Baseline expectation of responsiveness from political elites	Focus on the likelihood of unpredictable challenges
Central challenge	Minimizing free riding and activating likely supporters	Generating constituent loyalty, flexibility, and resilience
The Strategic Logic		
Focus of power building	Accrue resources needed to generate proximity or access to decision makers	Develop an independent source of power that does not depend on access to elites
Allocation of resources	Investment in tools to generate action	Investment in civic feedbacks, or the downstream consequences of constituency engagement that feed back to shape the strategic position of the organization over time
Nature of strategy	Unitary	Flexible and pragmatic
Style of learning	Individualistic and operational	Collective and strategic
Constituency Characteristics		
Nature of relationships	Horizontal relationships are mostly preexisting; vertical relationships are created	Horizontal and vertical relationships are shaped and expanded by the organization
Nature of engagement	Task-oriented	Distributed strategists
Nature of commitments	To outcomes: policies, candidates	To people, to one another; flexible about policies and candidates
Nature of identities	Fixed, bonding	Changing, bridging

political battles they were waging meant they were essentially engaged in a repeat game, or long-term relationship, with constituents. To prepare for contingency, leaders had to build their constituency in ways that allowed them to go back to their base repeatedly as political circumstances changed, creating a potential threat that forced decision makers to be more responsive. All of these organizations built learning loops into their work to enable this repeat game. Thus, representation in this context was not a simple matter of discerning what people wanted and then acting accordingly, but instead a mutual relationship of accountability between leaders and constituents that created both opportunities and constraints for both. Leaders who understood that their ability to continually move people is the source of their power had to build relationships with constituents that would allow them to go back to and regenerate that resource again and again.

Distinct assumptions about the contingent nature of political power thus led to distinct leadership choices. We develop a concept we call "civic feedbacks" (Han, Campbell, and McKenna 2019) to understand how leaders prepared for the uphill battles they knew they faced. The concept of civic feedbacks suggests that power depends on not just having constituents take action but also *how* leaders engage them. In particular, how leaders choose to engage their constituency feeds back to shape the strategic position of the organization over time by affecting the range of strategic options a leader has. Instead of focusing only on one election, policy change, or other outcome, these leaders developed their constituency with an eye toward the long, unpredictable fight ahead of them. Expecting setbacks, these leaders wanted to build an independent, committed, and flexible base, because that would enable them to exercise not only plan A but also plan B, C, D, and so on. Building a prismatic constituency maximized their chances for having multiple strategic options available when they faced obstacles.

Prismatic bases have a resilience that enables positive civic feedbacks, because they are more likely to exhibit the commitment and flexibility that allow leaders to independently exert power. In prismatic constituencies, people are power, not props. Individuals exercising the rights and responsibilities of prisms cannot be treated as interchangeable bodies. Instead, leaders cultivate constituents' capacity to exercise voice, thus constraining themselves via member accountability but also making it more likely their constituencies will stay loyal. Given this, the way that the organizations in our study engaged with constituents is distinct from the way that organizations that believe people need only be moved episodically engage constituents. The organizations in our study sought to build constituencies through a relational logic that gives people a sense of their own agency and makes it more likely they will stay involved over the long term by binding the fate of one to the fate of many. This means creating commitments that are more flexible across issues and candidates by (1) grounding the work in a set of values and relationships, (2) engaging people as strategic agents of change through distributed structures, and (3) seeking to shape people's identities through the work they do.

Prisms of people power thus link the practices of building a committed and flexible constituency base (one that is willing and able to weather the inevitable ups and downs of any effort to make change) to the effort to exert power in the public arena. In the cases we examine, a leader's ability to turn collective action into power depended on prior choices leaders had made about how to identify, recruit, and develop a constituency. These leaders could not always anticipate what challenges to their power would emerge in the campaigns they were waging, but they could prepare for the certainty of challenge. By enmeshing people in relationships, giving their base ownership over the work, and cultivating identities that enabled flexibility, leaders made these improbable bids for power more strategic.

RELATIONSHIP TO PREVIOUS ORGANIZING TRADITIONS

Some readers, looking at the prisms we describe, may argue that these prisms are synonymous with community organizing. Certainly, all of the groups in our case studies were rooted in the organizing tradition. Likewise, the leaders themselves were deeply embedded in interpersonal and organizational networks and were aware that they were part of a set of historical organizing traditions that have been constantly evolving as politics and society have evolved. In public and scholarly discourse, however, the word "organizing" has been commonly used to refer to any effort that organizations make to engage ordinary people in public life. Everyone, from those working in the tradition of Saul Alinsky to marketing-based social entrepreneurs, from union organizers to get-out-the-vote canvassers, has used the term "organizing" to describe what they do. It often seems like anyone seeking to engage the mass public in any sort of activity adopts the label of "organizer," rendering the term too vague for our purposes. We thus use the term "prisms" instead, to emphasize our focus on a particular kind of collective power building.

Our argument is not that any activism creates power but that a particular kind, in which people learn to stand with one another with the commitment and flexibility needed for political struggle, may very well do so. The practices we describe are akin to community organizing in many ways but also grounded in scholarly and practical traditions that emphasize the duality of the rights and responsibilities of collective action. The design choices leaders made to build constituencies in our prisms were not just about getting people to exercise their right to action but also about cultivating the responsibilities people have to act with others in community. These prisms become "strategic," we argue, because they enable the exercise of power.

SCHOLARLY SKEPTICISM AND STRATEGIC PRAGMATISM

Some skeptics may object to our argument about prisms, treating it as a biased and naive exaltation of insurgent examples of collective action. We seek to address possible causes of bias by gathering data from multidimensional sources that give us independent perspectives on what the leaders in our cases did. Instead of just taking leaders at their word about what power they built, we sought to develop independent measures of political power and get perspectives on their work not only from their allies but also from their opponents and political targets. We discuss the issue of potential bias at greater length in chapter 2.

To address the point about naivete, it is worth spelling out that we are *not* arguing that ideologues are more likely to win. In both academic scholarship and journalism, many depictions of community organizing, social movements, and other instances of collective action treat adherents and leaders of such movements as dogmatists, unwilling to compromise, and impractical in their arguments about how political change is made. These portrayals, however, conflate preference with strategy, assuming that preferences on an ideological continuum determine what kind of strategies people are willing to adopt. This framework thus often presupposes that moderate or centrist political positions are inherently more strategic. We challenge this assumption. While it is true that the ideological and issue positions of organizations in our case studies were, in many cases, to the left of mainstream public opinion, we found that holding ideologically left views did not preclude pragmatism or compromise. Our argument, in other words, partially unlinks preference and strategy.[7]

In fact, the leaders in our case studies exhibited a kind of political pragmatism that debunks commonly held perceptions of activists. This pragmatism emerged because the leaders recognized that their power came not from proximity to political elites but from their relationships with their constituency. These leaders understood that their ability to exert power in relationships with political decision makers depended on their ability to deliver a base repeatedly over time (Hansen 1991). While access to decision makers might have been an indicator of their power, it was not the source of it. These leaders had the most power when they were accountable to constituents. For these constituents, however, the fights were not abstract. These were people who had problems to solve; their pragmatism came from a desire to solve those problems.

As Tocqueville argued almost two hundred years ago, the transformative power of democracy is not only in the way engaging in collective action transforms people's interests, motivations, and capacities but also in the way leaders transform the resources of individuals into political power by strategically linking those resources to the interests and choices of decision makers (see, e.g., Fung 2003). This book describes the way leaders' choices about how to cultivate democratic proclivities in a constituency constrain or expand their ability to transform those proclivities into power.

An old adage argues, "Luck is what happens when preparation meets opportunity." We are not arguing that prisms of people power will lead automatically to power, but they are one compelling way organizations prepare for opportunities to exercise influence under conditions of uncertainty. Even as we describe the patterns that emerged in our cases, however, we recognize that the work these organizations and leaders do to realize democracy in twenty-first-century America is rare, difficult, and fragile. Nonetheless, instead of accepting the necessity of the probable, these organizations have made the possible plausible. Our job is to document how.

Previewing the Book

How do organizations translate the action and engagement of their constituents into political influence? What patterns do we see across our cases? Are the rare instances in which organizations break through to achieve meaningful victories for their constituencies completely idiosyncratic, or are there systematic choices that help explain how they achieved their goals? We observe commonalities, particularly in how the organizations in our study strategically translated people into power—even in highly contingent political circumstances. Our argument unfolds in five additional chapters. Chapters 2 and 3 detail some of the methodological choices in the book, including how we defined and measured political power. Readers less inclined to focus on such questions may want to concentrate on chapters 4 and 5, which describe the core characteristics of leadership and constituency that constitute the design choices at the heart of the prism.

CHAPTER 2: THE CASES

This chapter introduces our cases and the research design (methodological details are further elaborated on in appendix B). The study is a qualitative, inductive case-study project that seeks to elucidate the capabilities organizations can intentionally cultivate to make it more likely they will build the power they need to achieve their goals. Across all of our cases, we collected primary and secondary information, combining interviews and ethnographic observations with a close analysis of organizational and secondary data. We collected these data from not only the leaders and constituents in the organizations we were studying but also the political targets they were seeking to influence and the allies with whom they worked. We were thus able to develop a 360-degree view of these organizations. We also conducted in-depth fieldwork in each case, observing the organizations we were studying and the communities in which they worked. In addition, we fielded two surveys of political and corporate elites in Ohio and Virginia to understand network dynamics in the power-building campaigns we studied; we analyzed state-level legislative data from the National Conference of State Legislatures to understand trends in immigration bills in Arizona; and we used text-as-data methods to analyze the impact ISAIAH (one of the organizations we studied) was having on public narratives in Minnesota.

When selecting cases, we took a "most-different" approach (Gerring 2007; Seawright and Gerring 2008) to identify four sets of organizations in Arizona, Minnesota, Ohio, and Virginia that met two criteria: (1) they had built some measure of political influence, and (2) they were distinct from one another in terms of the geographies, issues, constituencies, and political targets they engaged. This selection strategy allowed us to maximize difference on the socioeconomic conditions, political opportunity structures, resources, and individual traits of constituents known to shape the ability of organizations to achieve their political goals. By maximizing difference on external conditions, we hoped to see what (if any) internal characteristics were shared across organizations that built power in varied circumstances. To select cases, in the fall of 2016 we interviewed a set of key informants and analyzed a variety of socioeconomic and political data (see appendix B).

In addition to the case study of immigrant leaders in Arizona that was introduced in this chapter, we had three other core cases: a statewide organization called New Virginia Majority that helped win voting rights for formerly incarcerated citizens; a faith-based organization in Cincinnati, Ohio, called AMOS that led the field campaign to pass a ballot initiative for universal preschool in 2016; and ISAIAH, a faith-based statewide organization in Minnesota that sought to influence narratives around race and class in the 2018 gubernatorial election. Two additional cases allowed us to go into greater depth on some of the internal organizational capabilities that made it possible for these groups to exercise the capacities of prisms: a case involving a coalition of organizations in Nevada that worked together in 2015 to counterbalance the power of corporations by advocating for (and passing) a corporate-profits tax law that would provide $1.5 billion of support for public education and services, and a case involving a group in Kentucky focused on multiracial organizing across urban and rural constituencies in the state. We selected the Nevada and Kentucky cases because of their unique internal structures and governance processes.

Our book analyzes the patterns that emerged across all six case studies. We aimed to select cases that would provide some analytic leverage in generating propositions about the way these organizations build power. Nonetheless, our design has inevitable limitations, which we discuss in chapter 2. While we work carefully throughout to describe and make visible the ways in which these organizations build power, we cannot definitely and precisely estimate the size of the causal impact these organizations had in any one case. All of them are working on complex issues in a contingent ecosystem of civic and political actors, and isolating the causal influence of any one organization in a given campaign is nearly impossible. Even so, studying the success of these organizations provides insight on key questions about the everyday practice of democracy.

CHAPTER 3: DEFINING AND MEASURING POWER

This chapter focuses on our assessment of the extent to which the organizations in question built power. Our study is premised on the idea that they did—so how do we observe it? After all, the question of how to define the extent to which interest groups and social movement organizations achieve political power is a topic of copious debate among both scholars and practitioners (e.g., Giugni 1998; Amenta 2006; Pierson 2015). These organizations are not only seeking to win elections, pass policies, and win executive orders that favor them—they are also seeking to rebalance power. This chapter builds on existing conceptualizations of power to provide some additional empirical ways to observe its shift.

Across all four of our core cases, we look for—and find—evidence of organizations shifting power. Given that the campaigns and goals of each organization were distinct, we use slightly different approaches to measure power shifts in each case study. What unifies our approach to each, however, is a focus on measuring power shifts not only in terms of the visible gains that were made but also in terms of changes that are largely obscured from immediate view. We examine data showing changing networks of power relationships in a community, shifting narratives around race and belonging in elections, and changes in state legislative agendas over time. We draw on network surveys, analysis of public statements and media coverage, and analysis of legislative action in state legislatures.

CHAPTER 4: THE STRATEGIC LOGIC OF PRISMS

This chapter analyzes the strategic choices that leaders in our cases made, given the uncertainty of their political environments. If we accept the idea that power is contingent, it necessarily puts a focus on leadership, because leaders are the ones who decide how to exercise power (or not). Thus, this chapter examines the choices leaders made to expand their strategic capacity. We divide our discussion of this into two parts. First, why is investing in prisms of people power strategic? Second, what leadership choices emerge from that strategy?

We ground our discussion of the strategic nature of prisms by distinguishing between the effort to build independent political power and the effort to gain access to power. Departing from dominant models of collective action that conceptualize the goal as gaining access to power, we argue that leaders in our cases wanted to gain access in ways that enabled them to build and wield an independent source of power at the negotiating table, much as Tomás and Alex did during the minimum wage campaign. These leaders wanted to be able to push decision makers without having to worry about jeopardizing their access. This desire for an independent source of power propelled them to focus on constituency as their key resource, even and especially when they made headway in institutional settings, and to focus, in particular, on building a constituency with characteristics that would maximize their strategic flexibility at the negotiating table.

We show that all of the organizations in our case studies engaged their constituencies with an eye toward the downstream (or feedback) effects of their actions. Instead of thinking just in the short term about the number of people they activated or the volume of action they generated, these organizations considered what choices they would have (and which would be foreclosed) down the road as a result of these actions. Leaders analyzed their political situations in terms of a long-term focus on political power and, as a result, decided to strategically invest in building their constituency to prepare for contingent negotiations over power.

CHAPTER 5: BUILDING PEOPLE TO BUILD POWER

Having examined the extent to which each of these organizations built power and the strategic leadership choices that made this power building possible, we turn to the implications for base building. In this chapter, we focus on four interrelated characteristics that we see across all of our cases.

First, the bases built by these organizations were populated by members in deep relationship with one another. A complex latticework of relationships undergirded all of this work and constituted the glue that held the base together. By creating settings in which constituents entered into relationship with one another, the organizations we studied invested in their most important source of influence (an organized base of people) and enabled the learning, action, and commitment that helped shift political power configurations. Second, these structures allowed these organizations to develop their constituents as strategists—the second characteristic we saw across cases. Constituents in these organizations were not just following directives from organizational leaders; they also acted as independent strategists.

Third, these practices led to constituencies that were simultaneously committed and flexible. A constituency base that is committed and flexible has made the choice to act together to build power for its members but is adaptable about the pathways to achieving that goal. The importance of social relationships in shaping civic action is nothing new (e.g., Sinclair 2012; Rolfe 2012). Our study, however, analyzes how relationality and the kind of commitment described above interact. The fourth and final commonality of the constituencies in our study is their ability to build bridging identities. We find that these organizations circumvented a kind of narrow identity politics (in which some groups of people build power to act in opposition to others) by drawing on relationships as sites of deliberation and learning. This approach unlocked people from rigid silos and created solidarity across racial, class, age, and geographic differences. As one of our interviewees said, "You are not doing your relational due diligence to other people in your community if you are not talking to those who are different from you."

CHAPTER 6: DEMOCRATIC FRAGILITY

Throughout the book, we try to be realistic about the challenges faced by organizations seeking to give voice to the interests of low-income constituencies of color in American democracy. Our final chapter zooms out from our specific cases to examine the broader context within which these organizations work. We begin with the idea of fragility: when we look across our cases, perhaps the most obvious observation that emerges is that power is often tenuous. For constituency-based organizations like the ones in our study, power is a constant negotiation. Given the long-standing asymmetrical distribution of resources in American politics, grassroots organizations are always fighting for their toehold on power. Moreover, the more powerful these groups become, they more they become targets for either co-optation or outright hostility from the opposition. If we imagine the effort to gain power as a scale these organizations are trying to tip in their favor, many factors tend to keep them on the losing side. Only occasionally can they move the fulcrum so that the scales lean in their direction—but when they do, they have to fight to keep the balance on their side. In all of our cases, we examine the ebbs and flows of power these organizations achieve over time, as well as the concessions they had to make along the way, showing how fragile their power is in the broader political context within which they are working.

The final chapter also discusses the ways our findings are distinct from previous research and conventional wisdom on collective action. Because the data in the book come from studies of a relatively small set of civic organizations, we discuss the external validity of these findings, examining publicly available data on other organizations to show there are important commonalities across them. We then discuss how existing research on social movement organizations and collective action might be recast in light of the findings from this book. The conclusion also discusses the implications of our findings for practice. We hope the book will provide actionable research that can inform the strategic choices organizers make. Our work illuminates a broad range of options that leaders of collective action have at their disposal, perhaps broader than they may realize, and, in doing so, helps address the failure of strategic imagination in much of contemporary politics.

The Challenge of Realizing the Democratic Promise

In documenting the implausible work of organizations seeking to give ordinary people a real voice in politics, we define an alternate logic of politics, expressed in the prism metaphor. Prisms of people power develop alternative pathways to power that are often underrecognized in twenty-first-century politics. Given this, the focus of this book runs counter to the political and scholarly contexts that shape modern-day democracy. The organizations we study all seek to accomplish the vision that is contained—but unrealized—in the promise of democracy. We accept the likelihood that the most probable outcomes will prevail, but nonetheless argue that there are some systematic ways to make the possible more plausible.

By probing the organizational foundations of people power, this book offers insight into ways the everyday practice of democracy can be realized. As we confront a long list of seemingly insurmountable challenges—from rising inequality to deeply rooted racism, from increasing social disenfranchisement to intractable issues of sustainability—the task of making democracy work seems simultaneously more urgent and more remote. When people take to the streets to agitate for change, reformers too often respond (if they respond at all) with attempts to manage or narrowly fix these problems. These attempts may offer temporary salves, but they ignore the underlying corrosion of people's ability to exercise voice in our political system. Our book steps into this gap and speaks to larger questions about revitalizing democracy.

The articulation of these alternatives, even if they are improbable, is important to making them more visible so that they can become more likely. The relationship between constituencies and the democratic system is a function of both supply and demand—the demands that people put on the political system shape the supply of participatory opportunities it affords, just as the opportunities that are supplied shape the demands people have. Lacking voice in the larger marketplace of politics, constituents become like fish wondering why they have no choice but to keep swimming. "Who invented water?" the old joke begins. "I don't know, but it wasn't a fish." A system focused solely on aggregating actions to build power creates a supply of participatory opportunities that simultaneously responds to and reinforces people's instincts for the thinnest forms of participation. Dominant models of collective action conceptualize it as the additive sum of individual behavior, thus shaping both what organizations ask people to do and what people expect to do. This approach, we argue, makes it less likely these organizations or individuals will build power. As constituents get locked into a set of invisible structures that deprives them of any real voice in the political system, the probable becomes inevitable.

With this book, we hope to shine a light on an alternative. Like Jeff, Michele, and many others in Arizona, all of the leaders in our case studies made strategic choices that may initially seem baffling to outside observers.

By digging deeply into these outlying cases, however, we are able to describe the strategic logic that knits these choices about how to engage people in action to their ability to build power. In doing so, we hope to recover a tradition of democratic self-governance and show how it can work in twenty-first-century America.

2 *The Cases*

AMOS is a faith-based grassroots organizing network focused on developing the power of faith communities and low-income people of color in Cincinnati, a city with sharp racial divides. In 2016, AMOS leaders ran the field operation for Issue 44, a $48 million municipal levy to create a universal preschool program and support K–12 education. If the levy were implemented, taxes in the city would go up by $278 for every $100,000 of a home's value—a tough sell in Ohio, a state that helped put Donald Trump in the White House in the same year the measure was on the ballot.

Winning this initiative was not a foregone conclusion. In one interview, a former Hamilton County commissioner and former Cincinnati City councilman recounted the long history of "big fights" over tax levies in the city and the stiff opposition that always came from COAST (Coalition Opposed to Additional Spending and Taxes), a well-resourced anti-tax group: "In a swing county—it's fifty-fifty—a tax increase is always close because there are 40 percent of people who will almost inevitably vote against a tax increase. That means you have to win five out of six votes. And if COAST comes around and says, 'We're gonna trash your levy for the next six months,' it can kill your levy."[1] Even in this context, however, Issue 44 passed by a twenty-four-point margin in November 2016, garnering 62 percent of the vote. It was the largest margin for any new education levy in Cincinnati's history.

Elected to the Cincinnati City Council in 2017, Greg Landsman was previously the executive director of the Strive Partnership, an organization that had been working for nearly a decade to advance early childhood education in the city. The son of two teachers, and a former teacher himself, Greg mostly exuded affability. His earnestness had a slick edge to it though, which might have come from his time in politics. He cut his teeth working advance for Bill Bradley's 2000 presidential run and also was the director of faith-based and community initiatives for Governor Ted Strickland. Most media accounts and many of our interviewees credited Greg with being central to making Issue 44 happen. Indeed, he had been toiling away on universal preschool for years, trying to patch together support from business and charitable leaders throughout the city. Despite their backing, however, the campaign struggled to garner the resources it needed from public officials.

Greg described meeting Troy Jackson, the executive director of AMOS, in a church basement in 2014. "That was one of the most important moments [in the campaign]," he said, "because that's when we went from trying to focus on elected officials and institution leaders to building this ground game." Greg's analysis of this turning point is particularly striking, because when he met Jackson he had just led a pledge drive to get five thousand signatures in support of universal preschool. The pledge drive had kicked off with a splashy press conference in June 2013, with business, philanthropic, civic, and political leaders in Cincinnati present, signifying everyone's joint commitment to universal preschool. "It looked like a presidential press gaggle," Greg told us. "Every TV station in the region showed up."

The early days of the preschool campaign in Ohio had followed a well-trodden path for advocacy campaigns that seek to leverage grassroots action: build scale and attention. Greg, like many other leaders, hoped that if enough people—or enough of the right people—took action, decision makers would respond. He thus developed a campaign focused on getting as much press and as many people as possible to act. By the end of the pledge drive, Greg had accomplished his goal—surpassing five thousand signatures—and generated many of the resources commonly associated with success for collective action. He had money, media attention, a large number of petition signatures, and a seemingly favorable political opportunity structure.

The problem with this strategy emerged when elected officials unexpectedly rebuffed Greg's pledge-card drive. "What was great, and what was amazing, was that all these people, all these elected officials signed [the pledge]," Greg said. "But we did not say, 'and secure the necessary public funding,' right, so [in the end] . . . [the pledge] had no teeth." When the city council refused to fund universal preschool, Greg had emptied his toolbox of strategies. He lacked the constituency relationships needed to reliably deliver a base again and again and again until those in power listened. Only then did he realize that he didn't have other alternatives or the power he needed—until he met Troy.

The contrast between Greg's petition strategy and the base-building strategy AMOS used exemplifies the distinction between the design choices at the center of mainstream models of collective action (the pledge drive) and the choices at the center of what we call prisms (AMOS). AMOS's approach built a set of capacities among its constituents, we argue, that helped the organization wield and negotiate power in a way that Greg's five thousand pledge cards could not.

Troy spells out his philosophy for building a base in a series of weekly reflection reports he wrote during his time as executive director of AMOS, which he shared with us. As a former minister and the leader of a faith-based organizing group, Troy quotes from the Bible often in these reports, including in one written on May 17, 2015:

> Every day Jesus was teaching in the temple, and at night he would go out and spend the night on the Mount of Olives, as it was called. And **all the people would get up early in the morning to listen to him in the temple**. Now the festival of Unleavened Bread, which is called the Passover, was near. The chief priests and the scribes were looking for a way to put Jesus to death, *for they were afraid of the people*. (Luke 21:37–22:2)
>
> My path through AMOS, the OOC [Ohio Organizing Collaborative], and in collaboration with regional and national partners is to build a powerful Peoples' Movement, deeply rooted in faith, and resolute in our pursuit of racial and economic justice. . . . This Peoples' Movement must be powerful enough to make the elite quake in their boots. (Emphasis in the original)

Reflecting on the Gospel of Luke, Troy underlines the commitment that people demonstrated to Jesus by their ongoing willingness to get up early to hear him speak. This commitment, Troy reflects, was what made the chief priests and the scribes "afraid." Notably, in the section Troy refers to, Luke locates the source of the establishment power players' fear as being in not Jesus but "the people." Troy states a desire to produce the same outcome in the work he is doing with AMOS, to build a "Peoples' Movement" that can "make the elite quake in their boots."

Throughout Troy's weekly reflections, we see that he understands power through commitments and relationships, not scale. The campaign he built, unlike Greg Landsman's, reflected these principles. The campaign began with a series of house meetings focused not on convincing people about the merits of preschool but on discussing the kind of community people wanted, the values they wanted that community to embody, and the relationships they needed to create to make it possible. As people's commitments to this community deepened, AMOS engaged increasingly large groups of constituents in a discussion about preschool that, though lively and contentious, eventually yielded the People's Platform, which was ratified in October 2015. "[AMOS] runs an exceptional meeting," one interviewee told us. "It is timely, it's intentional, it's meaningful, it's relevant, it's relational." The platform that AMOS leaders and members cocreated in their meetings enshrined a set of principles that they wanted in any preschool program: it had to target resources toward the poorest children, center racial justice, and include fair wages and benefits for preschool providers. Only after AMOS constituents created this platform did they consider the question of whether to support Issue 44.

That depth, and the capacity that AMOS and its leaders had to act strategically as a collective, moved them from the edge of citywide discussions about preschool to the center. Our network surveys with business, civic, and school-district leaders in Cincinnati show this progress, as we discuss further in chapter 3.

Thus, in March 2016, when the coalition for universal preschool got into a dispute about the funding mechanism for the ballot measure, Troy was able to withstand pressure to acquiesce to the demands of the corporate community. At one point in the campaign, business leaders balked at the idea of an income tax to fund the preschool measure. Knowing they could not win without the support of the business community, the other members of the coalition—school officials, philanthropists, and civic leaders from organizations like the United Way—thought they had to yield to the business community's demands. Troy faced intense pressure to go along with everyone, but he worried that doing so on this question would signal AMOS's willingness to compromise on other principles in the People's Platform.

As the tax issue threatened to destabilize the coalition, John Pepper, an AMOS board member and the influential and widely respected former CEO of Procter & Gamble, urged the CEO of the Cincinnati Business Committee and the head of the city's Chamber of Commerce to negotiate with AMOS to move the effort forward—which they promptly did. In his weekly reflection from this time period, Troy states, "They are meeting with me because they are afraid of the people, and know they must try to understand and navigate the power we have built." Although this reflection is a self-report from Troy, our interviews and surveys with other power players in the city reflect a similar analysis. One respondent not tied to AMOS told us that business leaders realized they could not "ride roughshod" over the organization.

After these meetings, and with the support of a diverse leadership board, Troy and AMOS staff members decided to organize a public assembly to force leaders of the preschool coalition to answer questions about the initiative in front of AMOS's base. With a little over a week's notice, AMOS organized more than three hundred people to show up to a public meeting at the New Prospect Baptist Church, where the CEO of the Cincinnati Children's Hospital, the chair of the school board, the CEO of the largest developer in Cincinnati, and other members of the city's power elite sat onstage and responded to questions from AMOS constituents for over two hours. According to interviewees, both business and school-board leaders said they had not realized how much of a constituency AMOS had built until the New Prospect meeting.

The business leaders' shift from believing that AMOS was not powerful to reaching out to Troy for meetings and publicly appearing before the organization's constituents exemplifies, in some ways, the distinct logic of prisms. From the perspective of people steeped in dominant models of collective action, AMOS lacked many of the traditional markers of power. The organization did not have a large budget—in 2014, when AMOS began the preschool campaign, its 990 tax form reported $129,000 in expenses—nor did it have the breadth of support across the city that would garner attention in the traditional political media. The organization's constituency was drawn from people of faith and low-income residents across the city and did not have the traditional, structural power of wealthy, white residents or business elites. AMOS, however, built its power using the logic of prisms, seeking to assemble a base of constituents who had a shared commitment to one another. Their willingness and ability to stand together when AMOS's power was challenged translated into the capacity to hold elites to account when it mattered.

To unpack the alternate logic that AMOS exemplifies, we conducted a multimethod set of case studies. This chapter describes the research design of our study, explaining the analytic strategy we used to get at some of our core research questions described in chapter 1. We use our discussion of AMOS to dialogue with research on collective action and identify questions that cannot be answered by the existing literature. We then dive even deeper into our research design.

Overall Research Design

How did we go about studying the work of people-powered organizations in Arizona, Minnesota, Ohio, Virginia, and elsewhere? In our experience, field-based research never unfolds in as neat and orderly a fashion as what is described in formal research reports. Our study is no exception. The process of case selection, data gathering, and data analysis did not evolve as linearly as it might seem in the description below. Nonetheless, to make transparent the logic and choices that undergirded our research, and the intention that we brought to the work, we describe the process with as much clarity and detail as possible.

From the outset of the study, our research objective was to assess whether there were any commonalities across otherwise disparate organizations that were able to build constituency-based political power. To examine this question, we designed a qualitative, inductive case-study project that stretched from the fall of 2016 to the end of 2018. The study generated propositions based on an examination of outlier cases—instances of success like AMOS's, when organizations were able to flout expectations and translate the participation of ordinary people into political influence. What could we learn by looking across these cases?

Our first challenge was to identify a pool of possible organizations to study. Which were the outliers? Where could we find organizations that had overcome the broken link between participation and power? We began by interviewing key informants who were positioned to have deep, comparative knowledge of grassroots, collective-action organizations in the United States. Over a six-month period in early 2016, we interviewed a total of thirty-six informants who brought a diverse set of perspectives to the work: leaders from the major national-organizing networks, leaders of statewide and local constituency-based organizations, leaders of digital organizing groups, labor leaders, researchers, academics, funders, and leaders of organizations that exist to support collective action (such as those that provide technical and training support).

We did these interviews in two phases. In the first phase, we interviewed approximately thirty people, with the aim of understanding the overall landscape of progressive civic engagement and power-building organizations in the United States. Our goals in these conversations were to develop an overall picture of the types of collective action that were emerging across the country, to identify people who were perceived by their peers as having particularly deep knowledge of or a good bird's-eye view on movement work, and, finally, to get a preliminary sense of places that might be good to study. In this first round of conversations, twelve names consistently emerged of people who were regarded by their peers as subject-matter experts on collective action. Six were names of people who were part of our initial set of conversations, and six were new names.

In the second phase of interviews with key informants, we interviewed or reinterviewed the twelve people who were nominated by their peers as experts. These conversations focused on trying to pinpoint particular instances of successful collective action for study. We started the conversation by describing the broad goals of studying outlier cases, and then asked the experts to identify organizations (broadly construed) across the country that they considered good candidates for this study. Some informants identified geographic areas (such as states) that contained ecosystems of organizations they thought would be good for study, while others identified specific organizations (including networks, coalitions, or individual organizations). Because states were the most common geographic unit of analysis people identified, we organized our investigations at that level. Collectively, our twelve informants identified twenty-one different state-based campaigns or instances of collective action. Within that group of twenty-one, ten different states came up in three or more conversations with our informants.

Throughout these conversations, we focused on organizations that sought to advocate for the interests of constituencies that often lack power in the political system. Our logic here had to do with our interest in studying situations in which David beats Goliath, so to speak (Ganz 2009). If we were to only study cases in which middle-class white constituents or small-business owners won victories, for instance, we would not be able to differentiate the extent to which those victories depended on the political privilege already associated with race, wealth, and business interests. Studying organizations that are organizing and advocating on behalf of low-income constituencies of color means that we are studying organizations working on issues in the face of structural biases. In that sense, it is harder for them to build the power we are examining.

Our second challenge, then, was to choose among these possible cases. Because ten examples of collective action came up in three or more conversations with informants, we focused most of our subsequent investigation of possible cases on those ten candidate states. How could we select among them? Our goal was to use a "most different" selection strategy, in which we identified cases that varied on dimensions known to affect "success" in collective action. For instance, previous scholarship tells us there is a set of structural or contextual factors that impacts organizations' chances of political success. Here, we use the terms "structure" and "context" to refer to macro or micro factors that are largely immutable or out of the control of the organization itself. A large literature examines macro, contextual factors, like political opportunities, state capacity, and countermovements, that affect a social movement's likelihood of success (Tilly and Tarrow 2007; Kriesi 1996; Meyer and Staggenborg 1996). A related literature examines microlevel factors, such as population-level predispositions for certain communication frames or public-opinion trends that shape the context a movement faces (Ferree 2003; Gamson 1995; Benford and Snow 2000). An overlapping literature similarly examines political and institutional conditions that shape interest groups' abilities to achieve their goals (see Baumgartner et al. 2009 for a summary).

Much of this literature would suggest that things like widespread media attention, support from institutional and corporate players, access to key decision makers, and political opportunity structures should condition whether

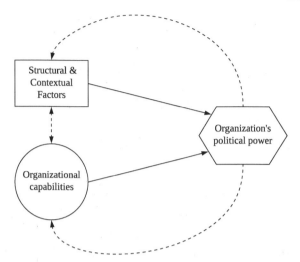

Figure 2.1. Contextual and organizational factors in relationship to political power.

collective action succeeds or fails. We did not want to only study organizations that were working in states with Democratic governors, for instance, or organizations that were all working on issues like same-sex marriage that had received widespread media coverage and a recent wave of public support. If we only studied organizations working in progressive states or on one issue, we would not be able to rule out the possibility that the main source of their success was, in fact, the favorable opportunity structure or the whims of national media coverage.

Instead, we wanted to see whether there were any explanatory factors over which organizational leaders might have more agency. A stylized representation of our logic is depicted in figure 2.1. In this figure, for the purpose of exposition, we group the factors known to affect the success of collective action into two simplified categories: (1) structural and contextual variables, including things like the demographic, ideological, economic, and civic context of a community, as well as the political context of the issue, the characteristics of the institutional arena in which the organization is working, and other structural factors that shape the organization's ability to achieve power; and (2) organizational capabilities, which refers to processes internal to the organization over which leaders have agency. As the solid arrows in the figure indicate, both of these factors affect the degree to which an organization achieves power.[2]

Following our most-different selection strategy, we intentionally varied the sociopolitical, economic, and contextual factors to see whether there were any organization-level patterns that helped explain outcomes. In other words, we maximized variation on the known contextual variables and held constant the outcome variable (political power). To ensure we were varying the sociopolitical and economic contexts, we gathered demographic, political, economic, and civic data on the ten states in question (appendix B shows this data and provides a more detailed analysis of the factors that varied).

The question, then, was whether there were any shared organizational choices that emerged across these cases of groups working on different issues, in different states, and in varied political contexts. The null hypothesis, so to speak, is that there are no shared characteristics. In other words, perhaps the outlying success of these cases is entirely idiosyncratic—it could be dependent in one case on a gifted leader like Troy and in another case on a unique set of political circumstances that created an alchemy that could not be replicated elsewhere. If the null hypothesis held, we would see no shared patterns across the cases we selected. As we describe throughout the book, however, we did see patterns that persisted despite the varied geographic, demographic, sociopolitical, and economic contexts within which these organizations worked.

Ultimately, we selected a pool of six cases in the following states: Arizona, Kentucky, Minnesota, Nevada, Ohio, and Virginia. Based on what we knew at the time, we divided these states into core cases (Arizona, Ohio, and Virginia) and what we called "extension" cases (Kentucky, Minnesota, and Nevada). We made this distinction because we knew the organizations in the three core cases had achieved concrete, visible victories on campaigns they had been waging, but we did not know how they had done it. Leaders in Arizona had won a series of defensive and offensive victories, beating back the excesses of anti-immigrant legislation and raising the statewide minimum wage. AMOS had helped expand early childhood education with Issue 44, and New Virginia Majority had led a coalition that won rights restoration for returning citizens. These cases thus met our criteria of having translated base participation into power over outcomes they cared about, and also varying on dimensions already known to be associated with power. Each of the three "extension" cases were organizations that informants told us exemplified some of the organizational capabilities we hypothesized might be worth exploring. As we got deeper into our data collection, however, we moved Minnesota into the category of "core" case, because our prospective examination of ISAIAH's role in state politics during the 2018 election clearly demonstrated the attributes of achieving power that we sought to understand.

Having selected the cases, we moved on to our next task, which was to collect and analyze the data.[3] We did so by engaging in an immersive, mixed-method data-collection process. We constantly toggled back and forth between the existing literature and our findings during regular check-in and analysis conversations with one another (twenty-four meetings in total over the eighteen-month period of the study) and two multiday, in-person retreats. Our data consisted of a combination of interviews, surveys, ethnographic observations (including those gathered after being added to one organization's digital chat applications), analysis of internal organizational documents and databases, and examination of publicly available data. We collected data between October 2016 and December 2018. All told, we conducted 232 in-depth interviews, which yielded 4,029 pages of typed transcripts. In addition, we produced 142 pages of typed field notes from visits to our research sites, conducted two network surveys, and triangulated data from each state with primary and secondary sources.

Throughout our data collection, we were careful to corroborate findings using as many data sources as possible. Because the kinds of internal organizational data we needed for the analysis depended on building deep relationships and trust, our research plan exposed us to the potential risk of bias. What if the relationships we formed with informants led us to present an overly rosy or uncritical picture of these organizations' work? To help guard against this, we tried, as much as possible, to develop a 360-degree view of the work and to confirm what we were told in interviews or observed during fieldwork with other data sources whenever possible. This meant that we were basing our analysis of these cases on the perspectives of not only the organizations under study but also their targets, allies, and opponents. Our network survey with political elites in Virginia is one example of this cross-checking. In that case, we asked state-level politicians to assess the range of power relationships they held, without naming the anchor organization in our case. We also sought, whenever possible, to confirm leader reports about the number of participants in a particular event by using data from their own organizational databases, media coverage, or other interviewees who were present. Our goal was to develop a picture of these organizations that was as holistic and multidimensional as possible.

The Cases

This book analyzes four core cases in Arizona, Minnesota, Ohio, and Virginia. The organizations in these four states vary substantially in terms of their sociopolitical, demographic, and civic context, yet all achieved some visible political victories in recent years. In addition, as we will demonstrate in chapter 3, these victories shifted underlying power dynamics. Each case study is, by itself, a compelling story of collective action, but our analysis focuses on commonalities across those cases. To provide some grounding in the basic elements of each story, we introduce the core facts—who, what, when, where—of each case here.

In the extension cases of Kentucky and Nevada we identified two organizations, Kentuckians for the Commonwealth (KFTC) and the Progressive Leadership Alliance of Nevada (PLAN); both have been organizing for political power in each state. The fact that they were not included as core cases should not imply that they have not achieved political influence; as we will describe further, both won important victories for constituents in their states. They did not, however, emerge through the selection process that we laid out above. Instead, our expert informers identified them because of a set of their unique organizational practices and structures. Given our interest in understanding these dimensions of collective action, we included them in our analysis as additional cases.

A summary of all six cases is included in table 2.1. As the table shows, we focused on one or more anchor organizations in each state as the subject of each case. Within this set of cases, the constituencies, issues, and arenas in which the organizations operated varied. The campaigns that we studied also varied in terms of their strategic focus. While one concentrated on shaping power dynamics around access to education in the city, another sought to shape the narrative around race and class issues in a gubernatorial election. While one organization focused primarily on building power relationships through lobbying in the state legislature and the governor's office, another moved municipal and county-level targets to align with its movement's agenda.

EMBEDDEDNESS IN ORGANIZING
NETWORKS AND TRADITIONS

It is worth noting that all of these organizations (and their leaders) are part of both formal and informal national networks. A picture of the range of these networks in the United States emerged in a map created by the Democracy Alliance that was leaked to the media. The Democracy Alliance is a network of wealthy political donors interested in supporting progressive causes and coordinating donations to Democratic campaign efforts (Skocpol, Williamson, and Hertel-Fernandez 2015; Hertel-Fernandez and Skocpol 2016). After the 2016 election and the groundswell of grassroots resistance activity that emerged in response to it, the Democracy Alliance created a map of progressive organizations, including those focused on litigation, rapid-response work, electoral mobilization, political bundling, media monitoring, and the like (*New York Times* 2017). One big section of the map contains a list of fif-

Table 2.1. Case Organization Summaries

State	Anchor Organization(s)	Constituency	Campaign Goal	Arena
Core Cases				
Arizona	Coalition of 501(c)(3) and (c)(4) immigrant-led organizations, including **OneAZ**, **LUCHA/ ACE**, **Poder in Action** (formerly CNL), **Promise AZ**, and **Puente**	Latinx immigrants, their families, and allies in AZ	Stop anti-immigrant legislation, put immigrant-friendly candidates into office, and pass a new statewide minimum wage law	Municipal and house district elections and campaigns Statewide minimum wage proposition (Proposition 206)
Minnesota	**ISAIAH**: a faith-based community organizing 501(c)(3). **Faith in Minnesota (FiMN)**: 501(c)(4) sister organization to ISAIAH	Multiracial base of people of faith in MN	Use 2018 caucus and convention process to pressure Democratic candidates to explicitly prioritize racial equity, immigrants, and universal health care	Faith delegate campaign to shape 2018 primary and general election for MN governor and selected legislative and city-level races
Ohio	**The AMOS Project**: a faith-based community organizing 501(c)(3)	Multiracial base of people of faith in OH	Pass a ballot initiative for universal preschool in Cincinnati and hold stakeholders accountable to equity outcomes (provider pay, parental involvement, and a focus on families living near or below the poverty line)	Municipal levy (Issue 44) to fund universal preschool and K–12 education in 2016
Virginia	**New Virginia Majority (NVM)**: statewide coalition of POC-led grassroots constituency hubs	Latinx immigrants, African Americans, and Asian Americans in VA	Change the electorate by restoring voting rights for returning citizens, registering people to vote, and getting them to turn out	Lobbying governor's office and state-level elected officials to restore voting rights for the formerly incarcerated

Table 2.1. Continued

State	Anchor Organization(s)	Constituency	Campaign Goal	Arena
Extension Cases				
Kentucky	**Kentuckians for the Common-wealth (KFTC)**: 501(c)(3) state-wide organization with 14 county chapters	Multiracial base of KY progressives	Build power for pro-gressives in KY; develop leaders through demo-cratic decision-making processes	Health care, taxa-tion, anti-racism, environment, and LGBTQ issues
Nevada	**Progressive Leadership Alli-ance of Nevada (PLAN)**: 501(c)(3) state-wide organiza-tion comprising 44 constituent organizations	Multiracial base of NV progressives	Build governing power for progres-sives in NV	Criminal justice and structural racism; economic and gender inequality; immigration reform; climate justice

Note: Throughout the book, we reference the work of the organizations in our study primarily through the name of their 501(c)(3) organization for the purposes of clarity, so as not to confuse the reader with too many organizational names. In their own work, however, all of these organiza-tions are very careful to adhere to IRS guidelines in terms of the distinction between their 501(c)(3) and 501(c)(4) work and the inability to coordinate therein. Our interchangeable use of the organiza-tions' names should not be interpreted as indicating otherwise.

teen national organizations focused on what the Democracy Alliance labels "organizing." Most of the groups listed in this category are actually federated networks that provide a national umbrella for a set of local and state-based constituency-based organizations.

Many state-based organizations in the United States are part of several of these national networks, and the groups in our cases are no exception. The anchor organization in our Ohio case, for instance, is AMOS. AMOS is a mu-nicipal organization in Cincinnati that is part of a statewide organization called the Ohio Organizing Collaborative. The Ohio Organizing Collaborative, in turn, works with three national networks: the Center for Popular Democ-racy, the Center for Community Change, and Faith in Action (formerly called the PICO National Network). ISAIAH, the anchor organization in Minnesota, is also part of Faith in Action. In Virginia, the New Virginia Majority is also part of the Center for Popular Democracy and works with the Center for Community Change. In Arizona, the leaders and organizations in our study have partnered with the Center for Community Change, the Center for Popular Democracy, Faith in Action, and a group called People's Action. All of these networks are rooted in long-standing traditions of community organizing, labor organizing, faith-based organizing, and so on that shaped their work. Importantly, the organizations in our study maintain their strategic independence despite being connected to larger networks. In some ways, the multiple and overlapping affiliations that most of these organizations have mean they are all relatively independent in the end even though they receive some support and training from the national networks.

It is worth noting that, despite this strategic independence, many of the leaders in our cases were personally networked to each other. As exemplified above, these leaders are all part of state and national networks of progressive advocates. Later, we discuss how these relationships created broader learning ecosystems that shaped some of the strategic creativity we observed in the cases.

First, we turn to a description of each case.

CORE CASE: ARIZONA

The Arizona case study examines a coalition of organizations that emerged after SB 1070 to form a new immigrant rights movement in the state. In the first decade of the twenty-first century, immigration reform dominated political headlines, intensifying an already harsh social and political climate for undocumented families. Racial profiling, raids, detention, and deportation were techniques the state used on immigrant communities. Like several other border states, Arizona was a hot spot for battles over immigration. Anti-immigrant sentiment provided latitude for people like Joe Arpaio, the infamous sheriff of Maricopa County who opened his Tent City Jail in 1993. The jail had a special outdoor holding area for "illegal aliens" and other inmates, who were exposed to Phoenix's extreme temperatures and forced to wear striped prison jumpsuits and pink underwear.

Despite and because of this hostile local climate, many immigration advocates spent much of the 2000s organizing around national immigration policy rather than state and local measures. In 2006, for example, harsh anti-immigrant legislation in Congress prompted mass marches across the country, representing what were at the time the largest national mobilizations since the anti-war demonstrations of the early 1970s. When Democrats won control of both houses of Congress and the presidency in 2008, immigrant

rights advocates thought the moment had come for comprehensive immigration reform. They organized a national campaign called Reform Immigration
for America (RIFA).

Momentum for creating a path to legalization seemed to be growing
around the country. In the fall of 2009, the New Organizing Institute (NOI)
led trainings for movement leaders in Florida and Colorado. In Colorado, two
Latina organizers from Phoenix "crashed" the training. According to (then)
NOI organizing director Joy Cushman, they said, "We want to organize, we
want more training. . . . We're going to take this back to Arizona with or without [your] help." NOI met their demand. In December 2009, one hundred immigrant leaders and activists packed an organizing training in Phoenix led
by NOI and statewide leaders from Arizona.[4] So many people showed up at
the training that the organizers had to improvise overflow breakout groups
that met in the bathrooms of the dilapidated airport hotel where they held
the training.

Interviewees told us that at the time of the training, in large part because of
initial Obama-era optimism that the DREAM (Development, Relief, and Education for Alien Minors) Act would finally pass, state-policy measures were
barely on their radar.[5] This changed radically in April 2010, when Governor
Brewer signed SB 1070 into law. The Supreme Court would later strike down
some of its provisions as discriminatory and unconstitutional. In the moment, however, immigration-rights organizers told us that they felt "blind-
sided" by the law. As we described in chapter 1, they responded by organizing
a months-long vigil on the Arizona Capitol lawn. Despite the large numbers,
national media attention, and intensity they garnered, they did not immediately develop the political power they needed to block SB 1070.

By 2016, however, the terrain had shifted. Despite being unable to stop
SB 1070, the 104-day protest had long-term consequences: it was a trial-by-
fire test of learning, leadership development, and formation that shaped the
growth of a statewide network of leaders and organizations that fought back
against anti-immigration policies. In the six years between 2010 and 2016,
a strategic coalition of immigrant rights groups emerged and won a series
of important local and state victories. They helped entangle SB 1070 in lawsuits, oust a key architect of the law through the first statewide recall in Arizona history, win five seats on Phoenix's city council, advance a municipal
ID policy, and win a new minimum wage law. In 2012, the coalition tried to
remove Sheriff Arpaio from office, but lost by six percentage points. By 2016,
however, this coalition had built enough power that they were able to help defeat Arpaio, beating him by a margin of more than eleven percentage points.
These victories were not only about policy and electoral wins but also evi-

dence of how the movement had earned immigrant groups a seat at the bargaining table, built collective capacity as a coalition, held elected officials accountable over time, and shaped the interests of national donors.

This is the only case within our study that does not have one clear anchor organization. Rather, the core organizations include LUCHA (introduced in chapter 1), Promise Arizona, One Arizona, Poder in Action (formerly the Center for Neighborhood Leadership), and their allies (we include interviews with people from organizations like Puente, even though we were not able to interview the head of that organization). All of these organizations are led by people who were activated in response to SB 1070. In this case study, we examine the way the bill's passage caused these emerging leaders to shift the way they organized, moving from a strategy promulgated by national leaders to one that prioritized building their own organizational and leadership capacities. Over time, we argue, this shift in strategy correspondingly helped change the overall policy agenda in the state, making it less hospitable to anti-immigrant legislators and legislation.

LUCHA (Living United for Change in Arizona) provides a glimpse of the size and organizational infrastructure of these groups. Like many of the other organizations in Arizona, LUCHA grew tremendously in the years just prior to our study. According to their tax filings, their budget swelled from approximately $240,000 in 2015 to $2.5 million in 2016. This was in large part because of the work they did in the 2016 election to lead the statewide passage of Proposition 206. A 501(c)(4) organization, LUCHA works in close partnership with ACE (Arizona Center for Empowerment), their 501(c)(3) counterpart. ACE's budget increased from $78,000 in 2011 to about $380,000 in 2016. The two sister organizations are widely recognized as key leaders in constituency-based organizing among the immigrant community in the state.

An umbrella organization within this ecosystem is One Arizona, a 501(c)(3) organization that acts as a statewide "table." This term is used to refer to organizations whose job is to bring together other organizations to coordinate funding, targets, and other activities. A table usually has a large budget but a small staff. For instance, One Arizona's budget in 2016 was approximately $3.5 million, but organizational documents listed only six paid employees. (The budget was likely unusually large in 2016 because 2016 was a presidential election year, and a large part of state tables' work is coordinating funding for nonpartisan get-out-the-vote efforts.) A number of the 501(c)(3) organizations that emerged from the SB 1070 fight were part of the One Arizona table. For instance, Poder in Action is a 501(c)(3) organization based in Phoenix, founded in 2013, whose executive director, Viri Hernandez, was first called to act in response to SB 1070. On its tax filings, the organization lists zero revenue and zero expenses in 2013. From 2014 to 2016, its budget was approximately $400,000 each year.

CORE CASE: MINNESOTA

The anchor group in the Minnesota case is a partnership between a 501(c)(3) organization and a 501(c)(4) organization, much like LUCHA and ACE. The 501(c)(3) is a faith-based organization called ISAIAH. They describe themselves on their 2016 tax forms as "a statewide coalition of congregations and allies" that acts as "a vehicle for people of faith to work for racial and economic justice in Minnesota." Among our four core cases, they are probably the most mature organization, as leaders in Minnesota have been working for over twenty years to build a statewide, multiracial, cross-class coalition of people of faith. In the five years spanning 2012 to 2016, their budget varied between $1.2 million and $2.5 million (largest during election years). Their 501(c)(4) counterpart is Faith in Minnesota (FiMN), formed in 2017 in response to a need they saw to develop greater political influence.

ISAIAH, like almost all of the organizations in our six cases, has a reputation within the state for being unpredictable and agitational. ISAIAH's longtime executive director is Doran Schrantz, a brilliant, charismatic woman in her early forties who does not shy away from uncomfortable negotiations. She and ISAIAH have been discomfiting establishment Democrats for years, agitating from the left for them to be more responsive to communities of color and low-income people in the state.

The campaign we studied was no exception. Unlike the data collection for our other cases, which were mostly retrospective, the data collection around ISAIAH's work unfolded in real time. We had initially seen ISAIAH as an extension case, based on prior work it had done in the state, but as we were digging into the data collection, it became clear that the work it was doing in 2017 and 2018 to influence the narrative around race and class in the 2018 gubernatorial and legislative elections merited further analysis as a core case.

This 2018 campaign emerged from lessons ISAIAH had learned in the final days of the legislative session of 2017. At that time, Democratic governor Mark Dayton was trying to pass a range of policies through a Republican legislature. Progressive advocates were pushing for things like bargaining rights for workers and driver's licenses for immigrants. Facing obstinacy from his legislature, Dayton was looking to cut deals. Eventually, he negotiated an agreement with labor that would protect bargaining rights but withdraw support for protections for immigrants. This prompted an angry response from ISAIAH, which accused the governor of "trad[ing] away immigrants for labor."

ISAIAH called for a boycott of a major Democratic-Farmer-Labor (DFL) party fundraiser, bringing allies from part of the labor community on board. After this incident, ISAIAH leaders and their allies reflected on what they needed to do to advance the cause of immigrants, communities of color, and people of faith in the state. They decided they needed to develop more political influence to get a seat at the decision-making table and forestall future deals like the one that labor struck with Governor Dayton.

In the summer and fall of 2017, ISAIAH did three things. First, it formed a 501(c)(4) counterpart (FiMN) to allow for more partisan political work. Second, it partnered with a professional communications firm (working with communications expert Anat Shenker-Osorio and Berkeley professor Ian Haney Lopez) to develop research on the best ways to construct a narrative around race and class issues in the state. Democrats provided funding for this research in exchange for ISAIAH calling off the boycott of their fundraiser. Finally, it organized a house-party campaign with its constituents, with the goal of developing a "faith agenda." The faith agenda was to be a statement of principles ISAIAH constituents wanted to see advanced in the 2018 state-wide elections. Central to the faith agenda was the broadening of the definition of "we" in Minnesota. In a challenge to a narrative that pitted different demographic groups against one another in the wake of Trump's victory in 2016, ISAIAH wanted to develop an alternative that presented a more inter-dependent sense of what it means to be a Minnesotan. The organization drew on the research it did with the communications consultant around how best to talk about race and class issues.

The faith-agenda campaign developed into what we call the faith-delegate campaign, which was an effort by ISAIAH and FiMN to influence the narrative around race, class, and immigration by running ISAIAH leaders as delegates to the Democratic-Farmer-Labor state-party convention. The faith-delegate campaign focused primarily on the state's 2018 gubernatorial race, but we also include analyses of other legislative and local races in which the campaign participated. In this campaign, FiMN recruited 500 leaders to run as delegates to the state convention and 3,800 people to attend the caucuses where delegates were elected.

The initial goal of this campaign was to use the caucus attendees and delegates to advance the faith agenda, not to support any particular candidate. The campaign was so successful, however, that the group unexpectedly captured about 12 percent of the delegate seats to the state-party convention. This prompted a strategic pivot in the spring of 2018, when FiMN realized it could shift to endorsing specific candidates in addition to working on narrative change. The faith delegates decided to vote as a bloc in support of Erin

Murphy for governor, giving her the votes she needed to win the support of the Democratic-Farmer-Labor party convention. The unexpected loss at the convention of the DFL frontrunner Tim Walz triggered a primary in August. At that point, FiMN had come out in support of Murphy, and they fought to aid her in the primary. Although their backing was enough to help her win the caucuses, she ultimately did not have enough support to win the primary. Tim Walz became the DFL candidate and won the governorship in November of 2018, with FiMN's eventual support.

Our study examines this entire campaign. We argue that even in cases where the efforts that ISAIAH and FiMN supported lost, the organizations nonetheless built power. As our data shows, they retained the ability to influence how candidates discuss the intersection of race and class issues, thus advancing their original goal (see chapter 3 for further discussion and evidence of this).

CORE CASE: OHIO

The Ohio case focuses on the 2016 municipal ballot initiative for universal preschool in Cincinnati (Issue 44) introduced at the beginning of this chapter. The anchor organization is AMOS, a faith-based organization seeking to build a multiracial, cross-class coalition of people of faith advocating for social, racial, and economic justice. AMOS played a key role in winning the ballot initiative in 2016, a victory that culminated a sixteen-year effort by a number of civic, political, and business leaders in the city to combat racialized, intergenerational poverty. AMOS's involvement was concentrated in the final two years of the campaign. We argue that AMOS's work building the constituency base gave the campaign the help it needed to get across the finish line in 2016.

In 2001, following a police shooting of a young black man named Timothy Thomas, Cincinnati experienced the largest civil unrest in the United States since the 1992 Los Angeles uprisings. This disturbance sparked a widespread discussion in the city about ways to combat persistent and deeply racialized poverty. Decades of research had demonstrated that early childhood education was one of the most effective possible interventions. As one interviewee told us, the United Way of Greater Cincinnati, a privately funded social-service organization, responded by "put[ting] a stake in the ground" in 2003 and publicly committed to making early childhood education its highest priority. It pledged to develop programming that would render 85 percent of Cincinnati children kindergarten-ready by 2020.

For over a decade, however, the United Way's effort languished. The organization led a campaign that, as interviewees described it, was "out-of-touch" and unable to generate private investments at the scale needed to make preschool universal. In 2012, leaders realized they needed public dollars to fund early childhood education. In the years that followed, the Strive Partnership and United Way led a coalition called Preschool Promise that used a variety of tactics to try to build support for public investment in early childhood education. They ran a pledge campaign, community forums, and press conferences that some interviewees called "corporate marketing." Lacking a real grassroots base, Preschool Promise was not able to generate the public will needed to pressure elected officials.

This changed when the AMOS Project became part of the coalition in 2014. As a group focused on multiracial power building, AMOS organized constituencies in Cincinnati most in need of universal preschool. Those constituencies would benefit the most from early childhood education but had largely been excluded from the prior campaign. When AMOS decided to partner with the Preschool Promise campaign, it did so conditionally. After a series of meetings with between four and five hundred constituents, AMOS drafted what its leaders called the "People's Platform." The platform's final version explicitly demanded that any universal preschool program should allocate funds to directly address Cincinnati's racial disparities and guarantee a minimum base wage of $15 per hour, paid sick time, and affordable health insurance for preschool providers.

Once AMOS and its sixty affiliated congregations got involved, they provided what an interviewee called the "old-fashioned organizing muscle" that the coalition needed. The campaign became so robust that the chairman of the Ohio Democratic Party told us he directed his staff to funnel resources to them because "they had the best on-the-ground operation of any effort in Cincinnati." But AMOS only provided its support to the extent that its constituency-generated platform was reflected in the levy language. Throughout the campaign, AMOS fought to hold business leaders and the United Way accountable to the People's Platform.

In November 2016, even as Donald Trump won Ohio by eight points, 62.2 percent of Cincinnati voters elected to pass a municipal levy to fund preschool, a levy that would raise taxes by $278 per year for every $100,000 of a home's value. The levy contained key concessions to AMOS's People's Platform, including guarantees that families living at up to 200 percent of the poverty line would be served first and that preschool providers would receive a $15 per hour wage. Had it not been for AMOS, these provisions likely would not have been included in the levy—although the fight to implement the raise for providers continued after the measure passed. Perhaps more importantly, as our data shows, the victory gave grassroots faith leaders a seat at the political decision-making table.

When Troy Jackson became the executive director of AMOS in April 2014, he had a clear and disciplined focus on rebuilding and expanding its base, which had atrophied somewhat during the years before he took the position. The organization's budget was about $120,000 in 2010 and grew to about $300,000 in 2016. In addition to addressing the group's financial assets, however, Jackson did considerable work to grow AMOS's constituency base, building a network of clergy, members, and leaders across the city. Our data shows that the work Jackson led in the preschool campaign not only put himself into greater relationship with power players in Cincinnati but also brought networks of his key constituent leaders into relationship with power as well.

CORE CASE: VIRGINIA

The Virginia case focuses on a statewide organization called New Virginia Majority (NVM), which worked closely with Democratic governor Terry McAuliffe and his predecessor, Republican governor Bob McDonnell, to restore voting rights for 173,000 formerly incarcerated citizens in 2016. Before then, Virginia was one of only four states in the nation to permanently disenfranchise people with felony records.

As an organization, NVM had grown quite a bit in the decade preceding our study. The 501(c)(4) portion of its organization had a budget of $5 million in 2016, according to its 990 tax forms. This is remarkable growth for an organization that had just formed its 501(c)(3) partner in 2010. As is the case with the 2016 budgets of several of the other organizations discussed in this study, NVM's 2016 budget was definitely an outlier. Nonetheless, this growth reflected the overall trajectory of NVM. It began as Tenants and Workers United, a group that organized primarily Latino immigrants around workers' rights and fair-housing issues in Northern Virginia.[6] After the 2004 election, Tenants and Workers' then executive director Jon Liss began to reflect on the organization's work and realized that if it wanted to advance the interests of its members, it had to build statewide power.

Jon decided to expand the reach of Tenants and Workers United by founding New Virginia Majority. His first employee was a woman named Tram Nguyen, a hire that was, as Jon put it, "the best decision [he] ever made." Tram turned out to be an extraordinarily gifted people's lobbyist and was able to develop a series of key relationships with state legislators and the governor's mansion while NVM built out its base in Virginia. Like many other such organizations, NVM started by networking preexisting local organizations to one another, including Tenants and Workers United. Jon and Tram wanted to expand NVM's base from just urban Latino immigrant communities in Northern Virginia (Tram told us that people often divide the state into NoVA and RoVA, for "rest of," to highlight this demarcation) to a broader, multiracial base that stretched across the state. Jon focused on building this coalition and strengthening grassroots organizing across Virginia, while Tram focused much of her time on building insider relationships at the state level. This turned out to be a potent combination.

For years, progressives and voting-rights advocates had been lobbying Virginia's governors to use their power to extend voting rights to returning citizens. Democratic and Republican governors alike, however, employed their clemency powers sparingly, reluctant to develop a "soft on crime" image. As NVM grew its base and increased its representation of African American constituents, its leaders realized that they had to address the issue of voting rights if they wanted to bring real power to these communities. NVM's constituents could not develop their voice without addressing the structural barriers to the participation of the many black Virginians who were disenfranchised because of a past criminal record. NVM thus joined the coalition of voting-rights advocates.

After many years of pressure, and after working closely with multiple governors, NVM now belonged to a coalition of advocates seeking to restore voting rights to returning citizens in Virginia, and eventually they succeeded. What had changed to prompt McAuliffe's willingness to act? Public-opinion data shows that public support for rights restoration had not shifted much between 2002 and 2014. So why did McAuliffe take the political risk? In the 2013 election, NVM worked in coalition to pressure gubernatorial candidates to take a stand on rights restoration. NVM did this work with a very clear sense of where its power to influence candidates was: "It's not enough to just rally and protest and do these actions, but at the end of the day a lot of these elected officials also care about who's voting and their power, right?" one interviewee told us. In the 2013 election, NVM sought—and earned—commitments from leading candidates that, if elected, they would use their authority to enact rights restoration. Then, NVM organized its constituency to turn out for the election.

When McAuliffe was elected in 2013, NVM worked to hold him accountable to his promises. During the first two years of his administration, McAuliffe issued rights-restoration orders in a piecemeal fashion. But, as an interviewee told us, NVM "[showed] up at every committee meeting, whether it was at 7 in the morning or at 8 o'clock at night. . . . We kept showing up because [we wanted McAuliffe's people to think], 'Okay they're not going to let us get away with anything.'" Through this work, NVM developed a close relationship with McAuliffe's office, pressuring him to take more sweeping action. When he did, he did so knowing that NVM would not rest until its constituent base had a voice in the political process.

In this case study, we track the work that NVM did around voting rights, but we also examine the way the group wielded power on a range of issues in the state legislature. NVM's ability to pressure the governor rested in part on its reputation in the statehouse, and on the coalitions it was able to build. Consequently, we examine both the specific work around the voting-rights campaign and NVM's general lobbying strategy. Among our four core cases, NVM focused more on elite lobbying than any of the others, thus giving us a window into how its leaders strategized and negotiated these kinds of power relationships.

EXTENSION CASE: KENTUCKY

In the Kentucky case, the anchor organization is Kentuckians for the Common-wealth (KFTC). Originally founded in 1981, KFTC is a statewide organization that is known among progressive advocates throughout the country as having very robust, democratic decision-making processes. Like many civic organizations that were more common in the early to mid-twentieth century, KFTC organizes its dues-paying members into a federated structure of local and issue-based chapters across the state. Each of these units is run by an elected leadership that comes together periodically to make governance decisions for the organization. We included KFTC as an extension case in an effort to better understand how this tradition of internal democracy helped the organization build a base that has political voice.

In thirty-eight years since its founding, KFTC has grown not only in numbers but also in the range of issues to which it is committed. Though KFTC began with a particular concentration on anti-coal campaigns and local tax policies, over time it developed a greater focus on social justice. KFTC's work is centered not around a single set of issues or a finite policy agenda, but on an overall vision that is codified in a statement, written in its annual meeting program guide, that grounds all of its work:

We have a vision. . . . We are working for a day when Kentuckians—and all people—enjoy a better quality of life. When the lives of people and communities matter before profits. When our communities have good jobs that support our families without doing damage to the water, air and land. When companies and the wealthy pay their share of taxes and can't buy elections. When all people have health care, shelter, food, education, clean water, and other basic needs. When children are listened to and valued. When discrimination is wiped out of our laws, habits, and hearts. And when the voices of ordinary people are heard and respected in our democracy.

Many KFTC gatherings begin with a shared recitation of the vision. However, KFTC's executive director, Burt Lauderdale, often says that although KFTC members are "vision oriented," they are careful not to be "vision-statement oriented." In other words, they treat their vision as a source of strategic dynamism instead of a source of constraint.

Structurally, KFTC has an elected statewide leadership and an annual convention where the group collectively sets its priorities for the year. Under this umbrella, fourteen chapters from counties all across Kentucky each elect their own leadership to decide their own strategic priorities. This commitment to local governance is rooted in a belief that KFTC should be responsive to the local needs of their constituents. The leader of one ally organization working alongside KFTC chapters to organize around new energy campaigns witnessed how engaging the local people who are knowledgeable of and directly influenced by any given issue increased the potential for repeated engagement. He explained: "The chapters worked on different challenges identified by their local leaders, and that work was an opportunity to build their leadership capacity and potential. I just think you can't have the sort of broad-based transition we envisioned in the region without lots of local leaders who have skills, awareness, recognize the public good, and are willing to advocate in their communities." But while each chapter has the ability to choose its own issue campaigns, those issues must be in alignment with KFTC's statewide platform. This foundational document, amended annually by the membership in what Burt called "the most exasperating, beautiful demonstration of democracy and wordsmithing," lays out KFTC's official positions on various issues. Members vote on the platform each year at the annual meeting. However, if chapters want to work on issues not included in the platform, they can petition the steering committee for permission.

Each year, representatives from across Kentucky convene for a KFTC steering committee meeting and retreat. At this annual meeting, each chapter decides whether or not to re-petition their membership into KFTC. A chapter representative then shares that chapter's accomplishments and its priorities for the coming year. After the chapters share their petitions, members vote on their inclusion. By making membership an explicit annual choice for each local chapter, KFTC exemplifies its commitment to constituency-based governance practices.

Throughout its history, KFTC has participated in dozens of campaigns to advance its agenda. One campaign the organization was involved in during our study focused on the RECLAIM (Revitalizing the Economy of Coal Communities by Leveraging Local Activities and Investing More) Act, federal legislation that would direct $1 billion to coalfield communities from a mine-site reclamation fund established in 1977. The fund receives fees from present-day coal mining that are then redistributed to tribes and states. However, Congress has never fully appropriated the resources, in part due to the difficulty of allocating funds among states with vastly different levels of historic and current coal mining.

In the face of continued steep declines in coal employment and production in Kentucky and across Appalachia, KFTC and other regional and national partners—including the Appalachian Citizens Law Center, Alliance for Appalachia, and Appalachian Voices—banded together to organize and advocate for passage of the RECLAIM Act. Even though the act simply accelerates the deployment of resources that the coal industry has already paid into the Abandoned Mine Lands (AML) fund, the National Mining Association opposes the bill, seeking instead to phase out its obligation to pay for environmental restoration. In response, KFTC and its allies leveraged their grassroots relationships, organizing campaigns and a coordinated communications effort to highlight the economic-development potential of the act and pressure Kentucky's congressional delegation to support the bill. Between 2015 and 2018, the organization and other regional groups collected more than ten thousand petition signatures; met repeatedly with members of Congress and their staff; organized to win local resolutions supporting the bill in twenty-eight small towns, cities, and counties in affected communities; held press conferences and demonstrations at congressional offices; and generated earned, paid, and social media to build pressure and a groundswell of support for passage.

The coalition secured several early victories. In 2015, KFTC and its partner organizations succeeded in persuading Republican congressman and Appropriations Committee chairman Hal Rogers to file the bill for the first time. A year later, KFTC members carrying Xerox cartons full of signatures in support of RECLAIM arrived at Mitch McConnell's office in London, Kentucky. McConnell initially opposed the bill, but on March 23, 2017, he introduced his own version of the act in the Senate. At first, this seemed like a victory, but as one KFTC staffer put it, "it soon became clear that [congressional] support for the measure was weak, at best. [We knew] the campaign would need to continue to grow."

In 2018, sensing the opportunity to do just that, KFTC built an even closer relationship with Appalachian Citizens Law Center, local black-lung associations, and other groups working on a separate but related issue: the need to protect funding for the Black Lung Disability Trust Fund. This federal fund provides health benefits and income support to miners with black lung disease and their immediate families. Like the Abandoned Mine Lands Fund that the RECLAIM fight revolves around, the Black Lung Disability Trust Fund relies on a fee levied on present-day coal mining. As of 2019, the fund faces insolvency due to a perfect storm of threats: a spike in the incidence of black lung disease, the decline of the coal industry, and a decision made by Congress decades before that the fee supporting the fund would drop by half on December 31, 2018.

KFTC and its partners did not give up. Their work was on display in July 2019, when 150 miners, their family members, and community supporters organized a bus trip to Washington, DC, to advocate for action on black lung disease. Of the eleven KFTC members and staff who participated in this trip, eight were retired miners or were close family members of miners with black lung, all of whom were also active in the RECLAIM Act campaign.

A testament to the nonlinear and protracted nature of most power negotiations, the combined campaigns had not yet reached a denouement by the time we finished our study. In fact, KFTC organizers told us that they were entering a new, critical phase: in 2019, the RECLAIM Act (HR [House Resolution] 2156) was reintroduced by Representative Matt Cartwright of Pennsylvania, with Kentucky congressman Hal Rogers as an important cosponsor. The bill was passed by the House Natural Resources Committee after a hearing in March 2019, and then was passed by the full House. Meanwhile, a bill to restore and extend funding for the Black Lung Disability Trust Fund (HR 3876) was introduced four months later. KFTC and its allies continue to organize and press for these measures to pass the House this year, setting up a major push to pressure Senator McConnell for support in 2020.

EXTENSION CASE: NEVADA

The anchor organization in the Nevada case is the Progressive Leadership Alliance of Nevada (PLAN), now led by Laura Martin as its executive director. The founder and now development director of PLAN is Bob Fulkerson. PLAN is a multi-issue, statewide umbrella organization that was founded in 1994 to advocate for a progressive agenda within the state. In 2015, PLAN participated in a campaign to pass the first statewide corporate-profits tax bill in Nevada, with proceeds from the bill dedicated to funding education and social services throughout the state. We included PLAN as an extension case because the organization began with a focus on environmental justice and matured to form a coalition that spans labor and other issues, thus bridging issue domains that are normally siloed in progressive politics. We wanted to understand the practices PLAN used to build these bridges.

In 1994, twelve progressive organizations in the state of Nevada joined to establish PLAN and create a single united force that could advocate for social and environmental justice. PLAN comprises a variety of different citizen-advocate groups, unions, and nongovernmental organizations (NGOs). Its member organizations represent anti-poverty activists, children's advocates, environmentalists, LGBTQ organizations, labor unions, racial-justice groups, and feminist organizations. Since its creation, PLAN has grown to represent over thirty advocate groups, unions, and NGOs in Nevada.

PLAN's initial goals focused on income equality and climate justice. Since 1994, PLAN has been organizing around water rights, and against nuclear waste disposal at Yucca Mountain, fracking, and transnational gold mining conglomerates. As part of this work, it has helped seed statewide environmental organizations. In addition, PLAN has always worked closely with labor groups to advocate for workers' rights and to address income inequality in the state.

As PLAN evolved, however, it developed a greater focus on racial justice and LGBTQ rights. Its leaders began to host "Dismantling Racism" workshops for its member organizations, encouraging environmental and other organizations that did not already have a racial-justice lens to develop one. This was part of a larger effort to identify, recruit, and develop the leadership of people of color throughout the state. As PLAN's leaders noted, their focus on issues of race was like a "waterfall." As PLAN recruited more people of color, especially immigrants, into the organization, the recruits brought friends and family members into the cohort, thereby widely diversifying the organization's base and leadership structure. Likewise, PLAN evolved to become a powerful advocate for LGBTQ rights in the state, recruiting its member organizations and other allies to support trans rights and other issues that had not traditionally been the purview of some of these organizations.

To support this coalition work, PLAN collects membership dues from its member organizations. In turn, PLAN offers these organizations access to resources, including some funding, training, volunteer leaders, and coalitional opportunities. In addition, member organizations have the opportunity to vote in PLAN's leadership elections, including elections for the board of directors. This setup allows PLAN to remain a self-governing organization with elected leadership.

PLAN runs a number of different campaigns, and observers of Nevada politics often think it anchors the radical left in the state. Nonetheless, despite a willingness to take what are sometimes perceived as ideologically extreme stances, PLAN also engages in a number of campaigns that have broader support. For instance, its work around the corporate-profits tax bill exemplifies the value of these kinds of coalition bridges.

Shortly before midnight on June 2, 2015, minutes before the last day of the legislative session ended, the Republican-controlled Nevada state senate voted in favor of the state's first-ever corporate-profits tax bill, allocating approximately $1.5 billion to education and human services in Nevada. Anti-tax conservatives had lobbied aggressively against the measure. Nonetheless, after what Republican Senate Majority leader Michael Roberson called "very hard work," Republicans also joined the vote. Republican state senator Joe Hardy called the deal "monumental," arguing that it showed that Republicans "can vote for a tax . . . and still get reelected" (Chereb and Whaley 2015).

This dramatic day of dealmaking represented the climax of a decades-long effort by a progressive coalition of PLAN, the Culinary Union, and other advocates. As PLAN wrote in a grant application in 2015, "Our communications and field efforts over the past two decades have helped reframe the debate in Nevada on corporate taxes. We helped create a new imperative in Nevada where even the Chamber of Commerce agreed new revenues must be found to fund education."

These victories in 2015 and 2016 were not preordained. In 2015, Republicans swept state offices, winning unified control of the governorship and both houses of the legislature. It was under these circumstances that the education spending bill and the 2016 victories took place. From a demographic standpoint, although Nevada is a state that is likely to be majority minority within the next decade, constituencies of color have little voice in the political system, lacking infrastructure to support them (including access to the vote). Nevada has the highest percentage of undocumented immigrants and the largest share of undocumented workers in the country. In 2000, Nevada ranked forty-seventh in the nation in terms of per capita density of civic organizations.

However, even in this environment, PLAN and Culinary Union 226 worked in alliance with each other and other grassroots groups to build capacity among immigrants and communities of color in the state. Their continued ability to bring grassroots pressure to bear on electoral and issue campaigns in Nevada helped them forge a close relationship with Democratic state-party leaders, including elected officials like Harry Reid. The ability of this coalition to engage traditionally marginalized communities, develop leadership within those constituencies, and leverage its grassroots infrastructure to elect its chosen leaders to office and to hold them and other policy makers accountable made PLAN worthy of study.

Limitations

We aimed to select cases and analyze the data in a way that would provide some analytic leverage in generating propositions about how these organizations build power. Nonetheless, our design has inevitable limitations, which we discuss here.

QUESTIONS OF CAUSALITY

First and perhaps most importantly, while we work carefully to describe and make visible the ways each of the selected organizations built power, we cannot definitely and precisely estimate the size of the causal impact these organizations had in any one case. All of these groups are working on complex issues in a contingent ecosystem of civic and political actors, and isolating the causal impact of any one organization in a given campaign is nearly impossible.

For example, consider New Virginia Majority's effort to restore voting rights to returning citizens in Virginia. Governor McAuliffe likely had many reasons for re-enfranchising the state's formerly incarcerated population, only some of which related to NVM's work. For one thing, because the state's electoral laws do not allow governors to serve consecutive terms, he was not up for reelection and would therefore not have to face the wrath of the GOP (Grand Old Party), which had put up a vociferous fight against the rights-restoration effort. Moreover, Virginia is a swing state, 2016 was an election year, the governor's close ally Hillary Clinton was on the presidential ballot, and the majority of those who would benefit from the policy shift were people of color who tend to vote Democratic. Qualitative case-study research nearly always lends itself to alternative explanations like these. Thus, like previous scholars in this tradition, we want to clearly acknowledge that all of the political outcomes discussed in this book are not reducible to social-movement activity alone but rather result from a constellation of forces that act on the proximate decision makers—voters, legislators, or other elites—which challenger groups do not directly control.

To address these concerns, scholars make an effort to appraise counterfactuals, trace causal pathways, identify mechanisms, and assess the evidence relative to the predictions of existing theory. In many of our cases, longitudinal within-case comparisons proved helpful. In Ohio, for instance, we can compare the pledge-drive campaign Greg ran to the one run by AMOS. Comparative historical research is also possible in the Virginia case. A set of factors and motivations similar to those experienced by McAuliffe had been present for Democrat and former civil-rights attorney Tim Kaine, for instance, who was governor of Virginia during the 2008 election but did not yield to the rallies, emails, and letter-writing campaigns that urged him to restore the rights of former felons before he left office. New Virginia Majority was a brand-new organization at that point. In fact, it was Republican governor Bob McDonnell—with whom NVM worked closely and whose party did not stand to gain as much electorally—who took the first major step on the policy by automating rights restoration for nonviolent offenders who had completed their sentence and paid all fines, fees, and restitution. As Tram observed,

> I actually credit Governor McDonnell for doing more for voting rights restoration outside of Terry [McAuliffe]. Everything that he did, and everything that we pushed him on, he did in a way that paved the way for Governor McAuliffe to do what we did. . . . When McDonnell first took office, we had a long application for people who needed their rights back. And so, through pressure and through conversations, a thirteen-page application became a five-page application. What used to be a requirement that people had to get letters of references, a moral letter—he did away with all of that. That's what I'm saying, we peeled back layer after layer, requirement after requirement after requirement—and that all started with Bob McDonnell.

Such historical comparisons between similarly situated political actors give us more confidence that AMOS and NVM were central actors in driving forward their associated campaigns. At the same time, however, we recognize that we cannot claim precise causality.

Instead of being dissuaded by the difficulty of specifying causation, we hope that study of these organizations provides insight on key questions about the everyday practice of democracy. Even though we are unable to define the direct causal impact of these groups, our sense is that their ongoing work in the democratic politics of the United States and around the world renders them important subjects of study. There are so many advocates who are constantly making strategic choices about how to act within our political system, and generating the resources to do so, and that is valuable to look at. Our data do not allow us to weigh in on debates about whether social movements are generally influential (Baumgartner and Mahoney 2005) or not (Burstein and Sausner 2005; Giugni, McAdam, and Tilly 1999). Our six cases do, however, permit insight into *how* such organizations might alter power deficits in ways not typically observed by existing methods.

EXTERNAL VALIDITY: THINKING ABOUT OTHER TYPES OF ORGANIZATIONS

How much can our cases say about other organizations? Are our findings generalizable? We study a particular kind of constituency-based organization and cannot make precise claims about whether and how these findings are valid for other kinds of organizations. There are certain characteristics that distinguish the organizations we study from other political groups.

First, the organizations in our study are all focused on collective action and people power as a pathway to social and political change. This distinguishes them from nonprofits where the primary goal is service provision. It also distinguishes them from many organizations focused on "social enterprise," where the goals often do not entail structural change (Ganz, Kay, and Spicer 2018). Thus, our argument about the strategic value of prisms may not apply to organizations that do not seek to build power in the same way.

Second, the organizations we study are all focused, in some way, on making change through state institutions. Although they operate in different political arenas (some are working on electoral campaigns while others are working on ballot initiatives, for instance) and at different levels (some are working at the municipal level while others work at the statewide level), they are all seeking to influence political outcomes. This distinguishes them from movements like #MeToo that are focused more on cultural change and thus have distinct theories of power. However, according to previous research, this focus on the state puts our organizations in line with most other protest movements. Walker, Martin, and McCarthy find that the vast majority of protests target the state and that "corporate-targeted protest is more likely to occur when the state is less sympathetic to public concerns about business" (2008, 54). Even movements that are focused exclusively on cultural or corporate change often have shifting goals that eventually focus on the state in some form.

Third, the organizations that we study are engaged primarily in offline organizing. This characteristic raises questions about the extent to which our cases are relevant in the digital world of the twenty-first century. All of these organizations have online components to the work they do, but none of them can be regarded as "digital-first" groups. We did not necessarily intend that our case studies would share this trait, but when we approached the case-selection process described above, this is the type of organization that emerged. Given the research about the challenges that digital movements face in building power, perhaps this is no accident (Tufekci 2017). Nonetheless, in the concluding chapter, we consider the extent to which these findings apply to digital-first organizations. In short, our sense is that the basic principles would apply across different technological media, but the mechanisms through which they do so might vary.

Finally, the organizations we examine are all based in the United States and are working on the left. Prior research on constituent-based organizing on the right (McGirr 2002; LaCombe, forthcoming; Skocpol and Williamson 2012; Skocpol, Williamson, and Hertel-Fernandez 2015; Teles 2010) provides some sense that the core logic of prisms—namely the idea that building constituencies that exhibit loyalty over time will enable an organization to better exercise power in the political domain—is consistent across the ideological spectrum. However, it is quite likely that the practices used to generate loyalty are distinct, given the varying ideological agendas. In addition, varied cultural contexts likely affect the way these practices are implemented. Nonetheless, given prior research on other national contexts, we argue that the core logic of prisms of people power may be consistent beyond the United States (Giugni and Grasso 2019; Anselm et al. 2019; Rasmussen and Reher 2019; Rasmussen, Reher, and Toshkov 2019; McKenna forthcoming). Future research should verify the validity of these claims outside our set of cases.

Defining a Research Agenda

Given the limitations, we see this as an agenda-setting and theory-building project that generates a set of propositions about how these organizations work. Further research is needed to deepen the propositions, understand their underlying mechanisms, and examine some of the causal questions inherent in our argument. Beyond that, we see our findings making several specific contributions to research in political science and sociology. First, the study opens up the black box of constituency-based organizations to illuminate whether and how the factors over which these groups have agentic control relate to their ability to shift power over time. In conducting this study, we hope to reinvigorate an older tradition of political science research on political organizations and their relevance to democratic outcomes (e.g., Wilson 1973). In addition, by focusing on the way internal organizational capabilities affect an organization's ability to achieve its goals, we seek to integrate insights from different disciplines, including sociology, political science, and management. Finally, we hope to deepen our understanding of how participation translates to voice for the individuals taking action.

Looking beyond the academic literature and from a practical standpoint, we hope the book will provide actionable research, research that can inform the strategic choices organizers make as they navigate the uncertain political terrain that defines the present state of US democracy, better enabling them to take action that builds voice for ordinary people.

Our case selection gives us the analytic leverage to examine patterns that emerge across outlying cases of powerful collective action. We know the success of collective action is unusual in contemporary democracy; is it also idiosyncratic? Using a most-different case-selection method, we sought to select cases in a way that would allow us to elucidate whether there were any consistent patterns across them. An additional ambiguity remains, however: How do we know whether the organizations in our cases actually built power? Our argument rests on the idea that they did. Yet, how can we examine this power?

3 *Defining and Measuring Power*

Here's the interesting thing that happens when you're president. . . . So, you start [as] a community organizer, and you're struggling to try to get people to recognize each other's common interests and you're trying to get some project done in a small community, you start thinking, "Ok, you know what? This alderman's a knucklehead, they're resistant to doing the right thing, and so I need to get more knowledge, more power, more influence, so that I can really have an impact." And so you go to the state legislature, and you look around and you say, "Well these jamokes"—not all of them, but I'm just saying you start getting this sense that this is just like dealing with the alderman. So, "Nah, I got to do something different." Then you go to the US Senate and you're looking around and you're like, "Aw man!" And then when you're president, you're sitting in these international meetings, and it's like the G20 and you got all these world leaders, and it's the same people . . . the same dynamics. It's just that there's a bigger spotlight, there's a bigger stage. . . . The nature of human dynamics does not change from level to level. . . . The way power works at every level, at the United Nations or in your neighborhood, is, "Do you have a community that stands behind what you stand for?" And if you do, you'll have more power. And if you don't, you won't.

FORMER PRESIDENT BARACK OBAMA, NOVEMBER 2018

Reflecting on his experiences as the president of the United States, a United States senator, an Illinois state senator, and a community organizer, Obama argues that "at every level" the key question to ask regarding one's own power is the question of constituency: "Do you have a community that stands behind what you stand for? . . . If you do, you'll have more power. And if you don't, you won't." In Obama's analysis, people become a source of power when they "stand behind" a leader negotiating for something.

Obama's analysis speaks to essential questions about collective action and how it gets translated into political power. Most fundamentally, what does it mean for a community to "stand behind" a leader? If we shift Obama's analysis of political power away from the context of elected officials and apply it to the context of organizations, a distinct set of questions emerges. How do community leaders gain access to the higher-level negotiations? Unlike the president of the United States, who is invited to the G20 summit because of the authority granted by his office, leaders of grassroots organizations are not automatically granted seats at any decision-making table. How do they obtain and hold onto those seats? And how do they use them?

These questions are at the heart of the analysis in this book. How do leaders translate collective action into political power—or not? How do they build a community that stands behind them, and then wield the power of that community in political negotiations? Most previous work in this arena—as well as common assumptions in the public sphere—assumes that the central challenge of collective action is to generate numbers: How do leaders overcome problems like free riding to get more people to take more action? The more people a leader like Obama has standing behind him, the more powerful he will be. We extend this work to further probe the meaning of "stand behind." A community that stands behind a leader does not just vote, rally, or march once. When Obama was negotiating with aldermen, state senators, US senators, or international leaders, he had to have confidence that his base would remain loyal over time. Understanding this logic illuminates additional pathways through which collective action can become powerful.

This chapter outlines how we made power shifts visible across our four core cases. Our strategy for identifying power rests on a definition of political power that examines how it is (a) interactional and dynamic, as opposed to static, and (b) present at multiple levels. Power is not only about winning elections or passing policies; it is also about getting a seat at the decision-making table, shaping the terms of the debate, and impacting the underlying narratives that determine the way people interpret and understand political issues. Given the dynamic and multifaceted nature of power, taking a unitary approach to measuring it across all of our cases made little sense. Instead, we developed context-sensitive approaches to making visible how power shifted in our cases.

"As a Citizen, I Didn't Feel Whole"

In 1902, state delegates gathered for the Virginia Constitutional Convention and proclaimed their intent to suppress the black vote. Representative R. L. Gordon put it bluntly: "I told the people of my county before they sent me here that I intended . . . to disenfranchise every negro that I could disenfranchise . . . and as few white people as possible" (Ford 2016). With support from the press—the *Richmond Dispatch* characterized the state's postbellum constitution as "that miserable apology to organic law which was forced upon Virginians by carpetbaggers, scalawags, and Negroes supported by Federal bayonets" (Heinemann et al. 2007, 276)—delegates ratified a constitution that permanently disenfranchised Virginians with felony convictions. Because the carceral state has always disproportionately targeted African Americans, stripping former offenders of the right to vote was and is one of the many tools used to disenfranchise the black population in Virginia and, indeed, across the United States.[1]

The Virginia constitution laid a foundation defining voting rights in the state that persisted throughout the twentieth century. By 2014, Virginia tied Kentucky as the two states with the highest disenfranchisement rate in the nation, and was one of only four states that permanently rescinded the political rights of former felons (Gibson 2015; Brennan Center 2018). Its constitution did, however, grant the governor the authority to restore the right to vote to individuals on a case-by-case basis. Between 1938 and 2014, Virginia governors used that authority sparingly, restoring voting rights to a combined total of 22,367 people over a seventy-six-year period (Fiske 2016). This number represented a small fraction of the total number of people disenfranchised. In 2014, advocates for criminal-justice reform estimated that 6.1 million Americans were disenfranchised by such laws, including nearly one in five black residents of Virginia, the nation's first slave state (Uggen, Larson, and Shannon 2016).

In August 2016, more than a century after the 1902 convention, Virginia governor Terry McAuliffe stood outside the capitol building where the state's constitution had been ratified. McAuliffe declared that he had individually restored the rights of more than thirteen thousand formerly incarcerated Virginians, more than half the number of people whose rights had been restored over a seventy-six-year period.[2] As he made the announcement, he stood in front of—but seemed overshadowed by—a civil-rights memorial. "It seemed like reaching for the moon," read the granite inscription above McAuliffe, a quote from legendary civil-rights organizer Barbara Johns, whose bronze statue had been cast in a defiant stance. Virginia's rights-restoration effort was part of the largest voter-registration drive in state history. By 2018, the McAuliffe administration had helped restore the franchise to 173,000 returning citizens. In an interview, the data director of Virginia's Civic Engagement Table called attention to the "unprecedented [number] of registrations" that had resulted from the rights-restoration campaign. It was unprecedented "both in raw numbers and percentage-wise," he continued, "outside of, like, women getting the right to vote when suddenly you doubled your eligible population. I think that's . . . something that will pay dividends for a long time."

By most accounts, New Virginia Majority and its coexecutive director Tram Nguyen were two of the key forces behind the rights-restoration campaign. At the organization's tenth-anniversary gala in February 2017, we witnessed NVM's other coexecutive director, Jon Liss, thank the "allies, elected officials, cabinet officials, and folks who'd organized thousands of voters" who filled one of the historic John Marshall ballrooms in downtown Richmond. Jamaa Bickley King, NVM's board chair, and his father—grandson and son, respectively, of the civil-rights attorney Oliver Hill, who helped overturn the "separate but equal" doctrine—presented the organization's inaugural Oliver W. Hill Freedom Award to McAuliffe for doing what Jon called the "difficult, unprecedented, but right thing." In McAuliffe's acceptance speech, he referred to NVM leaders on a first-name basis. The same thing happened at a national meeting of major Democratic Party donors nine months later. The meeting we observed took place just after the off-year elections, in which Democrat Ralph Northam was chosen to succeed McAuliffe as governor of Virginia. Occurring in the first major race after Trump's victory in 2016, Northam's election was a significant win for Democrats. At this gathering of some of the nation's biggest Democratic donors, governor-elect Northam videoconferenced into the meeting. After a rousing introduction and hearty round of applause, Northam began by saying, "The first thing I want to say is hi and thank you to Jon and Tram [the leaders of New Virginia Majority]." In the presence of enormous Democratic wealth and a collection of people who were undoubtedly donors to Northam's campaign, it was significant that NVM got the first shout-out.

It was not only NVM's allies who recognized the organization's leadership in voting rights and its political muscle, however. The same conservative newspaper that had reported on the 1902 convention (now called the *Richmond Times-Dispatch*) submitted a Freedom of Information Act request for McAuliffe's records related to re-enfranchisement of returning citizens after he issued a blanket restoration of voting rights. Local newspapers reported the revelations. One lede read, "When Gov. Terry McAuliffe announced that he was restoring the political rights of about 206,000 felons, it came as no surprise to New Virginia Majority, which had fliers already printed encouraging would-be voters to register immediately. The progressive activist group got an official invite days ahead of the April 22 news conference and Tram Nguyen, the group's co-executive director, had more than three weeks' notice that the order was coming" (Zullow and Moomaw 2016). Much of NVM's reputation came through its electoral work. The organization successfully filed 148,025 voter-registration cards in the 2016 electoral cycle, 1,524 of which were collected by a fifty-four-year-old NVM organizer.[3] Of the people this organizer registered, about eight hundred were formerly incarcerated citizens. "As an ex-felon, myself, I couldn't vote and I didn't feel—as a citizen I didn't feel whole," he said. "I was paying taxes. I had to follow laws, and I had no say in what these laws were." One man he had helped register had been convicted of a felony in the 1950s for stealing a chicken. "What they have done with mass incarceration, and by putting a felony on us [black men] every chance they got, is that they have froze us out of most of the world," the NVM organizer said. "They've created an underclass." In 2016, he voted for the first time in his life.

In this case, as in our other cases, we argue that NVM was able to achieve a visible victory—rights restoration for returning citizens—in a way that not only secured a policy win but also shifted the underlying power dynamics in Virginia. NVM did so by putting the organization and its leaders into relationship with power players, including the state's current and former governors. How do we make such shifts in power visible? Although many would agree that power shifts are often the goal of most collective action, making that power visible in consistent, measurable ways is no easy task. However, the research design and the arguments we developed as a result of it depended on our ability to assess whether power actually moved. Did the organizations in our study shift power in the ways that we are claiming?

What Is Power?

Our argument about why prisms are helpful for understanding power building begins with a definition of power that focuses on its dynamic and somewhat elusive nature. In defining power, we focus on two key attributes: (a) power is expressed as the interactional relationship between (at least) two political actors, and (b) power has, as theorist Steven Lukes argues, multiple faces, some of which are largely obscured from immediate view (Lukes 2005; Gaventa 1982; Pierson 2015). This approach to understanding power builds on multiple research traditions, including work on social-movement outcomes (Amenta et al. 2010; Giugni, McAdam, and Tilly 1999), a strain of which argues that a movement achieves power (or influence) when it alters the pattern of interests its targets use to make strategic choices (Luders 2010). Power is not a static good that organizations obtain; instead, it is expressed in relationships that constantly change as the context changes, because it is dependent on a dynamic and situational relationship between an organization and the interests of political decision makers. To obtain power, organizations must negotiate for it (Hansen 1991).

If power is dynamic, our theories must account for contingency. On the one hand, the importance of contingency in collective action may seem to be a facile point. Yet, on the other hand, scholars and practitioners alike systematically underestimate it (Staggenborg 2016; Ganz 2000; Tarrow 1998; Morris and Staggenborg 2004; Voss 1998; Morris 2000).[4] Often, our scholarly and practical analyses assume that resources—such as people or money—can be equated to power. The more supporters, voters, money, or expertise an organization has, the more power it has, this thinking goes. From a practical perspective, this means that the goal for constituency-based organizations is to aggregate as many of these resources as possible, summing the actions of individuals to form a winning majority.[5] From a scholarly perspective, this means that empirical models often use the relationship between resources (or head counts) and political outcomes as a proxy for impact (Vasi et al. 2015; Mackin 2016; Madestam et al. 2013; McVeigh 2009). Significant coefficients that describe the relationship between organizational activity (or characteristics) and outcomes thus become evidence of impact, even though they could mean many different things (Andrews 2001).

Empirical analyses and history alike show, however, that numerical majorities or simple accumulations of material resources are not always equivalent to power. In fact, research shows there is no linear relationship between any given resource and political power, whether that resource is numbers of people, amount of money, or intensity of adherents (Baumgartner et al. 2009; Hojnacki et al. 2012). Analyses of lobbying and social movement activity underscore the importance of organizations and leaders in strategically translating collective action—even collective action at scale—into political power (see, e.g., Clemens 1997; Ganz 2009; Hansen 1991). Just as we can point to data showing that having more people, more passionate people, or more people distributed across strategically identified locations was associated with movement influence (e.g., Madestam et al. 2013; Gillion 2013), we can point to numerous situations in which simply amassing resources was not enough to enact the change activists sought (e.g., Skocpol 2013; Ganz 2009).

In addition, constituencies of color and low-income constituencies face even more contingency because of the structural barriers impeding their bids for power. Poor people, constituencies of color, people at the intersection of multiple marginalized groups, and others have always had to struggle for recognition and legitimacy in politics, thus making their attempts to seek power more uncertain (e.g., Gillion 2013; García Bedolla and Michelson 2012; Piven and Cloward 1977; Piven 2006). These are the constituencies that are the focus of our study. In our cases, organizers like Jeff, Michele, Tomás, and Alex who work with low-income constituencies of color knew their bids for political power would be ignored or met with pushback, even from presumed allies. Expecting such reactions, they developed alternative strategies for collective action that prepared for the unpredictability of politics.

MEASURING THE OUTCOMES OF COLLECTIVE ACTION

In both academic scholarship and the world of practice, methods for assessing power range broadly. At one level, those interested in assessing power disagree about *what* should actually be measured. In other words, how should we conceptualize the outcomes of collective action? What does it mean for collective action to be successful?

Past efforts to assess social-movement outcomes include (but are not limited to) examining the visible policy gains or electoral campaigns an organization or movement can win (Uba 2009; Amenta et al. 2010; Andrews 2004); assessing the extent to which movements and organizations can influence agendas or dominant narratives (Polletta and Ho 2006); cataloging organizations' ability to develop capacities or resources (such as large numbers of people) known to make long-term policy wins more likely (McCarthy and Zald 2001); and tracing how organizations shift public opinion or media content (Ferree et al. 2002; Ferree 2003; Gottlieb 2015). These outcomes are often challenging to obtain (let alone demonstrate), and past scholarship has shown that collective action only rarely has direct effects on policy (Olzak and Ryo 2007; Giugni 1998; Burstein and Freudenburg 1978; Amenta, Caren, and Olasky 2005) in part because "there is so little of it" (Burstein and Sausner 2005, 413).[6]

Of course, movements do more than just win concrete policy and electoral victories. They can also influence broader cultural attitudes. For example, one undocumented leader in Arizona told us,

> I had a Lyft driver not long ago, and he came to drop me off and he's like, "Hey, your street isn't that lit up." And he was from like, I don't know, some other state, he had just moved here. And I was like, "Well it seems fine to me—what are you talking about?" And so that's kind of like an example of like, where it seems so normal to me because I grew up and I lived in those kinds of neighborhoods my whole life. But to someone from the outside they're like, "This

is not normal, why don't you have more light on your streets?" And then you wonder [about other things:] the crime rate and potholes or [why it] flood[s] when it rains. Our neighborhood streets are flooded and that's not going to happen in another place like Scottsdale. Their streets are not flooded there when it rains.

So, systems are in place to just maintain or, keep sorting the communities just to the side. You have the war on drugs that fuels the school-to-prison pipeline, and then you blame the kids that are in school for behaving badly ... that's been playing since the 70s, the late 60s, and it all goes back to like, what was there before? With immigration, the system [is] broken but also ... is it really broken? It [didn't] stop working the way that it's supposed to, with private prisons and the privatization of the whole process. Who's really benefiting from that? ... And then you get into it and you realize, "Man, it is working exactly the way that it was meant to be all along instead of actually solving a problem."

This leader was describing a denaturalization of her worldview, a recasting of what she believed was possible. The transformation she describes in her understanding of the world, repeated throughout a constituency and diffused into the broader public through social networks, cultural narratives, and sometimes art (Isaac 2008), is a crucial part of the power shift that can emerge from collective action. These shifts are very difficult to measure, but that difficulty does not make them any less significant.

At another level, there is also a debate about not only what should be measured but also how to measure it. Even if we were to imagine a world in which scholars agreed on the conceptual outcomes of collective action, they would still debate how best to measure those outcomes. This question of measurement is bedeviled by the fact that power operates in complex ways, often hidden from immediate view (Pierson 2015; Lukes 2005). Passing a policy or winning a campaign is a clear, measurable outcome. Beyond these visible victories, which are often the culmination of very long campaigns, how do we assess the extent to which a movement is making progress on its goals? How do we assess whether it has influenced agendas or developed the resources it needs? Scholars of social movements, interest groups, and other related forms of collective action have used a range of proxies for measuring "success" in the context of collective action, such as access to decision makers (e.g., Hansen 1991), scale of actions (e.g., Gillion 2013), media coverage (e.g., Earl et al. 2004), shifts in public opinion (e.g., Lee 2002), and self-reports (Han et al. 2011).[7]

In designing this study, we were eager to move beyond the most visible signs of power to address the less visible but potentially more transformative means by which collective action can produce change (Amenta and Caren 2004). We wanted to draw on the richness made possible by an in-depth case study to develop clearer measures of power shifts in the cases we examined. Each of the organizations in our study, for instance, took credit for at least one visible win in the form of a policy changed, an ally elected, or an adversary defeated. How could we tell whether those visible victories were one-offs or whether they reflected a broader, underlying power shift?

Because the approach we developed rests on the premise that power operates in ways that are both relational and often invisible (Gaventa 1982; Lukes 2005; Pierson 2015), we had to move away from examining power as a static trait or characteristic that any one organization can possess. Instead, the extent to which an organization has power is dependent on whether it has resources that can act on and shape a target's interests. In practical terms, organizations commonly define targets as the individuals who have the power to make decisions that can enact the change the organizations seek (Bobo, Kendall, and Max 2010; Ganz 2018b). Targets have interests that propel them to act in or against the interests of the advocate. We conceptualize the work of movement building as a process of attempting to shape the interests of the target in a way that makes them more supportive of the organization's stated interests (Luders 2010; Warren 2001).

However, the factors that shape a target's interests are not always obvious. Although we can empirically observe things like whether a target chooses to vote a certain way (such as an elected official's vote on a bill), there are many other, less visible factors that influence that choice. First, what alternatives were available to the elected official? What determined which alternatives were available? Would the elected official have made the same choice given a different set of alternatives? In addition, how did cultural factors, narratives about how the world works, or assumptions the target makes about what is possible affect their choice? In this framework, power may reasonably be analogized to an iceberg: we see only the topmost portion protruding from the water, while most of its mass remains submerged.

Taking these conceptualizations of power seriously implies that power is (a) interactional and relational and (b) largely obscured from immediate view. To study the extent to which an organization achieves political power, then, we must understand who the target is, what the interests of that target are, and how those interests shift—or not—over time. To assess these questions, we build on research that looks beyond firsthand accounts of social-movement actors to examine their interaction with targets.

We particularly draw on an interactional theory of social-movement influence developed by Joseph Luders (2010) in which success is measured as a function of the costs that challengers impose on their targets. Luders states, "The core argument is simple: the target of any social movement, interest organization, or other benefit-seeker must discern the threat posed to its interests and the cost of capitulating to demands, and then respond accordingly. A mugger's declaration, 'Your money or your life,' succinctly depicts a similar cost calculation" (2010, xi). Luders's framework, which we adopt and expand on, estimates influence not only by the ultimate outcome but also by the extent to which movement actors changed the cost calculations of their targets. These changing cost calculations rendered targets more or less likely to concede to constituency demands.

As we unpacked the work of the groups in our case studies, we observed underlying shifts in the strategic calculations of targets, similar to what Luders describes. Not only were these organizations able to generate concessions related to the state (winning visible policy gains or elections), they also altered other observable factors. We analyze these here along three dimensions: network surveys measuring shifts in power relationships, analyses of the legislative agenda measuring the range of the politically possible, and text-as-data tools to measure shifts in narrative.

Instead of trying to develop a one-size-fits-all approach to measuring power in each case, we tried to develop an approach that shared conceptual commonalities but varied measures based on the specific conditions in each case. The conceptual commonalities revolved around an approach to assessing power that focused on its interactional nature and the extent to which it operates at varying levels of visibility. Each of our core case studies, however, varied in terms of who the targets were and what sorts of invisible power shifts they were trying to effect. Our measures thus reflect that variance.

WHO ARE THE TARGETS?

Because we take an interactional approach to measuring political power, our investigation must begin with the targets. How do we identify them? What are their interests? And how can we observe whether their behavior or their interests change over time? We learned early in the interview process that it is easy to mistake the target of a power-building campaign. Relying at first on news reports and publicly available data, we sometimes misidentified who our case organizations were trying to influence. Across our cases, we found that the obvious and staunch opposition—GOP leaders in Virginia determined to preserve felon disenfranchisement, sheriff's deputies raiding immigrant communities in Arizona, anti-tax Tea Party groups in Ohio, and anti-immigrant legislators in Minnesota—were rarely the actors with whom movement leaders directly negotiated power.

Instead, the organizations' true targets were often other actors involved in the case who, at first glance, appeared to be allies with shared interests. This is due in no small part to the fact that all of the organizations in our case studies were representing either low-income constituencies or constituencies of color, or both. In other words, they were representing constituencies that are structurally disadvantaged in our political system and, as previous research shows, often marginalized even within progressive coalitions and organizations (Strolovitch 2007; Blee 2012; Phillips 2016). A key challenge for the organizations in our case studies, in other words, was to get into strategic alignment with other dominant progressive actors so that they could draw on more shared resources. These actors often included labor unions, the Democratic Party establishment, and progressive funders—groups that controlled many of the financial means, communication tools, and other resources the organizations in our cases wanted to access.

An example of the challenge of properly identifying targets emerges from our fieldwork in Arizona. When we first arrived at the offices of LUCHA, a relatively new immigrant rights organization in Phoenix, Tomás saw us take note of the padlocks on the building and on all of the organization's file cabinets. He explained that LUCHA doesn't advertise its address, because the organization has been harassed by opponents. For instance, roughly ten Trump supporters once heckled LUCHA volunteers, guns in their waistbands. Another time, someone—they don't know who—tried to break in and steal sensitive immigration-related files. "I didn't think I was going to make it to our interview today," Tomás then said, "because I thought I was going to be in court all afternoon responding to Prop. 206 challengers." LUCHA, in other words, did not lack direct opponents. Initially, we conceptualized these opponents as their primary targets.

Over time, however, we realized that LUCHA was working to develop power not only relative to anti-immigration forces, but also, as we described in chapter 1, within the progressive political system. From LUCHA's perspective, the primary obstacle in the Proposition 206 campaign was not business owners, right-wing voters, or GOP legislators, but progressive gatekeepers. "We knew as soon as we got [Prop. 206] in front of voters they would love it," Tomás said. "The challenge was getting it on the ballot, and getting [progressive] funders to believe that we could do it. . . . Initially [labor groups] were not supportive of the initiative. They didn't wanna fund it, they didn't think we were capable, and they also didn't think it was strategic," he said. LUCHA had to fight for the right to lead the campaign that had materialized because of the demands of their base.

Thus Alex and Tomás preemptively organized all of their grassroots partners to go to a meeting with labor and philanthropy leaders to demand that Tomás lead the minimum wage campaign—raising the cost of their targets' continued opposition to their leadership. By organizing their allies in a united front to challenge funders, LUCHA won the ability to lead the campaign. Alex further noted, "We actually went up a lot against the funders, to ensure that we were able to bring organizers, and that this wasn't just a digital-funded media campaign."

In 2016, Proposition 206 passed with 58 percent of voters' support—the single highest vote getter on the ballot. When the campaign ended, the progressive allies who had initially opposed the work changed their narrative. One leader in the Proposition 206 campaign noted,

> There was a local labor group here that was tied to a grassroots organization here, that did not wanna support the campaign. And they did not support it financially, like one of the few unions that did not give any money, although the grassroots organization that they helped seed did eventually do some of the door knocks and really help us do the persuasion and turn out for the initiative. And so at that award ceremony, the president of the union stood up and said, "And we won the minimum wage." But they were completely dragging their feet on it, completely against it the whole time.

Upon hearing this story, another leader recalled his reaction: "I was like, 'These mofos.'" There was no love lost between LUCHA and some of the allies with whom they worked to pass Proposition 206. As LUCHA leaders looked back on the campaign, their analysis of the power they had built in the campaign was in relation to the groups who were, on paper, their partners—and not the anti-immigrant forces who opposed them outright. "I've kind of created an analogy," Tomás said. "It is muscles versus brains. In 2016 we were fighting hard to be brain-led operations, instead of just muscle—just have people go out and knock doors," he said. From the perspective of shifting long-term power, LUCHA recognized that the anti-immigrant forces in Arizona were just as strong as they had been in the past. Their invisible victory in 2016, however, was to be recognized as a strategic leader within the progressive coalition in the state.

Table 3.1 captures our assessment of the range of targets identified in each

Table 3.1. Case Study Target Identification

Case	Campaign(s) and Arena	Target(s)
Arizona	Municipal and house district elections; statewide ballot initative (Proposition 206)	Joe Arpaio, Russell Pearce, moderate state legislators, and state (Democratic Party) and national (philanthropic) networks
Minnesota	2018 primary and election (includes MN gubernatorial race and selected legislative and city-level races)	Candidates for office, especially Democratic gubernatorial candidates Erin Murphy and Tim Walz
Ohio	Municipal levy (Issue 44) to fund universal preschool and K–12 education	Business and philanthropic community in Cincinnati seeking to pass the levy
Virginia	State-level rights restoration for the formerly incarcerated	Governors Bob McDonnell and Terry McAuliffe; Democratic statehouse delegates

of our cases. As reflected in the "Target(s)" column of table 3.1, the movement leaders in our study did not engage in struggle only with actors whose interests were orthogonal to their own. As with Arizona, in each of our case studies the targets included not only outright opponents of the work each organization was seeking to accomplish but also the allies the organization was trying to engage. Leaders often focused their limited resources on brokering exchanges with these would-be partners—whom they sometimes considered targets—whose concessions could yield meaningful results for their constituencies. As Marshall Ganz notes, "Both 'power with' and 'power over' are at work in organizing. Members of a constituency can create the power to achieve a shared goal by collaborating to use their resources interdependently in ways they had not done before. . . . On the other hand, where real conflicts of interest exist, organizing requires a claims-making strategy, mobilizing constituency resources to alter relationships of dependency and domination" (2018b, 18). In other words, imperfect allies were important because bringing them on board opened up access to the broader pool of political resources that the organizations needed to advance their campaigns to challenge power asymmetries.

We used three main strategies to measure power: (1) network surveys, which depicted the relevant shifts in power relationships in Virginia and Ohio; (2) assessments of legislative data, which demonstrated the shifting political agenda in Arizona; and (3) text-as-data tools, which measured the changing narrative around race and immigration in Minnesota.

Networks of Power: "Power Respects Power"

Lukes argues that a significant element of what he calls the second face of power is who gets to set the agenda (2005). Who determines what issues are discussed, what is considered relevant on the political agenda, and the nature of viable options? For New Virginia Majority and AMOS, being in relationship with power brokers was a significant part of what they were seeking to achieve, because those power relationships would allow them to advance not only the immediate campaign goals (passing a ballot initiative for universal preschool in Cincinnati and restoring voting rights to formerly incarcerated citizens in Virginia) but also their constituencies' long-term issues of concern.

In the beginning of our investigation of each of these cases, we found that leaders in both NVM and AMOS discussed their long-term goals in terms of shifting that underlying power dynamic in their communities. NVM was seeking to influence legislators in the Virginia General Assembly. AMOS wanted to influence the network of power players in Cincinnati—the business, philanthropic, political, and civic leaders who controlled many of the city's resources. To examine the extent to which NVM and AMOS were each able to access and alter these networks of power, we conducted two network surveys. We also did semistructured interviews with targets in each case to help us better understand the results of these surveys.

AMOS

In our study of AMOS's work in Cincinnati, we wanted to know whether the visible victory AMOS helped achieve—the passage of Issue 44, a ballot initiative designed to provide universal preschool—shifted the underlying power dynamics in the city. As described in the previous chapter, the campaign had been going on for over a decade when AMOS got involved. City leaders had been pushing for universal preschool through a coalition and campaign called Cincinnati Preschool Promise (CPP) since the turn of the twenty-first century.

At the height of the campaign, CPP's membership included the leaders of the education nonprofit Strive Partnership, the United Way, Cincinnati Public Schools, the Cincinnati Federation of Teachers, national partners, many prominent leaders in the local business community, and independent preschool providers. When AMOS joined, it brought along its multifaith network of churches, mosques, and synagogues.

To evaluate AMOS's role in this power network, in 2018 we conducted a survey of nineteen key Cincinnati leaders who were involved in the preschool campaign. All but one completed the survey, yielding a 95 percent response rate. Our list of respondents included key business leaders, school officials (the district superintendent and school board members), philanthropists, the levy campaign manager, and faith and grassroots leaders who were mentioned in the interviews we conducted for the case study. We asked respondents to retrospectively identify the people they had been strategizing, exchanging resources, and negotiating conflict with at two different points in time. By comparing responses for 2013 and 2016, we observe AMOS's changing role in the coalition. When analyzed as a network graph, the survey results give us a sense of AMOS's relative power position, though the data may suffer from some of the biases inherent in all surveys that rely on respondent recall and self-reports. Nevertheless, they provide some evidence of who power players in Cincinnati thought were the key players on the campaign.

Figures 3.1a and 3.1b (p. 80) show the results from the network survey in which we asked people to name those they strategize with regarding education issues in the city. The key thing to note in these figures is the movement of Troy Jackson and key AMOS leaders from the edges of the network map in 2013 to its center in 2016. From figure 3.1a, we can see that in 2013, AMOS and its leaders were at the margins of this power network. At the time, Jackson ranked twelfth (out of eighteen) on a numerical measure of influence,[8] and was hardly mentioned as someone with whom people in the coalition strategized. Most of the people who named him as someone with whom they strategized in 2013 were clergy connected to AMOS.

The situation had changed by 2016, however, as shown in figure 3.1b. By this point, Troy had the highest score on our measure of influence within the strategizing network, matched only by the levy's campaign manager, the executive director of United Way's early-childhood initiative, and the recently elected city councilman who had initiated the ballot measure (Greg Landsman). By the end of the campaign in 2016, in other words, key business, political, philanthropic, educational, and other leaders in Cincinnati regarded Jackson as someone who was brokering the flow of strategy on a key education issue in the city.

The strategizing graph shows that by 2016 Jackson's level of influence in the network matched that of the city's traditional elite. Another set of graphs, figures 3.2a and 3.2b (p. 81), provides evidence that the source of his power is very different from theirs, a distinction we elaborate on in chapter 4. These figures show the shift in the network maps on the measure "negotiating conflict." Again, by 2016 Troy and other AMOS leaders had moved from the edges to the center of the graph. Figure 3.2a shows that in 2013, as with strategiz-

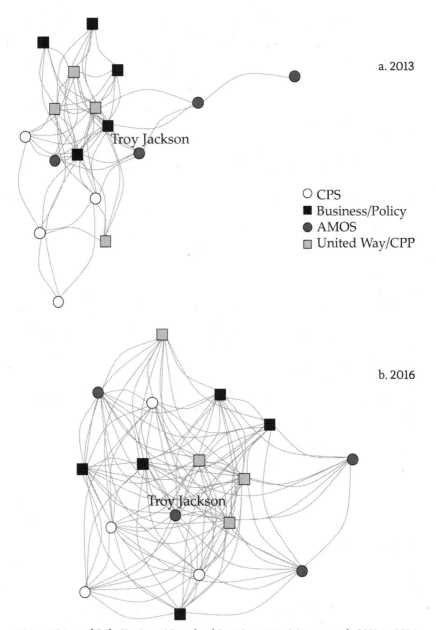

a. 2013

○ CPS
■ Business/Policy
● AMOS
■ United Way/CPP

Troy Jackson

b. 2016

Troy Jackson

Figures 3.1a and 3.1b. Cincinnati Preschool Promise strategizing network, 2013 vs. 2016. The graphs are based on data from a 2018 network survey of key leaders in Cincinnati regarding the people with whom they strategized around the preschool ballot initiative at two different points in time. All network maps were generated in R using the Igraph software package and the Fruchterman-Reingold layout, an algorithm that places nodes with more connections closer together.

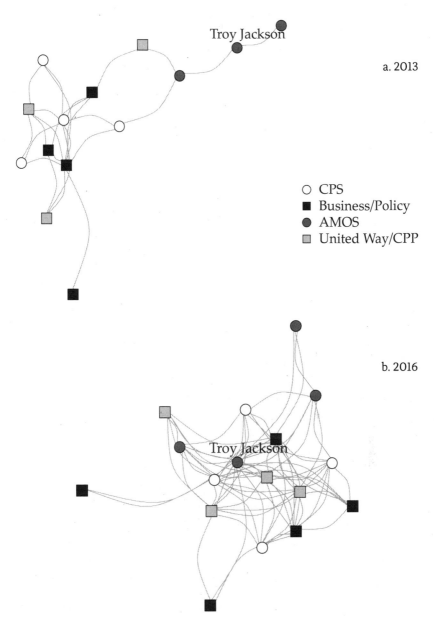

Figures 3.2a and 3.2b. Cincinnati Preschool Promise "negotiating conflict" network, 2013 vs. 2016.

The graphs are based on data from a 2018 network survey of key leaders in Cincinnati regarding the people with whom they negotiated conflict around the preschool ballot initiative at two different points in time.

ing, Troy was hardly named by any leaders as being a person with whom they negotiated conflict. Figure 3.2b shows that by 2016, in contrast, he was at the center of negotiating conflict within the coalition, as indicated by his location in the map.

Put together, the network graphs around strategizing and negotiating conflict show that, by 2016, Troy was at the center of the power networks in the CPP coalition. Importantly, his role was not to simply cede to the demands of the better-resourced business and philanthropic allies. Instead, he was constantly holding their "feet to the fire," as one interviewee put it, negotiating conflict around the campaign, and seeking to protect the interests of his constituency within the coalition.

When they joined the preschool coalition, AMOS leaders recognized the asymmetries in power between their constituency and the other members of the coalition. However, like LUCHA, they sought to articulate their base's desired outcomes before brokering an agreement with their coalition counterparts. AMOS's base decided to get involved in the effort to fund preschool for all Cincinnatians only after creating and publicly voting to ratify the People's Platform, the guiding statement of values about the kind of preschool policy AMOS and its constituents wanted.[9] AMOS members ratified the platform as an expression of their commitment to these principles.

The People's Platform was also a tool that allowed AMOS to be strategic in brokering its relationship with coalition partners—in other words, in negotiating conflict and disagreement with them. When AMOS's leaders perceived the coalition's commitment to the People's Platform to be wavering, they forced coalition leaders to answer to AMOS constituents. "There was enough of a feeling by the business leadership that they couldn't run roughshod over this because [AMOS] had already reached what they perceived to be a critical mass of [Cincinnati's] African American leadership, of the school community . . . they had tapped into a constituency that you wouldn't necessarily expect to get fired up but were captivated," a campaign leader told us.

Another interviewee with close ties to the business community said, "I don't think any of these big companies would want to be said about them that they were against the kids." This interviewee noted that Troy had the capability to rally "all the black ministers or the Jewish community—who are all the membership of AMOS. I mean you've got a pretty broad base and a powerful group there . . . and they could blast them, blast them, *blast* them and it would be a PR challenge for these companies." When we reflected this interviewee's sentiment back to Troy, he said it was "definitely hyperbole." Nonetheless, as Troy stated in a previous conversation, "Power respects power. . . . Bottom line is there was truth to the threat that if they did not respect us we would destroy [the ballot initiative]. We had that leverage. They saw that the threat was real." This power shift is visualized in the shift in network maps over time.

NEW VIRGINIA MAJORITY

In studying the work of the New Virginia Majority, we wanted to understand how the organization was able to position itself in the political arena relative to other organizations in the state. As mentioned above, NVM is co-led by Jon and Tram. Jon is an organizing expert who likes to read books about grassroots politics. Tram, by contrast, is an operative. She leads NVM's lobbying efforts in state government, and her short stature belies the attention she commands in a room. When we shadowed her in the state legislature, a colorful shawl adorned her shoulders as she maneuvered deftly through the halls, balancing multiple requests for attention from legislators seeking her help.

Nancy Rodrigues, a former cabinet official in the McAuliffe administration, said, "You know how sometimes advocacy groups can be their own worst enemy? I've seen it in so many settings where an advocacy group will start yelling or threaten, 'We are going to vote you out!'" By contrast, she continued, "[NVM] has been very professional in their delivery to the General Assembly. . . . 'It's just the fact, sir. It's just the facts.'" Then, Nancy said something we found striking: "I know that there are some people in the legislature right now who if Tram calls them up and says, 'I need you to carry this bill,' they probably wouldn't even ask what the bill is. They would just carry it because they have that kind of respect [for NVM]." This statement is similar to many others made by interviewees in the Virginia state government and by NVM's ally organizations.

How widespread are these sentiments, however? NVM claimed that the rights-restoration campaign helped build their statewide profile not only in McAuliffe's office but also among other elected officials. Do we have any evidence that this is true?

Rights restoration was not originally one of NVM's issues. As described in chapter 2, Tenants and Workers United focused initially on housing and labor issues in Northern Virginia. When Jon founded NVM, however, he joined a wave of statewide power-building organizations that grew up around the country in the early 2000s. As national politics became more gridlocked, organizations like NVM attempted to build stronger progressive bases in the states. Moving beyond local housing and labor issues, NVM sought to build constituency by canvassing in black communities around Virginia, focusing at first on just turning out the vote. As NVM was canvassing, however, it soon realized how many potential voters were unable to vote because the state had always disproportionately targeted black people for disenfranchisement. Thus, just as Troy decided to focus AMOS's efforts on childhood poverty and LUCHA chose to focus on minimum wage after each listened to and assimilated the demands of their bases, NVM pivoted from housing to rights restoration, giving or withholding its support for gubernatorial candidates depending on the public stance each candidate took during the campaign on the issue central to its constituents' interests. Terry McAuliffe won that race and vowed to make rights restoration a reality; NVM and its partners helped him make it so. Jon, Tram, and NVM were far from the only factors that enabled this restoration of rights, but their patient and strategic moves over the course of several years helped make it possible.

Curious whether we could corroborate interview data that spoke to NVM's influence in the statehouse—and hoping to better understand whether and how NVM wields power with respect to its Democratic targets—we designed a network survey, which we sent to all forty-nine Democrats serving in Virginia's 2018 General Assembly. We received twenty completed surveys, for a 40 percent response rate. Our cover letter to the delegates did not identify NVM as our research subject in order to avoid response bias that might favor certain answers over others. Instead, we requested delegates' participation "in a research project examining how grassroots and advocacy organizations interact with elected officials and exercise influence on behalf of their constituencies."

The first set of questions asked delegates to characterize the nature of their relationship with each of thirty-nine grassroots and advocacy organizations active in Virginia, along five dimensions: Had they (1) heard of them, (2) met with or exchanged information with them, (3) received electoral support from them, (4) strategized together directly or in coalition, or (5) experienced any form of opposition from them? We chose the organizations listed on the survey based on the responses of informants from multiple viewpoints (elected officials, progressive advocates in Virginia, and NVM organizers) who had identified influential grassroots organizations in the state.

As we expected, delegates indicated that they had "heard of" nearly all of the organizations in the survey. On these lower-barrier measures, we did not see much differentiation between the groups—delegates were as likely to have heard of New Virginia Majority as they were to have heard of groups with greater national name recognition, such as Planned Parenthood or Indivisible. We were more interested in the more intensive measures of movement-target interactions, such as the extent to which delegates indicated "strategizing with" a particular organization. Which organizations, in other words, were

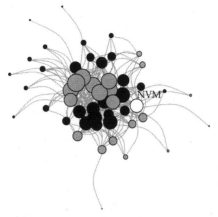

Figure 3.3. Virginia House delegate relationships with movement organizations on the measure "strategized together."

This figure is based on a survey of Democratic members of the Virginia General Assembly, collected in 2018, that asked about the organizations with whom they strategized. The node size is a function of the delegate or the organization's eigenvalue: the bigger the node, the higher the influence score (by this centrality measure).

Virginia state delegates planning about passing policy with? Figure 3.3 depicts the network map for responses to this survey item. The white dot highlights NVM's location in the graph; NVM is at the center with other delegates.

The graph shows that NVM was punching above its weight. Using a numerical score called an eigenvalue, which is a measure of a node's relative influence in a network (Bonacich 2007), we found that NVM had the fifth-highest score compared to all the other organizations. All four of the groups that had higher scores than NVM on this measure were national groups with state affiliates: the Sierra Club, Planned Parenthood, the League of Conservation Voters, and Virginia's teacher's union, a state affiliate of the National Education Association. By way of comparison, NVM was only ten years old, while the teacher's union was founded in 1863 and represents more than fifty thousand teachers throughout the Commonwealth.[10] Furthermore, three delegates reported that they only strategized with NVM and one or two other organizations listed in the survey.

NVM not only carries weight in the statehouse comparable to the weight

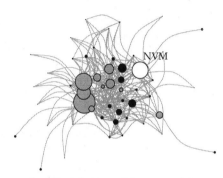

● Other Org
◉ Delegate
○ NVM

Figure 3.4. Brokerage network of Virginia House delegates and movement organizations on the measure "strategized together."
This figure is based on a survey of Democratic members of the Virginia General Assembly, collected in 2018, that asked about the organizations with whom they strategized. In this figure, nodes are weighted based on their betweenness centrality score, described in text.

carried by these national groups but also plays a brokerage role in the network. Our survey data show which groups help link, or create bridges between, delegates and organizations that did not otherwise share direct connections. On this centrality score, called "betweenness" because it measures the shortest path between nodes, NVM ranked higher than any other organization in the survey, a finding reflected in the size of its node, as shown in figure 3.4. The only two others in the survey with a higher betweenness score were elected delegates, not organizations (represented by the two larger grey nodes).

Figure 3.4 shows that, based on our survey data, NVM and its leaders have as much brokerage power as certain elected officials. The delegate with the highest betweenness score was first elected to the Virginia House of Delegates in the early 1980s. The second largest grey node represents a delegate who, according to her website, prides herself on working with both Republicans and Democrats to "get things done," a stance that would help explain the bridging role she plays in this network.

From all of this data, we can see that NVM was on par with the largest national groups and long-serving elected officials in terms of the role it played in shaping strategy on progressive policy issues in Virginia. NVM played a particularly important role in creating bridges and brokering the flow of information and strategy between elected officials and organizations in the state. In addition to substantiating the qualitative findings from our interviews, the network survey made visible the degree and kind of influence that NVM wielded among Democratic members of the Virginia House of Representatives. A decade before McAuliffe signed the executive order to restore voting rights, NVM did not exist. According to the statehouse delegates who responded to our survey, NVM is now among the most influential grassroots organizations in Virginia.

Arizona: "The Action Is Always in the Reaction"

In Arizona, unlike in Virginia and Ohio, the organizations we were studying did not work with a clearly circumscribed community of power brokers. Thus, network surveys like the ones we used in those cases would not have been appropriate. Moreover, the leaders in the Arizona cases were not pursuing a single victory—such as the passage of Issue 44 in the 2016 election in Cincinnati—but instead seeking to beat back anti-immigration forces at the municipal, county, and state levels. Thus, we needed an alternate approach to assessing whether there was a power shift. To capture the totality of the work that the leaders in Arizona were involved in, we focused on examining how the state's immigration-related policy making changed or remained stable over time.

In examining the evolution of the state's political agenda on the issue that mattered most to our cases' constituents, one relevant comparison was the quality and quantity of immigration-related legislation before and after 2010. Over and over again, interviewees made the contrast between, as one respondent put it, "that dark spring of 2010 when SB 1070 passed and the future looked quite bleak" and "today, where the same young leaders who led the fight against SB 1070 are now leading some of the most powerful organizations and campaigns in the state." SB 1070 was only one of a slew of anti-immigrant policies enacted in Arizona in the first decade of the twenty-first century. "The first thing to note," one longtime immigrant-labor-movement leader told us, "is that there was relatively nonexistent resistance to SB 1070 [in the early 2000s]." He continued,

> There was no, no even ACLU [American Civil Liberties Union], there was no Mexican Legal Defense Fund. There was just, frankly speaking there was a

lack of civil society. There was a lack of, you know, almost nonexistent civil rights bar in Phoenix. You know? I mean like you say, "Who were the civil rights lawyers in Phoenix and in Arizona?" There were none. . . . At the time [Phoenix] was like, the fourth-largest city in America. But it was one that sort of grew up so fast and without all these sort of these institutions and cultural practices that you'd expect in other places. And which contributed to this overall kind of dystopian environment that occurred. And as a result, yeah, there was a lack of political leadership from Latinos in particular . . . a vacuum of resources entirely.

For many of our interviewees, Arizona's "dystopian" political environment was most clearly manifest in state-level legislation that directly targeted the immigrant community. Raquel Terán, the movement leader who, along with Petra Falcon, brought the NOI training to Arizona and was elected to the state House of Representatives in 2018, rattled off a list: "I think from 1996, taking away the driver's licenses of people who didn't have their social security number. To making English the official language, to taking away bilingual education." Another interviewee remembered other legislative attacks on the state's immigrant community: "In 2006, they had another series of ballot initiatives. Prop. 300 being the one to charge out-of-state tuition, take away early childhood education, and take away adult education from undocumented people. There was another ballot measure that took away bond if you're undocumented. You were guilty until proven innocent if you were an undocumented person," he said.

After the SB 1070 fight, the political terrain seemed to shift. "We learned how to fight back," said Petra, now the executive director of Promise Arizona. "We [learned] you can turn fear into courage. [In] 2010, the people at the frontline were undocumented people—and they learned how to fight," she said. In May 2011, a group called Citizens for a Better Arizona submitted 18,315 signatures to the Secretary of State's office with a petition to recall Senate president Russell Pearce, the architect and sponsor of SB 1070 and the person the *New York Times* called "Arizona's most powerful legislator" (Lacey and Seelye 2011). In a special election months later, he lost to challenger Jerry Lewis, making him the first state legislator to be recalled in Arizona. In the following year's Republican primary, he lost again—this time to Bob Worsley—by twelve percentage points.

"The action is always in the reaction," said Raquel, who was actively involved in the Pearce recall. She was referring to how both Democratic and Republican legislators responded to Pearce's ouster, which, in itself was "something that people never thought was gonna happen," as she said.[11] Stephen

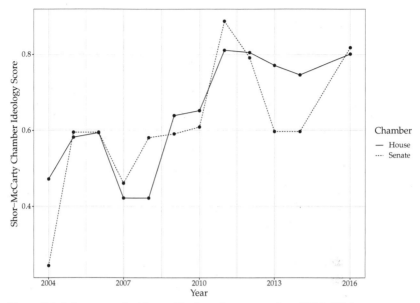

Figure 3.5. Arizona state legislature ideology change over time, 2004–2016

On the Shor-McCarty index, positive numbers are more conservative and negative numbers are more liberal.

Lemons, a journalist who had covered the immigration beat in Arizona for more than a decade, reported that even the state's top Democrats thought the recall would only embolden Pearce if and when it failed. As for the Republicans, Lemons continued, it was "the 'non-crazy' wing of the state GOP" that won out after they saw Pearce and the five additional pieces of anti-immigrant legislation he tried to introduce in 2011 go "down in flames" (Lemons 2011). The recall was the opening salvo in the movement's effort to change the interest calculus of their elected representatives. Sam Richard, the former executive director of the Protecting Arizona Families Coalition (PAFCO), agreed: "There's this realization that the giant has awoken and the giant is woke."

To examine the consistency between our interview data and other measures of change in the political landscape before and after 2010, we analyzed immigration policy making in Arizona pre– and post–SB 1070. If we examine the roughly seven years on either side of SB 1070, we can see that during that fourteen-year time period, the Arizona state legislature was becoming more conservative. Figure 3.5 uses the Shor-McCarty index (Shor and McCarty 2011; Shor 2018) to describe the ideological composition of the Arizona state legislature. From 2004 to 2016 both the Arizona Senate and House grew more conservative. In the years since SB 1070, the House became more conservative immediately after 2010, and then remained relatively stable. The Senate grew less conservative after the chamber's most conservative member was ousted in 2011 (Pearce), but then the score moved above 2010 levels in subsequent years. The 2016 Senate (.818) is considerably more conservative than the 2010 Senate that passed SB 1070 (.609).[12] In addition, until 2018, the state GOP retained at least a four-seat majority in the upper chamber and a ten-or-more seat majority in the lower chamber. In other words, Arizona GOP legislators have become more conservative, and they had the votes to continue to pass anti-immigrant legislation but have not.

Even though both chambers in the Arizona state legislature became more ideologically conservative over time, we do not see a corresponding increase in the number of restrictive immigration laws passed. This pattern emerges even though, as the leader of the state Tea Party told us, immigration is "the number one issue" for much of the conservative base in the state. Following prior research that uses data and classification schemes from the National Conference of State Legislatures (NCSL) (Anzia and Moe 2016; Birkland and Lawrence 2009; Hicks, McKee, and Smith 2016), we built a database using NCSL's year-end immigration legislation summaries, which report legislative activity by state for the years 2005–2017. NCSL data tracked and summarized immigration-related bills and resolutions. We also collected data on the partisan breakdown of the roll-call vote for each piece of legislation. Putting this information together, we coded each piece of Arizona statehouse legislation according to whether it expanded or restricted the rights of immigrant communities.

We coded as "restrictive" bills like HB (House Bill) 2592, which prevented the construction of day labor centers, which provide employment opportunities for undocumented immigrants, and SB 1035, which made proof-of-citizenship requirements for receipt of public benefits more stringent. The majority of these votes fell along party lines: Republicans were often unanimous or near unanimous in their support of the restrictive bills. We only coded five bills enacted during this time period as "expansive" in terms of immigrant rights; all of these had majority opposition from Republicans and support from Democrats. They related to overtime pay and other employer-sponsored compensation benefits for "aliens" (HB 2474 and SB 1125), tenants' rights after eviction independent of immigration status (SB 1376), the establishment of a state seal of biliteracy for graduates proficient in one or more languages in addition to English (SB 1239), and an exemption to the citizenship and residency requirements for liquor licenses (HB 2606).[13]

Figure 3.6 reports the pattern in immigration-related policy making in Arizona over time. Despite an increase in the ideological conservatism of the

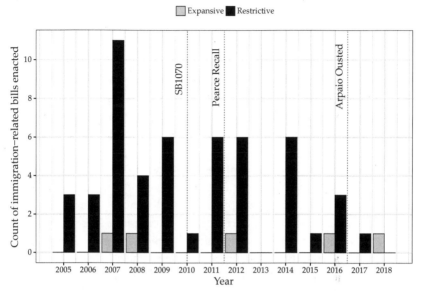

Figure 3.6. Timeline of immigration-related bills enacted in the Arizona state legislature, 2005–2018.

Counts and codes based on the National Conference of State Legislatures' Immigrant Policy Project annual reports and the Arizona state legislature's roll call vote archives.

chamber, the absolute number of anti-immigration bills and resolutions enacted in Arizona decreased—from thirty-four to seventeen—in the seven-year period before Pearce's recall (2005–2011) and in the seven-year period after it (2012–2018). If we remove 2007 from the data (an outlier year, with the largest number of immigrant-related bills enacted), twenty-three restrictive bills passed before Pearce's recall and seventeen afterward. Even without 2007, the pattern implies that conservatives were not able to push through as much legislation on what the Tea Party leader said was their "number one" issue even as the chamber became more ideologically conservative. In other words, the conservative majorities in the House and Senate and the growing anti-immigrant rhetoric with the election of Trump did not necessarily translate into greater momentum for their agenda in the state legislature.

Figure 3.6 accounts for the number of bills and resolutions enacted on either side of the temporal divide but does not, of course, account for the substantive impact of the bills. For example, in the 2010 session, only one bill regarding immigration issues was enacted—but it was SB 1070, widely considered to be the most extreme anti-immigrant omnibus legislation in the country. To get a sense of this qualitative pattern, we can examine bills that passed before and after SB 1070. Although one interviewee's assertions that "no anti-immigrant legislation has passed since 2011" is not strictly true, the comparison between the types of immigration-related bills that passed before and after the turning point is interesting. In 2005, for example, the legislature passed a law that allows judges to factor immigration status into sentencing (HB 2259) and another that prevents the construction of day-labor centers that aid undocumented workers (HB 2592). The next year, the legislature passed HB 2448/SB 2738, which requires US citizenship for patients to receive health benefits, effectively limiting undocumented immigrants to emergency medical services. Another bill that same year excluded persons without "legal alien status" from the state's Comprehensive Care for the Elderly program. In 2007, HB 2787 denied release on bail if law enforcement believed that there was "probable cause" that the accused was an undocumented immigrant. And so on. In contrast, examples of the restrictive immigration bills passed in the second period include a 2012 law that allows a police officer to impound a car that is "being used to transport, harbor, or conceal illegal aliens" (HB 2286), a law that "eliminates border crossing identification cards and voter cards issued by the government of Mexico as acceptable forms of age verification when purchasing liquor" (SB 1397 in 2014), and escalating "identity theft for work verification" to a class three felony (HB 2639 in 2014). The full list of bills is available in appendix C.[14]

When we put the data in figures 3.5 and 3.6 together, the pattern that emerges is one in which both chambers of the Arizona legislature were ideologically predisposed to pass more restrictive anti-immigration legislation over time, but the pattern of bills enacted shows either a decline or relative stasis in the restrictive bills passed. Part of this could be explained by an overall drop in the productivity of the state legislature that influences the number of bills introduced (Lee 2016). We found, however, that the number of immigration-related bills introduced in the six-year period before SB 1070 and the Pearce recall (thirty-eight) was similar to the number introduced in the six-year period after (thirty-three).[15] In other words, almost as many bills were introduced, but fewer were passed.

Meanwhile, Democrats have begun to close the representation gap at the state level. In the 2018 midterms, Arizona elected its first Democratic senator since 1995 and narrowed the GOP's lead in the lower chamber of the state legislature from ten seats to just two. One of the assemblywomen whose election helped narrow this margin is Raquel Terán. In that same election, Carlos Garcia, the executive director of Puente—who immigrated to Arizona at age five and has seen five of his relatives deported since 2009—was elected to the Phoenix City Council alongside Betty Guardado, a UNITE HERE! union organizer and former housekeeper (Santos 2019).

We are not arguing that the organizing after SB 1070 *caused* this decline in anti-immigrant legislation and this increase in Latino political representation. Instead, we show that SB 1070 catalyzed the action and the learning that developed the constituency's ability to exert its voice in the political system, and that played a part in processes of change. This constituency's visible victories—the recall of Russell Pearce, the eventual defeat of Sheriff Joe Arpaio, the passage of a minimum wage law, the election of a majority left-leaning city council in Phoenix, and so on—suggest a change in the immigration-related political priorities and possibilities in Arizona. While extreme legislation like SB 1070 and the bills leading up to it were viable prior to 2010, the goalposts seemed to have shifted after the emergence of an increasingly cohesive immigrant rights constituency in the state.

It is important to note that the movement organizations in the Arizona case do not take sole or even primary credit for this shift in state-level immigration policy making. Lisa Urias, founder of the business-led Real Arizona Coalition, which pressed for more "reasonable" immigration laws, described the economic impact of the national reaction to SB 1070. "I remember the exact figure being $860 million" in short-term losses, Lisa told us, "in convention business primarily. . . . We [couldn't] even calculate what the longer-term impact [was]." The Real Arizona Coalition wanted to use its corporate clout to "counter the [negative] mental imprint made by 'six million media hits'" after SB 1070 (Kallick 2014). Petra Falcon described other ripple effects in the economy: "You had two or three hundred thousand people walked away from their apartments, homes; the agriculture community suffered tremendously, the construction industry suffered, the hospitality [industry]—they were hurting. They were hurting for workers. Small Plaza shut down because people walked away and apartments went bare [after SB 1070 was signed]." Phoenix business leaders we interviewed believed that these economic impacts were the direct result of the public's response to the passage of extreme anti-immigrant legislation like SB 1070. In 2011, sixty Arizona CEOs wrote a letter to Russell Pearce opposing further anti-immigrant measures like the ones he had previously introduced.

Pressure from the business community almost certainly had an impact on the voting pattern we observed in figure 3.6, but movement organizers took advantage of what they saw as their newfound allyship with parts of the corporate community. As in our other cases, the immigrant rights organizers knew they had to work with better-resourced allies. The key, however, was that these organizers were able to do so on their own terms with the courage and capacities they had created in fighting SB 1070. "What I think was the beauty is," Raquel said, "that we were able to expose it [SB 1070]; we were able to build a narrative that it affected [Arizona] economically." "But," she continued, "if we wouldn't have set up [the vigil], if it wouldn't have been at the capitol, if we wouldn't have been building power, if we wouldn't have been as resilient as we were that whole summer, I think that law would have passed and would've gone under the radar, just like all the other [anti-immigrant] laws that [came before]. . . . What we have seen is that these crazy legislators, these, Russell Pearce type of people—their legislation just doesn't move forward as it used to." In 2019, Raquel was sworn in as an assemblywoman at the capitol she had sat vigil outside of nearly ten years earlier.

Minnesota's Shifting Narratives: "How Much Power Did We Build?"

In the final days of the legislative session in 2017, ISAIAH felt betrayed by the choice that Minnesota's Democratic governor, Mark Dayton, had made to broker a deal that protected bargaining rights for labor unions but made it more difficult for immigrants to get driver's licenses. ISAIAH saw this as yet another example of the constant marginalization of immigrants within establishment Democratic politics. After considering and trying several different methods of protest, ISAIAH and a coalition of allies decided to call for a boycott of an important upcoming fundraising dinner for the Democratic-Farmer-Labor Party (DFL), the principal branch of the Minnesota Democratic Party, in the summer of 2017.

To stave off this confrontation, the DFL Party agreed to fund a study on race- and class-based messaging to voters. ISAIAH leaders believed that investments in this kind of messaging would be helpful for fielding Democratic candidates in the 2018 and 2020 elections. This research, conducted by Anat Shenker-Osorio and Ian Haney Lopez in 2017 and 2018, supported a narrative that ISAIAH had been advancing for years. Shenker-Osorio, like ISAIAH, argued that confronting and openly talking about race is preferable to focusing only on "economic" issues without addressing race.

This research helped lay the foundation for ISAIAH's "faith delegate" campaign in 2018. Leaders from ISAIAH and its sister 501(c)(4) organization, Faith in Minnesota, sought to influence the way candidates in the 2018 election spoke about race and class issues. ISAIAH and its allies wanted to pressure DFL candidates to speak openly about the intersections of race and class, instead of speaking about the economy to the exclusion of race and immigration.

As we discuss further in chapter 4, this faith-delegate campaign turned out to be more successful than ISAIAH had anticipated. In Minnesota's second congressional district, for instance, Democratic candidate Angie Craig defeated Republican incumbent Jason Lewis by 5.6 points—Lewis had voted in line with Trump's positions more than 90 percent of the time. Craig became Minnesota's first openly LGBTQ person to serve the state in Congress. Throughout the race, Craig actively solicited the backing of ISAIAH, trying to demonstrate her support of their work in various ways, including in how she talked about race and class. As an ISAIAH organizer told us, "The day after she got the [DFL] endorsement, [Craig] texted me and her campaign manager texted me and said, 'Having Faith in Minnesota's support at the convention was really important.' Next week I'm sitting down with [member-elect Craig], one-on-one, and we're gonna talk through some of the research we've been doing about Greater Minnesota and how to bridge race and class."

Craig's text messages to ISAIAH staff are examples that speak to how the organization tried to shift power in the state by shaping narratives around race and class. However, as with our other cases, we did not want to rely solely on self-reported data and sought to test whether candidates' public statements aligned with ISAIAH's own narrative. Because the claim ISAIAH was making was about its impact on candidate narratives, we web-scraped the Twitter feeds of Democratic gubernatorial candidates Tim Walz and Erin Murphy, who were the main focus of ISAIAH's faith-delegate campaign. Tracking Walz's and Murphy's public statements on Twitter allowed us to examine the extent to which they adopted the language of ISAIAH. Both candidates were vying for the support of ISAIAH's faith delegates. We then compared that textual data to word bases drawn from ISAIAH's faith-delegate platform.

Figure 3.7 illustrates the number of times Murphy and Walz used one of the top twenty-five most-used words from ISAIAH's platform—words like "community," "justice," "family," "abundance," and "dignity." In identifying these words, we dropped terms like "campaign" or "Minnesota" that would not necessarily differentiate the extent to which candidates were adopting ISAIAH's substantive message over routine messaging. We wanted to focus on ISAIAH's overall narrative about a "community" of "abundance" in which all Minnesota families deserve to live with "dignity" and "justice."

Figure 3.7 displays the data, normalized by the number of tweets for that week. A score of 1 means that the average tweet contained only one of ISAIAH's top (most-used) twenty-five words. A score of 3 indicates that the average tweet contained three of ISAIAH's top twenty-five words. These time-series analyses allow us to compare the rates at which each candidate used a particular word throughout the 2018 campaign season.

The figure shows that, in the beginning of the campaign, neither Murphy nor Walz was using much language that mirrored ISAIAH's platform. The baseline narrative, in other words, was not consistent with the way ISAIAH

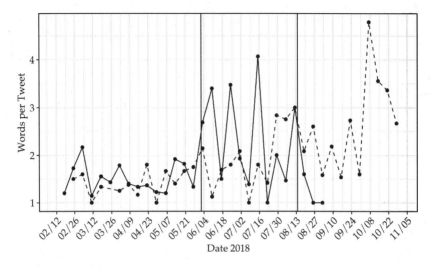

Candidate: — Murphy -- Walz

Figure 3.7. Minnesota DFL gubernatorial candidates' adoption of language from ISAIAH's platform, Twitter data from February to November 2018.
The data comes from code written to scrape all tweets composed by the Murphy campaign and Walz campaign Twitter feeds.

was talking about race and class in its platform. Over time, however, that began to change. In early June 2018, ISAIAH threw its support behind Murphy at the DFL state convention. Its support helped Murphy win the party nomination at the convention, a moment indicated by the first vertical line in the chart. Around this time, we see Murphy increasingly adopting ISAIAH's language. Murphy's unexpected victory at the DFL convention triggered a primary in August. Between June and August, when Murphy was battling the mainstream DFL candidate Walz, Murphy continued to build on ISAIAH's language. Walz did not—at least not until he got closer to the August primary (indicated by the second vertical line). In the weeks leading up to the primary, he incorporated ISAIAH's language into much of his online messaging, also laying the foundation for the general election.. Walz won the primary in August, becoming the party's official nominee in the November general election. We see that he continued to build on ISAIAH's narrative in the weeks leading up to the general election.

Using social-media text as data and textual-analysis tools, we were able to track the extent to which candidates in the gubernatorial election picked up on the narrative around race and class that ISAIAH sought to advance. Although ISAIAH's favored candidate in the 2018 election, Erin Murphy, ultimately did not win the nomination, this analysis shows that the movement nonetheless shaped the election in other ways, including by fostering new alliances between ISAIAH and down-ballot candidates like Craig.

Making Power Shifts Visible

The premise of our argument is that the political power of ordinary people is the product of contingent interactions between movement organizations and their targets. In this chapter, we employed original data to make visible these dynamic negotiations among the diverse sets of actors across our four primary cases: Arizona, Minnesota, Ohio, and Virginia. Even as we were able to document shifts in both visible and invisible power, the grassroots leaders we interviewed—who mostly stand to gain from positive accounts of their work—were wary of overstating their influence. We found that these leaders always sought to maintain a clarity about where they stand in relation to power. One leader with KFTC said, "I think that you can go into anyone's office in Frankfurt and tell them you're with KFTC, and they know who you are. That's powerful, I think, but they won't just roll over for you. We're not the NRA." Similarly, despite moving from the margins to the center of one power network in Ohio, Troy Jackson was realistic about AMOS's influence and lack thereof: "Our whole idea was, 'Who owns Cincinnati?'" he said. "I'm still convinced we didn't change that dynamic one iota in this campaign." This clarity about continued power asymmetries characterized all of the cases.

Despite these leaders' modesty, we argue that the power shifts documented here provide insight on the different ways scholarship can make the outcomes of collective action more visible and, thus, a more focused object of study. Scholars have good reason to regard a study of one visible political outcome— such as winning a vote, passing a ballot initiative, or securing an executive order—as an inadequate measure of movement success. Many other factors, such as McAuliffe's myriad motivations for restoring the voting rights of two hundred thousand Virginians, contributed to each of those victories. Without carefully considering those other factors, scholars can overplay their hands, making implicit suggestions that overstate the power or influence of collective action. While we acknowledge the fragility of these power shifts, this chapter also suggests that understanding movement influence *only* through the lens of visible wins or losses understates the level and type of change for which a movement may be responsible.

4 *The Strategic Logic of Prisms*

In the context of Minnesota right now . . . [other organizations say they] have 20,000 people . . . [or] 70,000 members. We don't have a base like that. But they can't deliver that base. Not even close. I mean not even close. If [those organizations] could deliver their 70,000 [members], they could run this state. But they can't.

ISAIAH LEADER, JANUARY 2018

Members of Congress alter their customary patterns of [access] only when events fulfill two conditions. First, new informants must prove their competitive advantage over old informants. Elections must demonstrate that their information and propaganda more accurately reflect the salient preferences of constituents. Second, the circumstances that made the competitive advantage of new informants possible must recur. Politicians must discern a persistent basis of interest mobilization and attention.

JOHN MARK HANSEN, *GAINING ACCESS* (1991, 108)

In 1991, University of Chicago professor John Mark Hansen published a book examining why certain interest groups had greater access to elected officials than others. His case study was the farm lobby in the twentieth century. Why, he asked, were farm lobby groups persistently able to gain influence in the US Congress disproportionate to their size? "Lobbies gain access when, in the judgment of congressional elites, they represent constituents," he concludes (Hansen 1991, 3). Constituency-based interest groups differentiate themselves from others when they are able to establish what Hansen calls a "competitive advantage" with "recurrence." These groups, in others words, must demonstrate to reelection-minded legislators that they can deliver their base.

As Hansen's work would predict, the leaders in our cases recognized that their power at the proverbial negotiating table with political elites depended on their ability to deliver an authentic constituency base. The quote above from the ISAIAH leader exemplifies this idea—ISAIAH knew that its influence rested on its ability to consistently deliver people, not just size or scale. Although none of the groups in the cases that we examine in this book were contesting for power in the halls of US Congress, they were all involved in similar negotiations with city leaders, statewide candidates, elected officials, business communities, and other power players. Across all of these venues, the leaders in our cases recognized that (a) exercising power required negotiation, and (b) their ability to build, maintain, and flexibly deploy a loyal constituency base constituted their power.

How did this recognition of the dynamic nature of political power and the need to link constituency actions to elite negotiations shape the strategic choices leaders made? This chapter examines the patterns we see in leadership choices in order to uncover the underlying strategic logic of prisms. Looking across cases that are operating in different political environments, on varied issues, and with distinct constituencies, what patterns emerge about how leaders identified goals, analyzed their options, and made strategic choices? When we began the project, we thought we might find patterns in the types of plans deployed. Instead, we found that the leaders in our cases shared a strategic dynamism and a clarity about sustaining that dynamism. There was no clear formula for power, no tactic, tool, resource, or action that would guarantee success. Leaders used online and off-line tactics, electoral and nonelectoral approaches, and coalitional and independent strategies. What was common was a strategic logic about how to cultivate people as effective sources of power and stay accountable to them when wielding power in the public domain. These shared patterns emerge through a careful analysis of leaders' considerations as they made choices.

In this chapter, we break our discussion of strategic leadership into two parts. The first part unpacks the strategic logic underlying prisms of people power. Why is it strategic for leaders focused on building power to invest in people? In uncertain political environments, people are the most independent source of power these organizations have that can enable them to earn a seat at the table and keep advocating for their interests. We describe the distinction between having an independent source of political power, one rooted in accountability to an authentic constituency, and having power that is dependent on access to decision makers. Based on this distinction, we then describe how leaders in our cases made strategic decisions with an eye toward their long-term, downstream consequences. Creating organizations that operated with the logic of prisms allowed leaders to engage their constituencies in ways that had positive civic feedbacks—that is, feedback loops that would strategically position the organization so it could more likely exercise power in the future.

The second part of the chapter describes particular characteristics of prisms that differentiate the choices leaders in our cases made from dominant models of collective action. Across our cases, leaders grounded their strategic decision-making in the needs of their constituency, thus maintaining a focus on power, an openness to a range of traditional and nontraditional strategic options, and a recognition of the long, uncertain battle they faced. An analysis that took all of these factors into account led them to a set of strategic choices that enabled them to act with the flexibility they needed in their David-like bids to beat their Goliath (Ganz 2009). We describe two particular practices that enabled this strategic dynamism: a pragmatic philosophy that balanced ideology and strategy, and a dedication to constant strategic learning.

The Strategic Logic

Our formulation of the prism metaphor examines the strategic linkages between the choices an organization makes about how to build its constituency and its ability to refract political power in the public arena. What are the conditions under which designing people's prisms is strategic for building power? We argue that designing metaphorical prisms of people power is the strategic choice when two intertwined conditions are met: first, when an organization needs an independent source of political power, one that is related to, but distinct from, access to elites or institutional channels; and second, when an organization needs to prepare for uncertainty—which, as we have argued, is almost always the case.

All of the organizations in our case studies were dedicated to building political power, as the previous chapter illustrated. Moving from a conceptual definition of power to a set of actionable strategic goals, however, is not easy. There are no formulas. Most people would chuckle at the idea of an instruction manual for democracy that includes a troubleshooting guide: "If you do not have the power you want, go through steps A, B, and C on page 8." Nonetheless, in the everyday chaos of politics, leaders like the ones in our case studies face numerous pressures to proffer a magic bullet for power. In a world where grassroots groups must constantly compete for resources, leaders face consistent pressure from funders, potential supporters, and the media to identify formulas for success. Worse, some of the leaders in our case studies told us that they often have to repackage their work, depending on funder fads. One executive director told us how she trains her staff to talk to funders:

"[I tell them] don't ever talk about process; the idea that you have 15 one-on-ones and then a meeting and all those people show up and were converted into leaders . . . [funders] don't care. It sounds so small compared to saying you had 10,000 contacts."

We found that the leaders in our study pursued their own strategic pathways for three related reasons: first, they recognized that the source of their potential power comes from, as Hansen observed, the ability to reliably and repeatedly deliver an organized base of people; second, they knew their bids for political power were uncertain; and third, they knew that whatever wins they did achieve would require constant protection. The leaders understood that simply having access to power brokers would not necessarily advance their constituents' interests, particularly when they were advocating for low-income populations of color whose needs historically have not been met by the existing system. They recognized that the only way they could use their access for influence was to maintain an independent source of power that sat outside their relationship with elite decision makers. This independent source of power was their constituency. Their understanding of the uncertain and long-term nature of political power building meant they were constantly making choices about how to invest in their constituency in ways that prepared them for unexpected wins and setbacks. Investing in the accountability structures, practices, and strategic orientation of the collective—what we liken to the internal design of a prism—was how these leaders prepared for uncertainty.

CONSTITUENCY AS AN INDEPENDENT BASE OF POWER

Social scientists studying political influence often use access to power as a proxy for power itself. Important studies have analyzed things like congressional testimony to identify the groups that are recognized by political decision makers as influential (e.g., Hansen 1991; Burstein 2003). While this approach provides a good look at one dimension of power—namely, who has a seat at the proverbial decision-making table—it does not differentiate between those who can use that seat to challenge the status quo and those who cannot.

We argue that investing in the internal design of a prism is strategic for organizations seeking to build power. Why is it strategic? Leaders accountable to and rooted in an active, engaged, and committed constituency can claim power at the negotiating table that leaders without that constituency cannot. One clear pattern that emerged across all of our case studies was the desire by our leaders to ensure that if and when they earned a seat at the table, they could continue to challenge the status quo without risking the loss of their seat. In part, this was because they recognized that their constituencies were often the kind most likely to get marginalized in political decision-making (Gillion 2013; Strolovitch 2007; Blee 2012). The only way they could maintain an influential position without compromising the representation of their constituencies was to earn their seat by developing what they often called an "independent source of power." Independent political power is strategic because it allows leaders to influence elite power without depending on it. In other words, with an independent source of power leaders had access to resources that they could use to influence decision makers, without those resources' existence depending on funders, party leaders, or other external decision makers. The constituency and its leaders themselves controlled that resource.

Doran Schrantz of Minnesota's ISAIAH described the importance of an independent source of power. In an interview from 2014, she reflected on the growing prominence of ISAIAH in movement circles in the United States. ISAIAH was becoming favored in particular among the large national philanthropies that financially supported much of the grassroots work that organizations like it did. Doran said,

> I'm of the opinion that there's not going to be a significant, people-powered, independent movement funded by foundations. . . . It's just that [the philanthropic world] has its own momentum and its own set of priorities. . . . The thing that's depressing is that you take . . . some of your most talented organizers and you turn all their strategic energy . . . on milking that thing [the world of philanthropy]. . . . And then, that thing can also defang you. It turns you into a celebrity, turns you into a commodity. So, I've also seen that happen to people—that they do really good organizing that becomes this big thing. . . . And then, you get positioned inside that whole system and all of a sudden you could raise ten million dollars 'cause you're the new celebrity. So then you build a big national thing and now you're a hustler. I mean, you hustle—you hustle and broker. But the minute you float up into that thing and you get ungrounded from the base, you turn into something different. And you're still dependent on the base, but instead of it being an authentic relationship, you're essentially buying it.[1]

Like the other leaders in our cases, Doran recognized the difference between having access to power that includes the ability to challenge it, and having access alone. In her analysis, once her relationship to her constituency becomes dependent on the money that foundations give her to organize that constituency, she no longer has an independent source of power. She can no longer challenge the donors, because she needs them to give her money (Reich 2018). She is, in her words, defanged. For an organizer to maintain her "fangs," she has to be in an "authentic relationship" with her base. In other words, she has to be in an accountable relationship with them, so that leaders and constituents alike remain committed to a shared agenda. With this kind of shared commitment, grounded in mutual accountability, the leader can deliver the constituency in the recurrent ways she needs to in order to influence decision makers.

Historically, this conversation around the importance of independent political power emerged from a discussion among organizations representing low-income constituencies of color. Many of the leaders in our case studies were part of a group of state-based, grassroots organizations that came into being in the early twenty-first century in an effort to build independent political power. Originally, most of these organizations were grounded in either community organizing or nonviolent direct-action traditions. The community-organizing groups and networks mostly grew out of Saul Alinsky's work in the 1960s,[2] which had traditionally rejected mainstream, electoral politics in favor of more locally rooted organizing based in existing community structures, such as faith communities. Organizers emerging from nonviolent direct-action work also tended to opt for more "outsider" strategies (mainly disruption), arguing that change was better made from outside, rather than inside, the system (e.g., Piven and Cloward 1995).

Leaders building the idea of independent political organization in the twenty-first century argued that the most powerful constituency-based organizations had to do both: blend both organizing and electoral work, and work both inside and outside. Changing organizational structures reflected this shift in priorities—while previous community-organizing or direct-action groups often did not have paid lobbyists or 501(c)(4) sister organizations, many of the groups in our study did. As Tram Nguyen from New Virginia Majority noted in an interview, she realized the importance of building independent political power:

[In] 2007, in the aftermath of the failure of comprehensive immigration reform, [it was] a time when immigration raids plagued our community much as they do today. A few very smart people realized that if we're really going to change things, for our community and our people, we had to engage in a much more deliberate and strategic way. It wasn't enough to attend rallies, or hold actions—we had to include voter engagement as part of the core of our work, and that the notion of citizenship and civic engagement for new Americans was going to be pivotal in changing the political landscape.

Across all of our cases, leaders like Tram recognized the importance of having what scholars might call a simultaneous "inside and outside" game if they wanted to build durable political power. Many of the leaders in our cases adopted a "both-and" approach. As Joy Cushman observed in an interview, "the organizations that are building more power are able to wield different types of power. It's not all voting, it's not all civil disobedience." Leaders in our study recognized both the value in articulating clear, measurable strategies for power and the need to do so in ways that maintained their strategic flexibility. Only with flexibility could they respond to the inevitable ups and downs that accompany any campaign for power.

These strategies for building independent political power were particularly relevant for and rooted in theories developed by poor people and people of color. Leaders from these constituencies have always understood that they have to fight for legitimacy and that they are likely to get blocked along the way. For these constituencies, any access to power has been, at best, ephemeral. These leaders therefore developed strategies that expect unexpectedness. And if they stayed grounded in their constituency, then they had a durable source of power they could leverage, distinct from any momentary attention or access they might get from funders, the media, or other power players.

One leader in Arizona gave us an example of the importance of staying grounded in constituency, as opposed to focusing on access to power: "We're no longer okay with a person just has to be Latino or have a Latino name or say good things but has no actual platform, no actual agenda and no actual policy ideas. . . . Even when [our allies like Danny Valenzuela] are elected, how are our community orgs, but also community people, involved [in the decision-making]?" Valenzuela was a city councilman and mayoral candidate who had been elected in 2011 with the pivotal help of a group of undocumented young people. Once in office, however, he did not respond to the constituency's needs in the way they expected. "I remember once we had a roll call protest, where we called all these names," the interviewee said. "[We yelled], 'Valenzuela where's your stance?' and [afterward] he called and was really mad. He said, 'Aren't you loyal to me?' And we said, 'No, we're loyal to our community, not to you.'"

Not all of the leaders from the organizations we studied were people of color or from low-income backgrounds. Yet, even those leaders who were not from the constituency groups they were organizing demonstrated this focus on constituency power as a hedge for uncertainty. AMOS's Troy, for instance, is a white evangelical Christian who is over six feet tall. He is a former preacher and has a PhD in history from the University of Kentucky. Based on his doctoral work, he coauthored a book about Martin Luther King Jr. Even with this profile, however, he focuses relentlessly on the potential uncertainty inherent in fighting for greater power for his constituents.

In a reflection written on February 7, 2016, that Troy shared with us, he remarks on his experience at a citywide meeting for business, political, and other leaders in Cincinnati:

> Most people in the room . . . have power that is vested and determined by their proximity to wealth and power via corporate leadership. They have to make certain trade-offs with their source of power, which means that they have to be careful what they say and how they say it, lest someone get upset with them and upset their career and livelihood. With organizing, our power does not come from networking or proximity and access to people of wealth and influence. It comes from a base, to whom we are accountable . . . that means we can be prophetic and bold in the public arena in a way that most . . . cannot.

Troy wrote these reflections every week, primarily for himself. His reflection from the following week contains a similar sentiment after he describes, in detail, all the business leaders who have power in the city and the origins of their power: "The biggest lesson I'm learning and reminded of week after week is that when your power comes from organized people and organized money, and is not dependent on proximity to powerful people or trading favors or keeping the elite happy, it frightens the principalities and powers way more than a one-off protest action that they can wait out."

Three notable points emerge from Troy's reflections. First, Troy distinguishes between power that depends on relationships to power brokers and power that sits outside that relationship. In his analysis, access is not the primary strategic goal for leaders seeking to build power in a dynamic environment. He wants a relationship with the decision maker to have emerged because he has an independent resource that the decision maker wants or needs. This independent resource would essentially act as a source of power that gives him the leverage and flexibility necessary to be able to negotiate more effectively with the "principalities." Second, in his analysis Troy recognizes that whatever the source of his power is, it has to be durable over time. It has to be more than something decision makers can simply "wait out." Because they have institutional power, those decision makers have time on their side.

Third and finally, in Troy's analysis, that independent source of power comes from "organized people and organized money." In other words, what matters is not the number of people or the amount of money, but the extent to which those people and that money are "organized."

Sometimes, an organization gains visibility by getting millions of people to sign a petition or to show up for an event. That visibility can, under certain conditions, grant it access to the corridors of power. But in these situations, the constituency base that helps the organization gain access to power often proves illusory. If political decision makers refuse, ignore, or bargain with the movement's requests, its leaders lack what Doran called the "authentic relationship" with their base that is required to move them, again and again and again, with the "recurrence" that Hansen (1991) argues is necessary. Instead, these leaders have to hope that mere proximity to power is enough to get them what they want. When it is not, the millions of names on a petition become mere props rather than collective agents of change. The lists, no matter how large, do not have the flexibility to constitute an independent source of political power.

For all the leaders in our cases, in contrast, a committed and flexible constituency makes up their key independent source of power. Their constituency acts as a self-governing base that has say over the organizational decisions that affect them and, as a consequence, say over the political decisions that affect their communities. The leaders and organizations in our study thus complicated the traditional tropes of mainstream politics through prismatic power. They recognized that power was not simply about having control over lots of some resource—people, access, expertise, or money. Instead, it was about having an "authentic relationship" with an "organized" base of constituents.

Another leader from Arizona further described why these authentic relationships matter:

When you asked [how big our] membership [is], I'm going to tell you 300 people, and I'm going to be super proud of those 300 people, because those 300 people come to the meetings, those 300 people, I know their children, they know my family. We know their stories, what they went through, and it's taken us ten years to develop those 300 people, and that's a powerful piece. We do membership meetings every Monday. The attendance there is 60 to 100 people every Monday. I could also tell you [that] we have 20,000 likes on Facebook. I could also tell you our email [list has] 120,000 [names], all those sorts of things, but those aren't real. I could also tell you thousands of people have walked through our doors, and at one point or another became members or not, or were part of one of our committees, or defense courses. We trained 600 people last year in the defense courses, it does not mean they're members. For us, it's 300 folks are actually super valuable, and we fought and we developed them, and that's membership.

This leader recognized that most organizations want to represent themselves on the largest scale possible. He knew that there were certain metrics he could use to paint that portrait of his organization: 120,000 people on the email list, or 20,000 people in the community on Facebook. In this leader's mind, however, it was the several hundred people with whom his organization was in deep relationship with that really mattered—the members whom he had to "get in front of every Monday and say, 'We've done this' or 'We haven't done this' . . . you're held accountable by the relationship," as he said. These were the people whose stories and families he knew; these were the people to whom he felt accountable, and the people who would be his source of leverage when challenges to his organization's power emerged. These organizations needed an independent source of influence because they wanted to hedge against their constituencies' uncertain hold on power.

CIVIC FEEDBACKS: THE DOWNSTREAM CONSEQUENCES OF CONSTITUENCY BUILDING

At the heart of the leadership choices we observed in our study was leaders' recognition that the effort they put in to build their constituency and leadership base would determine their ability to do the work they wanted to in the public sphere. In some ways, this statement seems so obvious that it is hardly worth saying: constituency-based organizations derive their power from their constituency. What was distinct about the leaders in our study, however, was their recognition that merely *having* a constituency is not enough. And, as the leaders quoted above noted, having an email list and having a constituency are not the same thing. These leaders recognized the importance of a constituency with certain characteristics (discussed in the next chapter), as well as the importance of building that constituency in certain ways. They were clear, in other words, that they needed an independent, committed, and flexible base in order to be able to exercise power in the public sphere.

As we examined organizations building power in the Midwest and the Southwest, in legislative arenas and ballot initiatives, and on issues related to voting rights and immigration reform, we noticed that they all shared the condition of unpredictability. In every case we studied, the leaders and organizations faced, at some point, an unexpected challenge to their power. Their choices about how to respond to these unexpected challenges revealed a great deal both about the way they understood the sources of their own power and about the extent to which they had the ability to wield it.

Unpredictability in politics may also seem so natural as to not merit discussion. Yet, when we examine the kinds of choices and investments that many political campaigns, organizations, and other investors make, we see that they often discount the likelihood of uncertainty. As Joy Cushman pointedly put it in a 2011 reflection on many organizations' (often funder-induced) obsession with what is often called "sustainable" and "systemic" change,

> There is nothing "sustainable" about change. . . . I am fatigued by campaign leaders I meet who are searching indefinitely for the perfect plan to which they can commit, coming back month after month with some revised version of their plan with little action at all in the interim. News flash: there is never a perfect campaign plan worth committing to. The world is chaotic and unpredictable. There is only the courage to commit to a change worth fighting for, the urgency to create enough of a plan that such courage is actionable in the real world in a purposeful way, and the humility to invite others to join us in action, and ask that they help us figure it out as we go.

Most progressive-change campaigns assume that, if enough people take action, the campaign can demonstrate sufficient power for change. Sometimes, these strategies even take the distribution of those people into account, trying to forecast how many of the right kinds of people will have to act in the right places. These strategies, however, are often too static for the unpredictable political environments in which they work.

Taking unpredictability and the dynamism of political domains seriously changes organizations' strategic calculus because it requires leaders to prepare for contingency. Given status-quo bias, the likelihood that their "Goliath" would win, and the inherent complexity of the political environments in which they were working, the leaders in our case studies never had the assurance that "If I do X, then I will get Y." How, then, could they act strategically?

The leaders we studied tried to maximize the set of strategic options at their disposal so that, when the unexpected challenge came, they would have as much flexibility as possible. For example, when the city councillors in Cincinnati refused Landsman's request to fund a universal preschool program even after he had gathered more than five thousand pledges, he had no further options. Troy Jackson, in contrast, could go back to AMOS's constituency when their first attempts failed and try again. Although neither leader could have predicted ahead of time precisely how their campaigns would unfold, a leader preparing for unpredictability would ensure that the resources he had built would enable him to switch to plan B when plan A failed.

Leaders' agency, we argue, is a function of the *size and quality of the strategic toolkit* they develop. They cannot control the complex and changing political environment around them. They cannot anticipate every challenge that will arise. But they can ensure that when those challenges do arise, they have many possible options for how to respond. In other words, they have the most agency when they maximize their choice set for down the road. To describe this strategy, we draw on the concept of what we have elaborated elsewhere as "civic feedbacks" (Han, Campbell, and McKenna 2019). The term "civic feedbacks" refers to the feedback loop that exists between constituencies and the groups that organize them. Not only do organizations shape the participation of these constituencies in collective action (Verba, Schlozman, and Brady 1995; Han 2014, 2016); the nature of participation among these constituencies also feeds back to shape the strategic position of the organization in subsequent negotiations for power. We argue that organizations operating with the logic of prisms have more options in their toolkit, giving them greater strategic flexibility that makes them more likely to be able to pressure decision makers in the ways they want.

ISAIAH's faith-delegate campaign is an example of how civic feedbacks work. To be clear, we are not arguing that ISAIAH's approach to building its constituency base determined the outcome of the campaign. A broad campaign-effects literature recognizes the importance of the sociopolitical and economic context (what political scientists call "the fundamentals") in shaping election outcomes (see, e.g., Sides and Vavreck 2013). Our argument with respect to civic feedbacks is that, given these contextual conditions, it is rational for leaders to prepare for uncertainty by maximizing the strategic choices available to them. Building a prismatic base has downstream consequences (or civic feedbacks) that allow leaders to have more strategic tools in their toolbox.

ISAIAH decided to act in the 2018 gubernatorial campaign because of losses at the end of the 2017 legislative session in Minnesota. At the time, Democratic governor Mark Dayton was facing a Republican legislature. In the chaos of the final days of the session, progressive advocates across the state objected to a flurry of bills. Three in particular drew progressives' ire: one that limited bargaining rights for public-sector unions, one that preempted legislation for paid sick days, and one that restricted driver's licenses for immigrants. ISAIAH was part of a coalition of progressive organizations fighting all three, but Dayton's office was resisting the idea that the governor could oppose all of them. Labor unions lobbied Dayton to protect bargaining rights, but not to support driver's licenses for immigrants. As an ISAIAH leader told us, "What's going to happen here is that everybody came together to fight this endgame and immigrants are going to be left out in the cold again—as usual." Another leader said, "He traded away immigrants for labor."

One ISAIAH organizer described their response: "So we did this protest. People marched to the capital, and then we decided to do a sit-in, right, outside of [Dayton's] office, and literally invited everyone that we could think of. And then through those sit-ins, those few days of sit-ins, we had people sleep overnight on the floor, and then we literally called a group of over 20 leaders that had been involved for years and sat on the steps and thought, 'What do we do?'" ISAIAH leaders recognized "trading away" one constituency group for another was nothing new. This was, in their analysis, part of a repeated pattern in which certain groups got preferred treatment at the expense of others.

The leaders were furious; for those who had been working on this issue for years, there was no small amount of despair. An ISAIAH leader who had been present that day told us how the experience helped her become clearer about what needed to be done in response:

> So, I'm sitting on the floor of the governor's office, and I am wondering where is everyone? Where is everyone from the sanctuary network? And I'm also wondering where are the 15,000 people who marched on the federal building in response to the announcement of the Trump administration's travel ban? Because this was also an attempt at a travel ban. A different kind of travel ban, but a travel ban of people traveling in their communities and living their lives. . . . [I realized] We're not clear. People are not clear about the policies and the laws that are brutalizing and crushing people and then throwing them out like they're garbage. They're not clear about what's happening, and we're not connected with each other.

One leader explained how she and about ten experienced ISAIAH leaders and allies from other organizations collaborated to figure out how to respond. Confronted with an unexpected rebuff from Dayton's office, they considered the range of tactics in their toolkit. She and other ISAIAH members considered more sit-ins, shutting down highways, organizing press conferences, and a range of other options. Finally, they realized they could organize a boycott of a DFL Party fundraiser, drawing on preexisting relationships they had with allies and party leaders to give this action the leverage it would need. They immediately got a meeting with Representative Keith Ellison and secured his support for a boycott. Throughout this process, ISAIAH leaders drew on a range of resources ISAIAH had cultivated for many years—from relationships with its base that could move them to action, to relationships with elites. Ultimately, these organizers planned a press conference at ten o'clock at night to launch a boycott of the upcoming fundraiser.

They got the unions on board with the boycott. Now threatened, the DFL Party paid attention, giving ISAIAH some of the concessions it wanted. Doran described the deal as follows:

> So one thing was we want 2018 to be a pro-immigrant election—not just silen[ce] [on immigration], but it should be pro-immigrant, right? And we know that that's hard. So we want you to put money into a set of research communications, you know, polling, that helps us figure out how to ensure that the candidates are running a pro-immigrant election in 2018. So we did that. And then the second thing is they formed like a commission to do audits of all the agencies, of like how can they be more pro-immigrant and protect immigrants? And so then this table got formed between all these different immigrant rights groups who then kind of ran with this commission.

As Doran reflected in our interview, however, the longer-term lesson for ISAIAH was that it had to build its own power base *within* the DFL Party to protect the interests of its constituents: "I think we and the set of the labor unions, a whole bunch of people, had this experience where it was like if we don't construct political power in the party in a radically different way, this is gonna happen again and again and again." Doran realized that without some measure of independent political power within the party, the pattern would repeat itself and ISAIAH would always be scrambling. Thus, heading into the 2018 election, ISAIAH started the process to essentially build what one interviewee called a "party within the party."

In the fall of 2017, ISAIAH leaders launched FiMN, a 501(c)(4) organization (below, we use ISAIAH to refer to both organizations). ISAIAH/FiMN started what leaders initially called a "faith agenda" campaign to influence the 2018 gubernatorial races.[3] Originally, the idea was to bring a group of ISAIAH leaders together in a series of house meetings around the state to articulate a shared agenda that would reflect the values and priorities of ISAIAH's base. To infuse this agenda into the 2018 elections, ISAIAH planned to invite five hundred leaders from Minnesota to run as delegates in the Democratic-Farmer-Labor (DFL) caucuses. Those who chose to run would have to organize their own base within their neighborhoods, identifying and recruiting enough people who could attend the caucus meeting and support them so that they could become delegates. Initially, ISAIAH told delegates they could support any candidate they wanted; their only job would be to try to get those candidates to pay attention to the faith-agenda platform.

The faith-agenda campaign gathered far more momentum than anyone, including ISAIAH, had originally anticipated. In the end, ISAIAH had about 3,800 people across the state attend caucuses and won 140 seats as delegates to the DFL convention. The "faith delegates," as they came to be called, caused a firestorm among the DFL candidates. None of the candidates had expected ISAIAH to control 12 percent of the delegates. Given convention rules, a candidate needed 60 percent of the votes to win the DFL nomination. None of the candidates had enough votes to win without the faith delegates. All of the campaigns thus entered into active negotiations with ISAIAH.

As ISAIAH came to an awareness of the political leverage it had with the faith delegates, it began to pivot its strategy. Its leaders realized that if they could get the faith delegates to vote as a bloc, they would have far more influence with the candidates than if the delegates fractured their support. This, however, required ISAIAH to convince delegates that they had to commit to collectively deliberating about whom to endorse, instead of supporting their individually favored candidates. This was not easy, particularly in the face of the pressure the delegates were facing. "Getting 140 people to vote as a bloc instead of as individuals, when they are getting called every day by candidates, is not easy. So far, we have had five delegate retreats and we are in constant conversation with the campaigns . . . these past few months have been the most intense few months of my public life," Doran said at the time.

ISAIAH and FiMN's ability to pivot from a sit-in at the governor's office to building a party within the DFL to the strategy of getting the faith delegates to act as a bloc would not have been possible without civic feedbacks. Because ISAIAH was in what Doran described as an "authentic relationship" with its delegates, it could ask things of its base that it would not have been able to had the relationship only begun with the 2018 electoral cycle. Had ISAIAH recruited ardent issue or candidate purists who were not in relationship with one another, it would not have been able to suture together a diverse group of delegates to act as a committed bloc.

An interview with one of ISAIAH's faith delegates who was involved in a congressional campaign in Minnesota's second congressional district reveals how ISAIAH built a prismatic base that fed back to shape its strategic options. This faith delegate's experience with ISAIAH came through her church. She told us that when she was first invited to be a delegate, she asked, "'Am I free to vote for whoever I want?' And they said yes at that point, not knowing how successful this was going to be." She entered the race and began organizing people she knew to support her in the precinct caucuses. Because her church congregation was not in the district where she was running, she had to go outside her church to find support. Nonetheless, this faith delegate entered the caucuses feeling pretty secure. She described organizing people to support her in the caucuses: "Because my church is not where my senate district is, I had to figure out other groups of contacts that I could make in order to [reach] my numbers. . . . I had the organizational muscle of ISAIAH behind me. I have some people that live in [the community] that attend my church, so I had that as a group. . . . That was many hours of organizing and phone calls and talking to people to try to get supporters." One thing that is significant about the work this woman did is that she was doing her own organizing; ISAIAH staff were not doing it on her behalf. In fact, she noted, "I met my staff organizer for the first time [at the Senate conventions]. I had gone there and I had my people lined up." Because of the work she had done with other ISAIAH volunteers through her church, she had a commitment to them that went beyond any loyalty to individual staff.

However, her commitments to the ISAIAH constituency were tested later in the process when she was not able to back the congressional candidate she wanted in the election. She was supporting progressive candidate Jeff Erdmann and had gotten involved with his campaign during the delegate process—she donated money to him, she volunteered at phone banks, and she attended house meetings on his behalf. At first, she thought that Erdmann was going to be the candidate ISAIAH advocated for. "Well, I'm really glad I don't have to make a hard decision," she said. In the end, however, ISAIAH asked its faith delegates to stand together in support of another candidate, Angie Craig, primarily because ISAIAH had determined that Craig had the votes to win, with or without the faith delegates. Craig had moreover demonstrated her openness to a deeper relationship with the organization, offering to create a faith-coordinator position on her campaign. The faith delegates decided, collectively, that supporting Angie Craig would put their constituency in the best possible position to have ongoing influence with a decision maker who would be elected to Congress in the 2018 midterms.

When we asked this faith delegate about her decision to vote with the other faith delegates despite her favored candidate not being chosen, she described the importance of being in relationship with the organization. "It was helpful just to be able to vent all of my feelings about that to a staffer, but there was no question[, of course] I was going with the collective." When we asked her why, she said,

> Well, if we don't stay as a collective, we don't have any power. I wouldn't have gotten to the point that I was if we didn't work collectively. It's a place of

hope. Being by yourself, that's not hopeful. I'm also doing this because my husband is a Trump supporter, and it's really been hard in our marriage. I can't be in that place where we don't share the same values. With people who view the world the same way, that's where I need to be. Like I said, it's just all about relationship building from the very beginning. . . . Also, I don't believe that any elected official is going to save us or our families.

ISAIAH's slow and careful building of its base enabled it to develop leaders, like this interviewee, who were prepared to act when the opportunity to be a faith delegate came along. With little prompting, this delegate was able to organize support for the caucus, get herself elected, and get into relationship with other ISAIAH leaders who had backgrounds different from her own. When ISAIAH asked her to support the other leaders' choice instead of pursuing her own candidate—a candidate she had actively supported—she chose to stand with the constituency in favor of the collective. Similar decisions made by many people like her made ISAIAH's faith-delegate campaign possible.

The kind of commitment that propelled this delegate to stand with the other faith delegates was not something that could have emerged overnight. Instead, it was the culmination of years of work. The ISAIAH staff organizer working most closely with this delegate noted the importance of having a set of leaders who had shared experiences that transcended the campaign. She described working with some of the leaders in that senate district on health-care battles in years past. At one point, they were combatting Republican Jason Lewis, who ultimately lost to Craig in the 2018 midterms and was, according to the ISAIAH organizer, "one of the faces of the repeal of the Affordable Care Act." She said that during that battle, "we were at his office at least once a week. At one point we had 100 people at his office. We had a banner of little people representing the 40,000 people in his district who would lose health care and we just unrolled it in his office and then we sat in his office for two hours and prayed."

The leaders who became delegates displayed variety in their movement experience and in how long they had been involved with the organization. ISAIAH/FiMN keep an internal database of leaders, recording, as much as possible, who comes to what events, how often, and what roles they take on. Although reporting into this database is not perfect, it represents the best picture we have of the kinds of trajectories these leaders follow within the organization. An examination of this data shows that on average the leaders who became delegates had been involved with them for five years and four months and had attended twenty-one events (as compared to an average of three events for the remaining 12,963 people in the database). Of the seventy-eight delegates recorded in the database, thirty-four had attended one or more of ISAIAH's intensive, weeklong annual trainings, the focal point of the organization's leadership-development work.[4]

Through this depth and duration of organizing, ISAIAH's leaders built a set of relational commitments that they could leverage to hold the faith delegates together. When the delegates were confronted with the challenge of deciding whether they wanted to stand together as a bloc, ISAIAH leaders brought them together to pose questions to them. An ISAIAH organizer would ask, "How much power did we build? Why did we build it? What do we want? And are we going to move as a collective, even if that means voting for the candidate we don't want to vote for?" She would then let the group decide and debate. ISAIAH was holding these meetings, trying to keep the delegates loyal to the organization even as those delegates were being courted by the candidates asking for their vote. In addition, gubernatorial candidates were explicitly asking staff leaders what concessions they wanted, as we described in chapter 3.

Throughout this entire campaign, ISAIAH leaders were very clear that they were operating under a political logic distinct from other campaigns. When we spoke with Doran in May 2018, in the heat of the period leading up to the DFL convention, we asked her what she wanted. "What would success look like?" we said. She replied, "The thing that we're asking for is so different from what they're used to people asking for. They want to know what transaction, 'What do you want? Like, what horse do we trade? Let's trade horses and then you'll give me your people.' That's the conversation people know how to have." But ISAIAH wished for something other than just that transaction.

Doran continued,

> I mean the most obvious answer is we want to have significant amounts of political power in relationship to the next governor's administration. And that looks like, more than access, it looks like shaping, you know? . . . It would be, okay, let's say we want to make a major leap forward on family care infrastructure. . . . A governor doesn't come in and wave a magic wand and make that happen. You partner [with the governor], and say, "Over the next four years, what is the scaffolding [we need] for that kind of structural change? And what's our role and what's your role and what's other people's roles and how are we in a strategy together?" Because doing something like that is very hard. It's not just, it's not an issue campaign.

Although ISAIAH's work in the 2018 gubernatorial and congressional races is one of the clearest examples we have of the kind of flexibility and commitment these organizations built, the prismatic approach is not limited to ISAIAH. Through all of our cases, we saw leaders making choices about how to develop their constituency, with an eye toward the long-term feedback loops those choices would create. The ways in which they engaged their base early on enabled greater strategic flexibility when they met unknown challenges down the road. These leaders' investment in constituency was rooted in a recognition that their ability to negotiate for power depends on not only their ability to get access to the decision-making table but also their ability to gain and hold that seat at the table using a source of power independent from their relationship with elite decision makers.

Pragmatism: "It's a False Choice"

Another sign of the focus on strategy and power that pervaded our cases was leaders' rejection of a set of false dichotomies that they described as dominating the thinking of many other political actors. In both the scholarly literature and the popular press, constituency-based activist organizations are often portrayed as extreme ideological purists. Because the groups in our cases are all working on progressive issues, they are part of what establishment politicians will sometimes describe as the "left flank" of the Democratic Party. But instead of being pushed into "you can either do this or do that" mentalities, the leaders in our study pursued alternative approaches. They rejected the idea that you have to make a choice between purism and pragmatism, and sought to ground themselves in a source of power that enabled them to be both ideological and pragmatic.

We found that just as the leaders in our cases argued that they could be in relationship with power while also challenging it, they also argued they could work pragmatically for pure political ideals. They thus rejected a long-held assumption in the social-movement literature that organizations become more moderate as they professionalize or get "channeled" into the arenas of institutional power (e.g., Piven and Cloward 1977; Jenkins and Eckert 1986). Instead, like the groups Elisabeth Clemens (1997) describes in her analysis of women's organizations at the turn of the twentieth century, these leaders saw themselves as using conventional political repertoires to advocate for unconventional stances. Many of the leaders and organizations in our study continued to hold views that are to the left of the mainstream even as they used pragmatic political strategies to realize those views. The idealism, in other words, was grounded in a pragmatic view of how power operates.

For instance, we asked one statewide organization's leader in Arizona how he walks the "tightrope" between "going with the insider strategy and losing credibility with your base or losing credibility with the electeds." He immediately replied, "I think it's a false choice." He continued at length:

It's what fucking Wall Street does, right? They go work for the Fed or whatever and then go back to . . . Goldman Sachs. . . . Yeah, they just go back and forth. That's what we need to do. Like you can work for [government] then you go back to [the movement organization] and then you work for [government] and you go back to [the movement organization] and you just do that over, so you're not fighting [government], you are [government]. . . . [When we are in government, we have to recognize that,] "You're not going to have perfect choices, you're going to have to make compromises and you're never going to get everybody, but you are going to do your best to serve and solve and save as many as possible." Then you go back to [the movement organization with people] who are all human beings knowing that it's not a perfect world. And you say, "Guys we did our best and this is what we're dealing with." . . . If you really want to build the power to govern, governing is not simple and clear. It's full of compromises and full of half measures and incrementalism and all that stuff and so what you want is not to send your pragmatist like me into the office. You want to send your craziest, most radical believer and that's the person that then has to figure out how to solve these really complex problems full of imperfect solutions, and to do it in partnership with all of us in the organizational side that are trying to build the power to keep them in so they can keep doing good shit.

He was not alone in his orientation. During our data collection, we spent time shadowing Tram Nguyen at the Virginia statehouse and observed the way she maneuvered among elected officials, advocating her constituents' views while simultaneously inserting herself in the middle of a number of different debates, as revealed in the network maps in chapter 3. At one point, NVM had organized a small protest in which activists advocated for driver's licenses for immigrants. At the time of the protest, Tram was in a conversation with the chief of staff to Mark Sickles, a moderate Democrat who was the ranking House Democrat on the Appropriations Committee. "Why are they fighting for driver's licenses?" the staffer asked. "They can't win this." Tram responded, "[But] this is what the people want." NVM's strategy was to put the issue on the agenda, even if its leaders knew they could not win a vote at the time.

Yet, even as NVM publicly pushed positions that were ideologically to the left of most of the chamber, we also saw the organization operate at the center of other, active negotiations. On the same day as the protest, the Virginia House and Senate were attempting to reconcile bills involving Medicaid expansion. Tram had worked with two other organizational partners to create a Google spreadsheet of the changes, with each row identifying line items cut from the state house version in the state senate bill. The Democratic caucus then used this spreadsheet to coordinate its members and push back against the Virginia Senate's proposed changes. In this setting, we saw elected officials looking to NVM for talking points and strategy, giving NVM influence over the terms of the debate. NVM was advocating for its values but also making itself indispensable by providing elected officials with practical advice.

At another point that same day, a staffer for one of the ranking members asked to meet privately with Tram. We waited outside while they talked. When Tram emerged twenty-five minutes later, we asked, in broad strokes, what the meeting was about. Tram responded that this staffer was asking her to "clean up" after some other immigration advocates who were creating what the staffer perceived to be unnecessary "drama" around some legislation. She noted, "This is one of the roles I play sometimes, working out issues caused by people who are not as experienced or who are new to the work and don't have the relationships and don't behave in strategic ways."

In March 2018, we observed Tram speaking on a panel at a national gathering of progressive organizers. Panelists from around the country were discussing how they build what they called "governing power" in the settings in which they were working, contrasting this idea with electoral power. One panelist said elected officials want to know "that you understand politics; you're not just an ideologue." Tram agreed quickly: "I cut deals all the time," she said.

However, the willingness of the leaders in our case studies to play the inside game did not preclude outside-the-box strategies. In Nevada, for example, PLAN is known for sometimes blocking traffic in their protests, for their executive director going to trial (during which he faced up to six months in jail for trespassing) for disrupting a meeting on fossil fuel lease sales, and for high-profile bird-dogging actions that target lobbyists as well as elected officials. In one primary-source document from the early 2000s that PLAN leaders gave us, the president of Nevada's AFL-CIO (American Federation of Labor and Congress of Industrial Organizations) sent a dramatic letter dissolving its affiliation with PLAN for what the AFL-CIO saw as the organization's "abandonment of the principle of the 'multiple use' of resources" and "engage[ment] in the process of promoting the interest of PLAN"—in this case, what PLAN viewed as a nonnegotiable environmental-conservation issue—"to the detriment of all others." For these and other reasons, PLAN has earned what one top Democratic official called "one hell of a progressive brand." At the same time, PLAN has its own statehouse lobbyist on staff.

The leaders in our case studies resisted being boxed into a specific kind of strategy, refusing to state either "I am an insider" or "I fight from the outside." They wanted to be able to tack back and forth as the conditions warranted, using their ambiguous position to generate productive tension that would move their agenda forward. Categories such as "insider" and "outsider" set up rules for behavior that work against the interests of marginalized constituencies. To identify with one or the other is to close off possibilities because there are institutional myths and scripts for how "insiders" and "outsiders" should act. These leaders implicitly recognized that the "correct" way of doing things tends to align with the interests of those already with power (Meyer and Tarrow 1998). Our case organizations were not willing to restrict themselves in this way, and their clarity around the need for flexibility emerged from their commitment to their constituencies. The needs and desires of their bases, rather than the advice of political consultants and experts, were the lodestar that guided their work.

These unconventional choices sometimes mean that these leaders' work is not very legible to outsiders. The ISAIAH leader quoted in the epigraph to this chapter noted, "I think that ISAIAH doesn't fit the boxes that the political world understands. . . . So it's not uncommon for [another grassroots organization] to get the kind of credit in the press that really should go to ISAIAH. Because the press has some ability to understand what [that organization is]. It's a set of individuals who align themselves with a progressive block of activists in Minnesota. It's essentially the progressive wing of the Democratic Party. ISAIAH is not so easily understood." One cost of not fitting into existing political boxes is that it is more difficult to be recognized as legitimate by other institutions, including the media (Meyer and Rowan 1977; DiMaggio and Powell 1983).

There is nonetheless significant power in ambiguity, in not being able to be put into an easily interpretable category. In their analysis of the dominance of the Medici family in Italy, Padgett and Ansell state, "Locked-in commitment to lines of action, and thence to goals, is the product not of individual choice but at least as much of others' successful 'ecological control' over you" (1993, 1264). If the leaders in our cases had accepted existing frameworks for political action, they would be submitting to the rules of, and thus be controlled by, powerful political interests. While our case organizations did not necessarily hide their motivations in the same way Cosimo de Medici did, their actions were driven by multiple motivations because they were always working at building an independent base while advancing a campaign. The organizations in our study thus maintained significant flexibility in terms of the types of messages they promoted, the campaigns they undertook, and the tactics they used to win. Their commitment to their constituency instead of to the political sphere itself rendered them unpredictable to allies and opponents, thus allowing them to maintain a broad array of strategic options. Those actors whose behavior follows more conventional political practices find their possibilities for action more limited.

Of course, the challenge in maintaining such flexibility is having the capacity to do so. How were these leaders able to make these moves? We argue that strategic flexibility was a function of these leaders' most precious resource—their constituencies. A commitment to power became manifest in specific strategies, not through any one tactic, tool, or resource. These organizations unified their goals by combining a pragmatic approach to political strategy with accountability to an independent constituency, thereby generating the precision and flexibility they needed to attain and influence power.

Learning Loops: Finding Sources of Creativity

As leaders sought to maximize the size of their strategic toolkits, how did they identify the range of options at their disposal? Strategy does not emerge out of nowhere; instead it depends on the narratives people create about what happened in the past, what opportunities for action are in the present, and what is possible in the future. These interpretations, narratives, and explanations are shaped by a complex range of lenses and experiences that people bring to how they view and understand the world around them (Emirbayer and Mische 1998). In the *Harvard Business Review*, Henry Mintzberg argues that, while many people think of the process of creating strategy as being one of "rational control" and "systematic analysis," it is better understood as a "craft" that requires "not so much thinking and reason as involvement, a feeling of intimacy and harmony . . . developed through long experience and commitment" (1987, 66). Strategy is thus, as Marshall Ganz teaches, a verb and not a noun (2018b).

Many advocacy organizations draw the range of their strategies from a familiar repertoire of commonly accepted political techniques. Research shows that repertoires are often shared and legitimated across political organizations, implicitly defining the range of possible alternatives (Tarrow 1998). Petitions, marches, rallies, calling campaigns, letters to the editor, voting, community meetings, and house parties are many of the familiar techniques organizations for collective action use. The leaders in our case studies drew on many of the same repertoires but also sought creative ways to deploy them. They sought new techniques that were less familiar to broader audiences. To operate outside the range of commonly accepted techniques, the organizations had to develop the capability to exercise the "craft" that Mintzberg describes above. Where did that craft originate?

Our data show that the leaders were intentional about building a set of capabilities that would make strategic creativity more likely. They wanted themselves and their peers to learn skills that were not just technical or operational but also focused on the idea that successful collective action is a craft that accounts for the dynamic nature of political power. Their focus on this craft became most evident in how they approached learning processes, building capability, and strategic relationships (such as those within national organizing networks). As Doran put it, "What is missing from [most] power conversation[s]? There are resources required to do this kind of work different than the resources required to organize a base, or the resources required to do civic engagement around an election, or resources required to run a campaign. Money matters, but also leadership. What is the tissue building needed across organizations that make new things possible?" Doran's description of "leadership" and "tissue building" is consistent with what management scholars call "second-order capabilities." Zero-order capabilities are about mastering a set of operational procedures that any organization needs—human-resources management, for instance, or (in the case of constituency-based organizations) coordination of mass communications to members. Second-order capabilities, in contrast, require a level of judgment that can only be taught over time and, as a result, are harder to imitate. That judgment thus becomes the resource that gives certain organizations competitive advantage over others. These distinctions are consistent with Michael Burawoy's (2005) differentiation between "instrumental" and "reflexive" learning. "Instrumental" or "technical" learning is about creating solutions to problems or solving puzzles in service of clients or particular outcomes. "Reflexive" knowledge is "concerned with a dialogue about ends" and thus "interrogates the value premises" that are offered (Burawoy 2005, 11).

We find that all of the leaders across our cases were intentional about cultivating a set of second-order capabilities among themselves and their leadership teams. This commitment became manifest in several ways. First, many leaders had explicit mechanisms for intentional introspection. Troy, for instance, shared with us three years of his written weekly reflections. The entries are organized into sections, such as "Meetings This Week," "What I Am Reading," and "Reflection." For the first year or so of entries, Troy also included a section on "Risks in the Past Week" and "Risks Not Taken." The former would include things like "Biggest risk of this week is the decision to [vote on] the People's Platform—we have our meeting this afternoon at 3:30.

We have RSVPs for the decision-making gathering. While all the people in the room are in relationship with at least one of the AMOS organizers, there are people who will be in the room whom I don't know." A risk not taken might be something like "I went into my one-to-one with [a member of] the board of elections for Hamilton County and a key bundler for Governor Kasich's presidential run without a clear proposition or ask. I thought it was a good [meeting] but I should have gone into it with a clearer sense that this was a power one-to-one. That said, hopefully I've set myself up to lean on [him] for connections to key legislative Republicans at the city, county, and state level in the future." The mere fact that Troy would record weekly risks and reflect on them shows the serious attention he paid to his constituency's uncertain hold on power and the need to reflect on the craft of his own leadership as a way of negotiating that power.

Just as Troy wrote weekly reflections that forced a disciplined consideration of his strategy, other leaders had their own mechanisms for learning. All of the organizations in the study had collective meetings after major moments in a campaign in order to reflect on what had happened, what they had learned, and what that meant for their work going forward. They also had formal processes for cultivating leadership among new volunteers and younger leaders, processes that are very common to community organizing (Warren 2001; Han 2014; Smock 2004; Gecan 2002). They trained leaders to ask particular kinds of questions that forced them to wrestle with tension, make sense of the world, and develop a complex analysis of where they were going.

Burt Lauderdale, executive director of Kentuckians for the Commonwealth, described the centrality of learning in his organization:

> Everyone says KFTC is so great, but we are always in learning mode. We are really proud of what we have done, but it is entirely insufficient. I think we are a pretty interesting case study around decision-making . . . [we have a] strong belief around shared decision-making—[it] makes our friends and allies crazy. But we already know how we make decisions. [We need research on] how that might restrict us? What opportunities are we cutting off? Are there other ways we could do these things better that would help us get to authentic grassroots power?

The leaders in our cases were deeply interested in self-critique and learning as means of constantly renewing their strategic capacity. This focus on learning was also evident in the way these organizations processed defeat. In all of our cases, we found that the characterization of certain events—the passage of SB

1070, the failure to oust Arpaio in his first twenty years as sheriff, Murphy's loss to Walz in Minnesota, PLAN coming up short on the mining campaign, AMOS losing on tax mechanism, and so on—as movement failure might have been misleading, even though at face value they appeared to fit that framework (Voss 1998). What distinguished the organizations in our study from other familiar cases in which high-profile defeats caused protesters to go home or accept loss is that the leaders in our study used these moments as opportunities for deliberate reflection and restrategizing. Win or lose, they only took on a fight if they could do so in a way that built their capacity.

Second, in addition to instituting deliberately reflective practices, these organizations devised campaigns that constantly developed their strategic capacities, particularly through cultivating new leadership. Those capacities were usually named as core objectives of the campaign itself. Joy Cushman described this approach:

> And so these leaders are fiercely committed, not afraid of tension, in deep relationship with a base, a people they respect and treat as equals and not as people they're advocating for. . . . You know, they have a moral framework that they are operating from. They believe in good and evil. They want to take on evil. . . . What's interesting to me about the decision they made to run the Arpaio campaign [in 2012] was that the odds were not zero, but they were very, very low, but the environment was moving in the right direction. So they basically made the decision to run the campaign knowing they would probably lose, but to do it in a way that they got more voters registered, they developed more leadership, they built their credentials, so they could take him on again down the line. So it's not just that they were willing to do a losing campaign, because people could take lots of weird wrong messages from that, but since they were likely to lose it, they did it in a way that they built just a lot of capacity.

Joy is describing work among the immigrant rights advocates in Arizona, but her point can be applied to any of the cases in our study. As she indicates, even an unwinnable campaign can be strategic for these organizations if it presents a good opportunity for them to develop the kind of long-term, second-order capabilities that will maximize their strategic choice set down the road.

Another example of this approach comes from PLAN's work helping to pass the corporate-profits tax bill. That victory, in 2015, came after the organization had advocated for over a decade on behalf of a tax on the mining industry. Mining is an enormously powerful industry and lobby in Nevada; PLAN was taking on a behemoth. The first time they tried to tax the mining indus-

try, PLAN and its allies lost by 1 percent. Although this campaign was puta-
tively a loss, it paved the way for the corporate-profits tax bill in 2015. As one
key organizer and political operative remembered, "We lost that [mining bill]
as well. But the good thing was that we at least got it in the popular mindset
and imagination so that no defeat is made up entirely of defeat." She noted
that a key result of their earlier fight over the mining bill was that they began
developing their constituency's capacity to act on the issue. "I like to think,
and I do think, that the work that we did up until that had some impact."

Throughout our case studies, organizational leaders were clear that one of
the biggest strategic investments they could make, in any setting, was to develop other leaders. They would intentionally design all meetings, events, and
campaigns with an eye to how leaders and members could learn through the
process of planning, executing, and reflecting on their actions. For instance,
as part of AMOS's Preschool Promise campaign in Ohio, teams of volunteers
did research visits with a variety of public officials and other stakeholders relevant to the campaign. We attended a debriefing meeting in a church lounge
where thirteen volunteers who had participated in these visits sat in a circle
and shared what they had learned. The lead organizer asked participants to
break into small groups and discuss the following questions: "What was your
experience during the conversations? What did you learn from this? What is
their self-interest, what do you think their power is?" After these small-group
discussions, each group reported back to the full group. The organizer then
asked the full group, "What did you learn about yourself? We were in meetings with people in power in the city, what did you learn about how you act
around people in power?" Thus, leaders pushed each volunteer to reflect on
both the power and self-interest of the stakeholders they had met as well as
their own behavior when confronting power.

An organization like AMOS has the option of having professional staff
conduct these meetings with public officials, and then having the staff use
the information they gathered to determine a course of action. That approach,
however, would have limited leadership-development opportunities for volunteers. The leaders in our case studies chose a different path. The discussion
at the AMOS debriefing meeting described above surfaced important insights
that helped volunteers grow in their own leadership capabilities. For instance,
one leader described what she saw during the meetings with public officials:
"There are two different goals—people who are advancing their own agendas
and people who come from poverty and know what it feels like." She said that
the former group is "not going to shift easily" and therefore "something has
to give." Through this debrief, this volunteer was practicing political analysis

and strategy. She and the other volunteers in the room were evaluating their own power and others' power. They reflected on their own behavior, got feedback, and, in the process, built stronger relationships with one another.

Third, and finally, in addition to cultivating learning and reflection within their organizations and selecting campaigns with an eye toward long-term capabilities, the leaders in our case studies all forged relationships with national learning networks outside their immediate cities and states. This meant that the leaders in our case studies were not completely independent of one another. Many of them knew each other, and some had even strategized together. In addition, they were part of shared conversations focused on interpreting the political moment and thinking about different strategies for challenging the status quo. We found that these ecosystems created a broader learning environment where leaders could consider new strategies they might not have been able to identify on their own.

Because the leaders in our case studies conceived of power as dynamic and recognized the inherent uncertainty their constituencies would face in building and maintaining power, they understood learning as a key component of strategy. Through a focus on learning—their own and that of other leaders and constituents in their organizations—these leaders built the craft of developing careful strategy. In other words, when building the metaphorical prism, they made learning part of their design choices because it would help them develop the insight and capacity to act strategically in moments of uncertainty (Ganz 2000, 2009). If there was any practice that was universal among our cases, it was the practice of creating learning loops. Leaders sought to enmesh themselves and their leadership teams in ecosystems of learning that facilitated the kind of strategic creativity they needed to make their improbable bids for power more likely to succeed.

What Makes Prisms Strategic?

In this chapter, we sought to show why it was strategic for the leaders in our case studies to follow the logic of preparing for uncertainty. In other words, what makes the investment in constituency strategic for these leaders? We argued that understanding the distinction between a constituency as an independent source of power and a constituency as a tool for access was key to answering this question. For organizations representing constituencies like the ones in our case studies, the bid for political power does not stop with access to power. Our case organizations knew they would have to constantly work to hold decision makers accountable, and that would necessitate an ability to wield resources that the organizations controlled. The key resource these leaders could control was their own constituency.

Leaders in our cases thus constantly built their constituency in a way that focused on civic feedbacks, or the downstream consequences of the choices they made about *how* to engage people. It was not enough to get people to take action; rather, they had to get people to take action in ways that would enable these leaders to exercise power in the public domain. These leaders were so deeply aware that their constituencies formed the basis of their power that many interviewees expressed anxiety about anything—including their biggest successes—that distracted them from constituency building. One long-standing ISAIAH leader told us, "I feel like the seeds of our destruction are in our success." The pace of political work is so fast, he was arguing, that it is hard to find time to do the slow work that base building requires: "What I really want to do is have like fifty clergy that I'm actually developing, and like they're becoming, not just better ISAIAH leaders but better human beings, and better clergy, and better pastors," he said. The next chapter explores exactly what it means to do this slow work of cultivating a base that serves as a durable and independent source of political power rather than an ephemeral ingredient of political stagecraft.

Leaders' focus on strategic constituency building led them to make distinct choices about not only how to build constituency but also how to think about leadership. All of the cases in our study had at their helm individual leaders who were at once pragmatic analysts of the political terrain and fiercely committed to the agendas that mattered to their base. The one compromise the leaders in our study would not make was that of undercutting their base, which they recognized as their most important and most reliable source of power. Their investment in this source of power was evident not only in, as Joy put it, "the humility [they had] to invite others to join [them] in action, and to ask [for] help," but also in their commitment to establishing organizational learning loops and civic feedbacks with every tactical decision they made.

5 *Building People to Build Power*

This conversation is happening in a context of who we are, who we have been as ISAIAH, even before we begin to talk about issues that are affecting our lives. There is a lens that we are approaching these issues with as people of faith. . . . Many of you have been part of this organization for a long time, that's the foundation that we are standing on, that's who we are, that's still there. When we talk about issues, like climate change, we are looking at them through those lenses. . . . We're going to brainstorm demands for the next governor. The question isn't just about climate change, but is connected to the relationships that you are building through the house meetings.
ISAIAH STAFF LEADER

I talk a lot about how I think KFTC was really formative in my identity as a Kentuckian and thinking of myself as a Kentuckian and wanting to stay here after school.
KFTC LEADER

It takes investment. . . . It takes a while, for, like a person like myself, who's even been doing this sixteen, seventeen years now, to learn both how to develop an infrastructure, how to create an organization, how to effect policy change, how to do all these things, how to build power, but there's an authenticity, and a value in having it be ourselves, coming in from our own, because me fighting for my mom, me fighting for my family, is very different than another person who has a theoretical connection to the work, rather than the heart, mind, and complete embodiment of the fight.
ARIZONA STAFF LEADER

What does constituency building look like in the context of prisms of people power? We have argued that the leaders in our case studies were able to trans-

late the participation of their constituents into political power by paying attention to not only *whether* the constituency was engaged but also *how* it was
engaged. Departing from dominant models of collective action that focus
only on how many people take how many actions, leaders designing what we
call prisms focus on *how* that constituency is involved. Constituencies with
particular characteristics exemplify the feedback effects that give leaders
more room to negotiate strategically for power with elite decision makers.

How, exactly, did these leaders engage their constituencies? This chapter
unpacks several patterns that we saw across our cases. By building their bases
in particular ways, the leaders in our case studies were able to help their constituents develop specific "lenses" through which they came to view the world.
As the ISAIAH staff leader quoted above noted, unlike most political analyses
that focus on issues, these lenses were more about people. "Who are we and
who do we want to become?" ISAIAH leaders saw their challenge as putting
constituents through what they called "a formation process that allows them
actually to think of themselves as part of a collective." For ISAIAH, actions
like voting were not about their individual outcomes but instead about the
idea that "I'm going to have a voice and then I'm going to operate with a collective."

The leader in Kentucky that we quoted likewise discussed her own transformation through KFTC. When she first got involved with KFTC, it was focused on trying to stop fracking and mountaintop removal and develop more
clean-energy sources for the state. This leader came from a community where
mountaintop removal was not a salient issue. Through KFTC, however, she
became invested in it. She said, "There's this motto, 'We all live downstream,'
so we all as Kentuckians worked to do our part in that work." Instead of framing the issue as being about the climate or the land or a distant community,
KFTC framed it as being related to people regardless of place. That approach
reflected the broader consciousness KFTC was seeking to build.

In Arizona, a number of the immigrant leaders we interviewed, like the
organizer quoted above, talked about the importance of having leaders who
emerge from the constituency they are seeking to organize. These interviewees were not just speaking about the superficial commitment to visual diversity that often dominates liberal discussions of race and leadership. They
were not referring to a token nod to allowing immigrants themselves to
speak on behalf of their constituencies. Instead, as the leader quoted above
argued, having indigenous leaders is, in this case, a strategic move. By grounding their work in people who have a personal stake in the outcomes of the
problems being tackled, organizations ensure that these leaders bring their
whole "heart and mind" to the work. These leaders become "embodied" in

the fight in a way that forces a strategic creativity, which we saw across our cases. These constituents were not content to color within the lines of strategic choices drawn by others. Instead, because the fight was about "my mom" or "my family," they were determined to get it right and were willing to make significant investments to build the capacities they needed.

In the organizations we studied, then, building a constituency entailed creating constituents who are loyal enough to do the work of exercising voice inside and outside the organization over time. In this chapter, we describe the characteristic patterns we saw across our cases. In particular, we describe four interrelated characteristics of the work that organizations in our cases did: first, the organization grounded constituents in a constantly expanding network of relationships; second, leaders developed the constituents as independent, distributed strategists, so that they had sufficient motivation and skill to strategize independently instead of constantly needing direction from centralized staff; third, the constituencies were simultaneously persistent and flexible; and fourth, the constituencies cultivated bridges across groups and types of people who are not normally connected in US society. We unpack each of these practices and characteristics in turn, drawing on examples from each of our six cases. We start, however, by grounding our description of the constituencies in a discussion of why the types of prisms they constructed allowed leaders to achieve the strategic goals outlined in the previous chapter.

Why Prisms of People Power?

Our argument about prisms links the practices of constituency building with organizations' efforts to move power. We argue that investing in building constituency helps organizations seeking to build power in uncertain political environments accomplish their goals. How? Put another way, why would certain base-building practices lead constituencies to stay committed and flexible in the ways these leaders want?

In describing the benefits of adapting practices from ancient self-governing organizations for the twenty-first century, organizational theorist Brook Manville and classicist Josiah Ober note that many modern-day businesses use the language of empowerment and create group decision-making practices that operate in localized ways but also exclude most members of the firm from key strategic decisions within the organization (Manville and Ober 2003b). Manville and Ober reach back to the earliest days of Athenian democracy to describe what they argue is a better model of self-governance than the contemporary one. They argue that effective self-governance rests on three intertwined elements: a "participatory structure" for decision-making, a set of "communal values" that define people's relationships to each other, and a set of "practices of engagement" that ensure broad participation. Understanding how these principles operated in the past can help counteract what they call "our emaciated modern conception of democracy" (Manville and Ober 2003a).

Like Manville and Ober, we conceptualize constituency building not merely as a process of bottom-up decision-making but as a set of structures, values, and practices rooted in mutual accountability between leaders and constituents. Self-governance is not a thin version of government "of, by, and for" the people in which leaders merely reflect the preferences of those they represent. Instead, it is a set of processes and practices through which constituents and leaders each foster constituency capacity, even as they are constrained by the constituency's voice. As scholars of civic associations have long argued, leaders cultivate the capacities of citizenship among members (Verba, Schlozman, and Brady 1995; Putnam 1993, 2001; Andrews et al. 2010; Han 2014). In such associations, however, leaders are also constrained by the voice of constituents who exercise the very capacities these leaders helped create. For example, Troy refused to cut a deal with other members of the Preschool Promise coalition without first gaining support from his constituents, knowing that acting otherwise would bring negative consequences. Similarly, LUCHA felt compelled by its constituents to press forward on a campaign for minimum wage even as funders and other power brokers tried to dissuade the organization from this path.

Constraint is not only for leaders, however. Constituents are also constrained by the internal democracy that makes up a prism. Democratic theorists are careful to note that giving constituencies a voice is about not just rights (their right to a voice) but also responsibilities. People who participate in self-governing organizations are constrained by the mutuality of their relationships to one another; to partake of the benefits of voice, they must also participate as members of the community, heeding the concerns and interests of their peers instead of acting as isolated agents (Anderson 2017). In Hirschman's (1970) language of exit, voice, and loyalty, members of organizations are implicitly making the choice to exercise loyalty, because loyalty makes them part of the collective.

The design choices that lead to constituencies equipped to exercise voice are core to the strategic exercise of power, because they engender constituents who are committed to acting with one another. That commitment is what makes the kind of strategic flexibility we described in the previous chapter possible. When leaders who have built such constituencies are sitting at the negotiating table, they have a keen sense of the limits and possibilities of their negotiation. This deep understanding of their constituents' wants and needs makes them better advocates for their organization's interests. Across our cases, we saw four key characteristics that distinguished these constituencies from the norm.

A Growing Latticework of Interconnected Relationships

The importance of social relationships to sustained participation is no secret. Scholars have long recognized the social bases of participation and, in particular, the importance of social ties in making participation stick over time (Sinclair 2012; Green and Gerber 2015; Rosenstone and Hansen 1993; Munson 2009; Nepstad and Clifford 2006; Nepstad 2008). As a Lutheran pastor and ISAIAH leader told us, "I guess the other reason that I've stayed involved in ISAIAH is that there have been leaders that I've known since the beginning that are still connected to it. . . . The number of leaders in the organization that I've known for five, ten, fifteen, twenty years and, you know, I trust them and know them. So you stick with people that you trust."

What we found to be distinct about our case organizations was that they were not only drawing on people's preexisting social networks (McAdam 1982; Morris 1986) but also engaging their constituencies in ways that constantly built new relationships, while also transforming previously private relationships into shared public commitments to act. People would reach out and recruit new people, and also ask people in their existing social networks to join them in action. These new relationships included both horizontal relationships between constituents and vertical relationships between constituents and leaders or staff. Figure 5.1 provides an example of how this works, showing how organizations can achieve both depth and scale by investing in relationships and intermediate tiers of volunteer leadership. The graphs in this figure are based on ISAIAH's internal data tracking of volunteers and supporters during a 2019 municipal ballot-referendum campaign in Saint Paul. This campaign followed on the heels of the faith-delegate campaign and was part of a bid by ISAIAH to not only win the ballot referendum but also demonstrate the strength of its ground game in order to enter into a deeper relationship of shared power with the mayor and city council. The three evolving network graphs show how a single ISAIAH organizer (the center node) was able to relationally activate more than two thousand voters in just three months' time. This was possible because of ISAIAH's long-standing investment in its highly engaged volunteer leadership base (the second tier of leadership, top graph). Over the course of the campaign, these seven leaders recruited eighty-nine additional volunteers, or "democracy builders" (the third tier of organizational

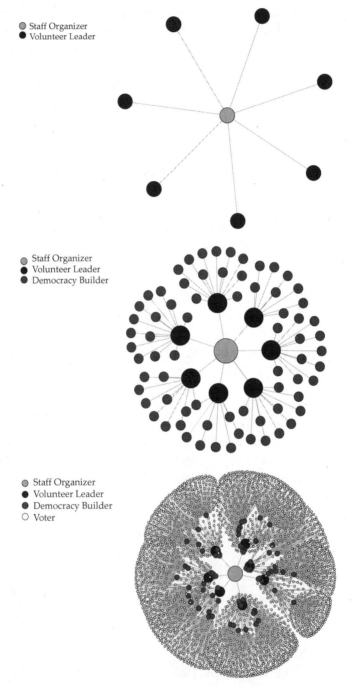

Figure 5.1. Growth in ISAIAH's relational leadership network and constituency base in Saint Paul during a 2019 municipal ballot-referendum campaign.

These graphs were created using the Kamada-Kawai algorithm and are based on ISAIAH's internal tracking of volunteers and voters during the 2019 campaign.

leadership, center graph) and cultivated their leadership and their capacity to build and strengthen their social networks. Those democracy builders, in turn, built relational lists of between fifteen and one hundred people they knew in Saint Paul. When it came time to vote, ISAIAH activated this relational infrastructure to mobilize supporters to vote in favor of the referendum—which passed by a twenty-six point margin, winning 63 percent of the vote.

The Arizona case shows how horizontal organizational relationships can grow as well. In Arizona, people who had not known one another before their shared involvement in the statehouse vigil chose in that moment to link arms and take action together. Afterward, they continued to collaborate with one another as movement strategists. That was one of the most durable effects of the 104-day vigil outside the Arizona statehouse: the network of immigrant leaders that emerged, many of whom now head the organizations that constitute the progressive ecosystem in Arizona (and one of whom was elected to the legislature in 2018, while another joined the Phoenix City Council in 2019). In other words, our qualitative data indicate that network ties were created among not only constituents but also leaders. We mapped these peer-leader relationships to show the number of relational ties among organizations in the Arizona progressive ecosystem after the fight around SB 1070. Before SB 1070, organized labor dominated progressive politics in the state, with other organizations sporadically working alongside labor to engage their constituencies. After SB 1070, however, the number of immigrant-led groups in the state grew, as did the ties between them. Over time, they decided to formalize two coalitions to strengthen the ability of these organizations to align resources and strategy: Arizona Wins, the state's progressive 501(c)(4) table founded in 2011; and One Arizona, the state's 501(c)(3) founded after the vigil in 2010. These alliances created new strategic venues and a very different political ecosystem by 2016, in which a number of immigrant-led organizations with strong ties to one another worked alongside national groups (see appendix C for a list of these affiliations). Thus, the mosaic of organizations shown in figure 5.2 turned constituencies that had previously been treated as atomized voters into an organized base capable of acting, learning, and growing together.

Given the intense forging of these cross-leader—and subsequent cross-organization—ties, these leaders frequently speak about the deep commitments they share with one another. One leader in Arizona reflected on his fellow movement leaders:

> Yes we come from different places, we come from different countries, but at this time right now, we have the same struggle. I've been prepped so many

○ One Arizona
● Arizona Wins
◐ Both

Figure 5.2. Network ties between immigrant rights organizations in Arizona in 2016. These graphs were created using the Fruchterman-Reingold algorithm and are based on Arizona Wins and One Arizona organizational membership data from 2017. A glossary of these organizational abbreviations and the national networks with which they are affiliated is included in appendix C.

times to talk to media, on CNN—how to do your "pitch" and share your story to "win the hearts of the moderates, win the hearts of the voters." That's different from winning the hearts of the community of your peers, and your soldiers you know, because we're the soldiers in the field and we need more soldiers to fight this fight . . . our stories are mainly the same, we struggle economically, financially, educationally. . . . I'm a person that I think I'm in this fight alone, that it's only happening to me, that I'm the only one that can't go to college, I'm the only one that can't get a job. I'm the only one that's afraid my dad might be deported.[1]

This organizer was not alone in sharing this sentiment. Another interviewee told us, "[Right after SB 1070 was signed], my neighbor . . . he invited my mom to a house meeting, and I don't even know why I went, but I went. It was a house meeting . . . It was a house meeting in his living room. In [his] living room. I was just like, 'Oh my God.' They started talking about their stories and their struggles. Everybody was undocumented. Most of the people there were undocumented. In that moment, I felt like, 'Oh my God, there's more people like me.'" These kinds of experiences locate people's individual experiences in a broader movement, reminding them that they are not isolated but part of a larger collective struggle.

Not all of our cases presented such a catalytic moment as SB 1070 and the subsequent vigil in Arizona. Nonetheless, across all our cases we see evidence of organizations creating new relational capacity. Drawing on principles of community organizing, all of the groups in our study placed a high premium on and devoted a number of resources to creating opportunities for people to be in relationship with one another. One of our interviewees in AMOS, for instance, described feeling some initial reluctance when he first encountered the congregation that he is now part of. Yet, he continued to stay involved. When asked why, he said, "They do a good job of just saying, 'If you want to do something, do it. Come in here, and we'll find something for you.' . . . In my previous experience that was not the situation—it can be kind of cliquish. If you wanted to be part of a group you had to know that clique before you could do it." He kept getting invited to different activities and eventually became enmeshed in the organization through the social relationships he created. Like all of the organizations in our study, AMOS was constantly focused on creating these social ties.

Once these organizations created social ties, they worked to reinforce them. Some organizations, such as AMOS, ISAIAH, PLAN, and KFTC, draw on a set of shared rituals to create a basis for relational solidarity. KFTC, for instance, begins many of its meetings with a shared recitation of the group's vision statement. Burt described the importance of the vision statement and the organization's other foundational documents: "[They] describe why we do what we do and the way we do it. So there's culture that is developed and then reinforced and then sustained with [the documents]." At the annual statewide meeting of KFTC leaders that we observed, the retreat opened with everyone in the room reading KFTC's vision statement aloud, in unison.

The vision becomes manifest through the relationships that these rituals help foster. Burt said, "People come because they want to work on restoration of voting rights, let's say, but they stay because of the vision [and] the relationships, the family atmosphere, the team. It's the culture of the organization . . . that holds people." The relationships become a way of making manifest the shared values the organization espouses. According to Burt, these commitments come to transcend people's original commitments to issues: "There are times when people get, 'My thing is most important,' but incredibly little of that."

The shared rituals in other organizations may not have been as explicit as those at KFTC, but many of our cases had them. AMOS and ISAIAH leaders, for instance, both noted the importance of their annual "weeklongs," their term for weeklong trainings. Unlike trainings that focused solely on developing a set of skills among participants, these weeklongs also focused on developing peer-to-peer relationships and a commitment to the organization. PLAN had monthly meetings that served the same purpose of building social relationships as well as disseminating information and skills. Many of the organizations in our study displayed a strong set of norms around the structure of meetings and other shared gatherings. These norms functioned like rituals that reinforced people's sense of commitment to one another.

Several organizations used art and culture as motivation. In one of our visits to LUCHA—whose logo is of a Mexican professional wrestler who is known for being "small but powerful," as Tomás told us—they held a *voteria*, a play on *loteria*, which is a wildly popular game similar to bingo. One Saturday morning, staff, volunteers, and their family members set up the *voteria* canvass launch with banquet tables, streamers, water balloons, and a piñata that said "5K new Arizona voters!" (the number of voters LUCHA had registered in the past month). The volunteer coordinator's mom was there setting up a delicious-looking pulled-pork taco spread in the already baking Arizona heat. The atmosphere was one of a political community in celebration.

Another common ritual across our cases was the intentional sharing of personal stories in group settings, particularly stories that highlighted difficulty, pain, or oppression. Prior research on community organizing has identified this as a core practice in the field (Braunstein 2012; Oyakawa 2015). These stories are told in a variety of organizational settings, including one-to-one meetings, house meetings, meetings with public officials, and large-scale public meetings. For example, in the house meeting that laid the foundation for ISAIAH's faith-delegate campaign, people were directed to draw out stories about what they were struggling with, such as health care, housing, fear of the future, and so on. ISAIAH trained hundreds of ISAIAH leaders to host these house meetings. Organizers created a packet of materials for that training that broke the purpose down as follows:

The Heart of the "Pain to Power" Conversation
1. Sharing How We Are Struggling
2. What is the lie/story that gets told about your struggle?
3. What do we say as people of faith instead?

4. These struggles and pain are part of a designed system and story that we can change if we lead together
5. Invitations to Take Action
   a. Some activity in their political context (ex. Invitation to a public meeting)
   b. Commit to lead a House Meeting in your own community and have the same conversation
   c. Commit to attend the Caucuses on February 6, 2018 to claim your vision for MN.
   d. Invest financially in this Path.

ISAIAH trained leaders to not only draw out personal stories but also connect those stories to the "lies" or false cultural narratives about why people struggle (e.g., not working hard enough). In doing so, ISAIAH sought to generate an alternative narrative of struggle rooted in faith and oriented toward justice. Importantly, ISAIAH leaders also explicitly connected this practice to an orientation to thinking about social structure and change that emphasizes collective agency: "we can change if we lead together."

One leader who belonged to a church that had been involved with ISAIAH for over twenty years described the way ISAIAH intentionally creates spaces for new stories and new relationships to emerge—even in communities that have been working together for an extensive period of time. She reflected on her experiences with the 2018 house meetings:

We were telling stories to one another that we had never told each other. I went to weeklong with somebody and we'd been trying to build a core team at [our church] for sixteen years or something. He shared a pain that I did not know about which felt like "Well, I've really been not going deep with him," but the same. I was doing the same. There were many of us that were sharing stories that [we] didn't know about each other. Some people say "Basically, I've never shared this with anybody." It deepened our own relationships with one another and it also helped everybody in those rooms see that "Yeah, hey, we all are part of this," you know? It did identify new people.

The house meetings thus served multiple functions for ISAIAH. Longtime leaders built stronger relationships with one another by sharing personal stories. Potential new leaders could participate, were encouraged to develop their political consciousness, and were invited to further events.

These rituals acted as patterned expressions of people's commitment to one another and the values of the organization. Research on religious organizations has articulated the importance of rituals in shaping people's shared faith commitments across difference (Braunstein, Fulton, and Wood 2014; Delehanty and Oyakawa 2018). In addition, historical research on civic associations in the United States reveals a similar importance given to shared rituals—historic organizations like the Elks and the Masons, for example, had elaborate joining rituals and particular hats or vests that members would wear to meetings (Skocpol 2003). In our cases, the rituals were a way for people to express and reinforce their shared commitments to one another.

However, the rituals were just one part of a larger effort to constantly focus on relational capacity. Marshall Ganz (2018b) argues that social-movement organizations are distinct from other kinds of organizations in that they not only draw on people's existing resources but also are constantly regenerating them, or creating new ones. Those relational ties, we found, formed an important basis for ongoing commitment.

Distributed Strategists

A second feature of building a people-powered prism that we saw across our cases was organizations' efforts to engage constituents as independent strategists. Previous research has examined the value of distributed strategy and leadership (Warren 2001; Gecan 2002; Smock 2004; McAlevey 2016; Han 2014). This is often a key feature of community organizing: instead of engaging people in ways that leave them reliant on a set of core staff or leaders for negotiating power, these organizations seek to build the capacity of leaders throughout the organization to engage in power negotiations.

We argue that building a network of distributed strategists is central to how these organizations build power. Because their philosophy of power relies on not numbers or proximity to decision makers but the ability to engage in an ongoing and dynamic negotiation, they have to be prepared for the unexpected ways—and places—that the negotiation can unfold. KFTC, for example, engages its base in deep education and analysis about the issues around which they advocate. When they bring these leaders to the statehouse for lobby days, the leaders are equipped to go toe-to-toe with elected officials or other lobbyists about the issue.

One organizer with KFTC recalled a story from her early days of being involved with the organization. She was working with a group of low-income women in Kentucky who were resisting a proposed new policy to put welfare recipients on a forced budget: "What they would do is put the [welfare] money on a debit card, which at the time was new. . . . They would assign each public benefits recipient a quote 'upstanding' member of the community as a mentor. Together, they would create a monthly budget and that would get logged into the debit card so that if you were trying to purchase diapers and the purchase went over your monthly diaper budget, the purchase would be refused at the register." This organizer began meeting on a weekly basis with a group of women organizing to resist this policy. Much of their time focused on what she referred to as "leadership development." At first, she said, a lot of the women would introduce themselves by saying something like, "'I'm not one of *those* people.' Right, I'm worthy, you know don't look down on me. I work hard. I'm not the one milking the system." She describes a process through which these women began to reconsider their assumptions of their own worthiness, to begin to consider the idea that all people have the right to have their basic needs met.

Part of why this organizer found this work so valuable was that these women were then able to act strategically when challenged:

There were moments early on. We took a trip to DC to lobby around welfare reform that was . . . being proposed. We had a meeting with Mitch McConnell's chief of staff. When we got to the door, you know this was a big deal for all of us, myself included, to be able to walk in. It was not something I had done before and the chief of staff met us at the door and said, "There's no way we're taking this meeting after what you all did last week." What we had done last week was that KFTC members—other people, not this group—had had a protest outside McConnell's office about defunding the Office of Surface Mining. I sort of held my breath because I thought, oh you know this meeting means so much to this group and it would make a lot of sense for them to say, "Oh no, that wasn't us." They really had no connection to that other set of constituents within KFTC or those other issues related to strip mining. Instead, just with no preparation, the woman sort of in the front of the group put her hands on her hips and said, "You need to take this meeting with us so we can tell you why we did that." It was super powerful.

All of the organizations in our cases were working in uncertain political environments in which their bids for power were constantly being challenged or rebuffed. In all cases, the professional staff played an important role in designing responses to these situations, but in many cases, the goals were for the volunteer leaders to step into those roles.

One member-leader within KFTC described her own development:

When I think of my time as a member, I think of being trusted with responsibilities even though I was young. I know a lot of people talk about the lobbying work we do as leadership development. I think most people think of lobbying as put on your best pantsuit and walking in with reports in your hand, and we go lobby with members all the time. Members are [often] reluctant to [step up in these conversations]. They want the organizer to lead the conversation. . . . For me, when I was doing fair housing legislation work, I thought, "I'm not the best person to talk to my city commissioners because I'm twenty-one-years old, and I don't know much about economics and whatever." But I had . . . valued lived experience.

Reflecting back on this she noted how important it was to be "trusted to do important things." "A lot of times I'd be like, 'But isn't that your job?' [The organizer would] be like, 'No, this is.'" By constantly pushing responsibility out to members, and equipping them to step into these roles, staff and leaders in the organizations distributed the responsibility of acting strategically out to an increasingly wider network of people. This incident was not a unique occurrence at KFTC, or indeed, across our cases.

In Ohio, the ability of AMOS leaders to strategize independently was manifest at the meeting at the New Prospect Baptist church. Incensed by a meeting that had happened in his absence at which AMOS's coalition partners made changes to the campaign, Troy Jackson knew he had to act quickly to hold the leadership of the coalition accountable to the People's Platform. When he called the meeting at the New Prospect Baptist Church, AMOS had only a little over a week to fill the church, ensure that coalition leaders would attend, and plan the meeting. A week would not have been enough time to recruit, educate, and prepare three hundred people to strategically negotiate with the city's power elite, but AMOS had laid the groundwork well before through house meetings and the cocreation of the People's Platform.

AMOS's constituents' deep understanding of the issue was evident in the questions they asked of the panelists and the comments they made on Kiwi-Live, a synchronous meeting software that AMOS used to allow leaders to share thoughts and ideas with one another while the meeting at New Prospect took place. Some comments evinced constituents' deep understanding of the details of policy and the funding mechanism: "We can talk [about] the need for preschool, but until we put an appropriate amount of money behind our effort—then we are NOT living our values. I do not believe a combined levy will put the appropriate money behind this effort." Other comments focused on the power dynamic in the room: "We have called the bluff of ruling elites and got their attention. I am still wary of being sold out by these same ruling elites. My prayer is that AMOS can hold all power brokers accountable." "End result needs to be the same. We can't let business leaders and CPS [Cincinnati Public Schools] make the decision. It's time for bold decisions and risks," another message read.

In other situations, moments of urgency forced constituents to make choices they did not anticipate. In those moments, the groundwork that organizations have laid can powerfully shape how constituents respond. One Arizona leader recalled the youth-led school walkouts that coincided with Brewer's signing of SB 1070:

> I remember those days having extra security around campus and . . . I remember talking to different individuals in the school and we knew that we were [going to be] locked inside of our schools. We [weren't going to be] able to protest a law that was going to profile us and was injecting a lot of fear in our communities. I remember a young woman. She was my age. We were in seventh grade and she looked at us and she's like, "I know what to do and they're not going to stop this." She didn't tell us what she was going to do, but around ten, fifteen minutes later we have the fire alarm going on. And we were able to walk out that day.

This young woman could not have anticipated what she would need to do on this day, nor could the organizations who were seeking to support the youth. Yet, in that moment, she found the courage and confidence to act because of the solidarity she had created with her peers. Constituents who were not equipped to act autonomously may not have had the emotional and strategic capacity to act in that moment the way she did.

Another Arizona leader remembers when he was recruited to the movement in 2011. He was at a meeting about the recent increase in community-college tuition for out-of-state students. The bill meant that he and his undocumented peers would have to pay 600 percent more for their classes. "Even though I lived my entire life in Arizona, I still qualified as an out-of-state student because I didn't have a state ID," he said. He gave a PowerPoint presentation about the economic impact of the new law, in which he noted that he was undocumented. "After presentation was over, [an organizer] . . . tapped me on the shoulder and she said, 'Hey, do you mind if we talk after the vote?' And I was like, 'Yeah, absolutely.' And it's almost like my life changed at that point because I met with [her] and we just had like this two-hour-long conversation outside of school. And she was like, 'Hey, are you pissed about this?' I'm like, 'Hell yeah. This is crazy.'" Both of these leaders went on to get deeply involved in a city-council race and then in progressive politics across the state.

Simultaneous Commitment and Flexibility

An important consequence of relational organizing in our cases was that people expressed their commitments in terms of the constituency rather than issues. When confronted with the challenge of SB 1070, the first question that Michele asked was, "What do the people need?" Putting constituencies at the center of strategy had important consequences. As one interviewee told us, "I learned to think about the people and the work, the people and the work, the people and the work, and so if we only think about the people, or we only think about the work, we're not actually building an organization or power. And so when people only talk about developing leaders, to me it's only talking about the people. . . . [The best organizations] build capacity through the work. They didn't build capacity as something separate from the work." This commitment to a constituency instead of an issue enabled a kind of flexibility across campaigns, political domains, and issues that is rarely recognized in the academic literature. Much research on collective action depicts activists as committed ideologues, driven by sometimes maniacal dedication to particular policy outcomes. Think here of the stereotypical pictures we have of single-issue abortion voters, gun-rights activists, tree-hugging environmentalists, or animal-rights extremists. Research on activism often substantiates these stereotypes, showing activists as driven by purposive, policy-oriented incentives that make them unwilling to compromise on policy solutions or candidates (Stone and Abramovitz 1983; Stone and Rapoport 1994). While some of the constituents in the organizations we studied undoubtedly fit this profile, in most cases, we found the opposite to be true.

In our cases, the key choice that organizational leaders sought and that constituents made was to stand with one another. As longtime organizer Marshall Ganz (2018a) wrote, this choice reflects the etymological roots of "constituent." The root of the word "constituent" is *constare*, "to stand together." This is distinct from other words that are often used to describe organizational adherents, like "client," whose root is *inclinade*, "to lean on"; "citizen," whose Latin root *civitas* refers to city; or "consumer," whose root is *consumere*, "to use up." Constituents are defined not by their needs (clients), their rights and responsibilities (citizens), or their choices of what to purchase (consumers). Instead, they are defined by a choice they make to stand with others. Because the constituencies that the organizations in our study sought to cultivate were committed to one another and not to a particular candidate or policy, they demonstrated an unexpected flexibility across candidates, changing policy outcomes, and campaigns.

For example, PLAN's constituency in Nevada displays this juxtaposition of commitment and flexibility. By design, PLAN is a coalition organization comprising forty-two advocacy groups and unions representing a wide spectrum of issues. Their constituent organizations include groups ranging from the Sierra Club to the Nevada Teachers Union to Gender Justice Nevada to the Comstock Residents Association. They bring a wide range of constituencies to the table—often groups not known for working collaboratively with others. Environmentalists and labor, for instance, have often found themselves on opposite sides of the negotiating table. Racial-justice and gender-justice organizations are often wary of mainstream environmental and labor groups, which often do not share their views or their commitments to diversity. PLAN, however, has not only been able to hold this coalition together, it has also moved it toward working cooperatively on a number of racial, economic, gender, and environmental-justice issues.

One of PLAN's leaders described her trajectory with the organization: "I came into this work because I am undocumented. I currently have DACA [Deferred Action for Childhood Arrivals] but at the time there was no DACA. I had graduated high school and I couldn't really work." A friend of hers invited her to a PLAN meeting, and she decided to attend. At first, she was not sure what it was about, but she eventually got hooked: "One of the things I truly do love about PLAN is that they invest a lot in their volunteers, volunteer leaders, and the people who are directly impacted. As I was coming in, I would be invited to different trainings, to different meetings, and just being able to be part of, just not like another body that's coming to events but actually part of almost like the team even though I wasn't staff." For the first time, she began to see herself as someone who could exercise voice: "For so many years I was told, 'You're not supposed to tell anybody that you're undocumented.' My parents from a very young age told me that. . . . Then, going through those trainings [with PLAN] and understanding the power behind our stories and what that meant. . . . and how that helps change the perception from the idea that we're bad immigrants into 'we're just human beings.'" She is now a staff leader with PLAN, working not on immigration issues but instead on environmental justice: "I specifically work on mining justice, which was something I didn't really know about. Taking on that role was really a challenge for me because even though I was really passionate about immigration, [I didn't know much about the environment]." She attended a training with PLAN, though, and "built some relationships that really opened [her] eyes." Through her relationships with other staff and leaders in PLAN, she began to work on a broader range of issues. Senior PLAN staff told us that they appreciated her involvement because her presence signaled to other young leaders of color that they have a place within PLAN, and that the organization is willing to put them to work on a range of issues.

We found this juxtaposition of commitment and flexibility to be key for organizations seeking to build a prismatic constituency that could translate into political power. By building this kind of flexibility over time, the leaders cultivated civic feedbacks (Han, Campbell, and McKenna 2019) that they could leverage in campaigns. Another example of how these feedback effects can redound to organizations comes from Arizona. A leader there talked about a recent campaign that a coalition of organizations had run to get municipal-identification laws passed in Phoenix:

> Undocumented communities were not in front of the defense of this [municipal ID] bill because the other communities that it supports are people who experience homelessness, domestic violence survivors, and a whole variety of other people that unfortunately, the people in power probably in the state capitol are more sympathetic to. So those populations really led the charge at the front, and that helped make the fight a little bit better, more palatable to some of those more moderate [decision makers]. And there's no way we would have been able to do that without the trust of the [immigrant] community.

The deep ties these immigrant rights advocates had with their constituency allowed them to maintain the community's support for the municipal ID campaign even though the public dialogue around it did not highlight the needs of the immigrant constituency. Instead, the campaign foregrounded the importance of municipal IDs for other constituencies that were likely to garner greater sympathy from lawmakers in the statehouse. Yet, this organization still maintained constituents' support for the policy, even galvanizing them for action around it. This kind of flexibility and trust in leadership was made possible by the relationships that connected leaders to their constituents.

Bridging Identities

One of the dangers of building a constituency that chooses to stand together in the ways we've described is that constituency can become insular, or develop parochial tendencies that can be normatively and strategically challenging in democratic contexts. In contemporary political discourse, the term "identity politics" is sometimes used pejoratively to emphasize a narrow definition of the role of identity in politics, but the broader problem of cliquishness threatens any organization that emphasizes relationship building. The juxtaposition of commitment and flexibility guards against this danger in some ways, but we also found that most of the organizations in our cases did additional work to explicitly build collective identities that are bridging instead of bonding.

The concept of bridging and bonding identities originates in the social-capital literature. Bridging social capital refers to social ties that link people across social divides (such as race, class, religion, and so on). Bonding social capital refers to social ties that operate within existing social groups and strengthen a sense of shared identity and belonging (see, e.g., Woolcock 1998). The groups in our study attempted to build both kinds of relationships. Bonding social ties were necessary for people to develop the kind of within-constituency links that produce a sense of commitment to one another. But, organizations needed to build these ties in a way that opened people up to engaging with others rather than closing them off from it. In other words, people needed to be strong enough in their own sense of collective group identity that they could see the strength to be gained by bridging to others. For the purposes of our analysis, the concepts of bridging and bonding provide a useful tool for understanding the idea of building collective identities that are explicitly focused on transcending difference.

Building bridging identities can be a strategic choice, particularly for organizations working with low-income constituencies or constituencies of color. A plethora of research demonstrates that there are persistent structural biases against poor people and people of color. As a result, these groups might not have success using political strategies that work for higher-income people or people with other forms of structural privilege (García Bedolla and Michelson 2012; Lee 2008). Indeed, the history of social change in the United States finds that social movements representing low-income constituencies or constituencies of color often reached their tipping point once they were able to galvanize the support of sympathetic groups with greater privilege. Some have argued, for instance, that key events in the civil rights movement, such as the march in Selma, were effective because the brutal response of law enforcement drew moderate whites into the movement (Lee 2002; Carmines and Stimson 1981; see also Morris 2003 for a counterargument). The organizations in our cases sought to generate this kind of cross-racial, cross-class sympathy without having to provoke such outsized responses. The anchor organizations in our study all worked intentionally to cultivate bridging identities in their constituents, particularly in Minnesota, Ohio, Nevada, and Virginia.

A leader from New Virginia Majority, which draws much of its base from returning citizens, talked about the importance of building unity across difference: "We're on the outside agitating, organizing, doing local campaigns, building up a base of . . . really, folks from jail. Or just out of jail or whatever. And building undocumented [folks]. That's who I'm trying to organize and meanwhile Tram [our coexecutive director] is in [the statehouse] having conversations in the power quarters. So we're trying to figure out how to bring those together and we do." Jon Liss described meeting with a "very strong progressive" state legislator and pushing him to reconceptualize his understanding of the group because of its cross-racial base:

> He's in a room that we brought half incarcerated people and half Latino people. . . . [At first,] he starts to go, "Oh you're a Latino group, you're into immigrant rights." But we're talking about driver's licenses and rights restoration and we're building unity among our people as we're talking to him and he . . . he just lost his words . . . he's looking around and I'm wondering how he's going to talk himself out of this one. And he goes, "I get you're helping all the economically disenfranchised, uh, I just stepped on my toes. I'm trying to figure this one out." It was all very fast. . . . We are trying to create a bloc where people understand that we have a greater sense of unity and can move at a greater level. . . . So my point is that [in the past] there was nominal unity. People have been to meetings together. But it was actually shoulder to shoulder doing these [legislator] visits that (a) the delegates are learning that actually, if you don't figure out at a state level how to build this kind of bloc, we're not going to win, and (b) at the micro level of our members, they're shoulder to shoulder.

Across all of our cases, NVM probably had the strongest lobbying presence; its success relied more than our other cases on its ability to mobilize around elections. When asked about the source of their authority in the statehouse and in elections, NVM leaders were quick to point to their ability to engage unexpected constituencies. Tram noted that legislators view NVM as the "people's people": "People want our endorsements because they know that . . . it might not come with a check, but it will come with programs that allow them to connect with a constituency of voters that they might not be able to naturally on their own. And then, they also know that we bring along coalition members." In other words, NVM leaders viewed their ability to bridge different types of constituencies in unusual ways as part of their influence.

There are two important points to note about this process of building bridging identities. First, in order for the organizations to build bridging identities, they have to recognize that people's individual and collective identities are constantly in formation, rather than fixed. Doran, for instance, argued that "behind every single choice you see of a leader who chooses to stand with us [like our faith delegates] is a relationship someone has built with them. And at some point in that relationship, someone has invited that leader to cross a bridge with them." For Doran, this metaphorical bridge is the choice to reject the "zero-sum politics" that characterizes many narrower approaches to identity. A view of identities in formation accepts the idea that we live in what ISAIAH leaders called a "world of abundance in which everyone can and should have dignity." A KFTC leader described it as such: "KFTC's vision is [realized] when we are able to see our realities connected to the realities of people across the state and across the country and across the world." Both ISAIAH and KFTC realized, however, that people do not arrive at these conclusions alone; they need to be in relationship with people who invite them across that bridge.

Second, the process of building bridging identities often forces people to rethink their own conceptions of themselves and their relationships to others. In talking about her early experiences with an organization in our study, one leader described the questions she was asked to think about before and during a leadership training:

> I got sent this form that I had to fill out that . . . introduced the word power, "Do I want power?" I was like, "What, do I want what?" [So they go on to define power,] how it plays out, how it operates in the world and [they frame] a decision: Do I have any and do I want any? Am I going to take responsibility for getting some and using it? . . . [The experience] gave me a new vision of myself in relationship to my own vocation—not just career vocation but . . . my vocation in terms of who I could be in the world.[2]

Because these organizations acknowledge that people's identities are fluid, they recognize the importance of crucible moments for shaping how their constituencies interpret the sociopolitical world. These unsettled, unpredictable moments offer the organizations an opportunity to build their base. One black leader with NVM described to us the work she was doing in southeast Virginia:

> This is a community that is largely African American, and there are parts where there's certain neighborhoods where the median or average income per family for the year is like $19,000. . . . And religion is a really huge part of the cultural life of the African American community . . . so I knew schools

and churches would be our main gateway to larger audiences. . . . So I utilized my connections with the pastors, we got invited to Bible studies . . . and we did this great registration event, we registered tons of people and then we got them excited. After [Trump's] election in 2016, however, many of these constituents felt turned off by political engagement, saying, "Oh no, not again. We're never going to depend on government for anything."

The leader continued: "And I felt the moment and the interest we had been building slipping through our fingers . . . the next morning, a room full of pastors called and were like, 'we've got to get you back out.'" She went to southeast Virginia after the 2016 election to help constituents interpret the election, to recognize their disaffection and try to turn it into a commitment for change.

In ISAIAH, we saw the work of building bridging identities play out most powerfully in the work ISAIAH was doing to build a constituency of Muslim leaders. In August 2017, the Dar al-Farooq mosque in Bloomington, Minnesota, was bombed. Catalyzed by the event, two Somali Muslim leaders attended ISAIAH's weeklong training in the last week of October 2017. Inspired by the training, these leaders sought to engage others in the Muslim community around a power-building strategy, but they found that most Muslim leaders were reluctant to take what they perceived to be a risky approach. These two leaders returned to ISAIAH, seeking their help in beginning to organize the Muslim community. These Muslim leaders became involved in ISAIAH's faith-delegate campaign, building Muslim constituencies in particular pockets of the state. One of these leaders said,

I'll just say traditionally, doing things across faith means for most mosques, doing an interfaith dinner or interfaith dialogue. Just kind of having a discussion of how we can come together and how we can eat together and how we can be friends and things like that. I think with what ISAIAH is doing, it's more of a concrete and more powerful than that. What ISAIAH is doing is that first of all, I recognize you're a human being and I'm a human being and we're going through the same suffering. . . . And now, I want to work and stand with people who are getting mass incarcerated and people who are, you know what I mean, their health care is taken away.

Prior to getting involved with ISAIAH, this leader did not recognize the power of commonality across difference; he found ISAIAH's use of the concept eye-opening. A white faith delegate in ISAIAH described having a similar reaction when she met the Muslim delegates:

I find out for the first time that there were Muslim delegates also in my district that have been organized separately, trained and stuff. We had a little pre-meeting before the delegation. . . . We introduced ourselves and we talked about how we're going to help as many of us move forward as we could. . . . When we broke up into sub-caucuses, at one point I had twenty people in my group. The viability number was sixteen. I was able to give four of my people to one of the Muslim delegates so they could become viable as well. That felt really good.

From the start, in other words, this faith delegate had a commitment to the other ISAIAH leaders who shared her values. Despite their differences, she shared precious political resources—namely votes—simply because they were in the same organization. In describing her relationship with the Muslim leaders, she said, "Just listening to them talk about what their issue was, Palestinian-Israeli issues, and I didn't really know that much about [them]. I was taking notes and I looked it up online and stuff. Their issue became my issue. There was no such thing as, 'This is not my problem,' because we're in relationship with each other. My issues were their issues." Given the context of contemporary US politics in these states, much of these organizations' bridging work focuses on building connections across race. As the Muslim leader's comments suggest, such work often begins by moving people to a place where they can empathetically see one another. He said that ISAIAH's week-long training, which involves people telling one another their stories in one-on-one meetings and workshops, helped him to understand how he could connect to white people. He told us, "I didn't know white people had pain . . . [weeklong] wakes you up to that. That like hey, wait a minute, this person, although they have a lot of privileges but there is pain there as well." That empathy becomes the basis on which new, shared identities are created. This philosophy is not inconsistent with what existing research tells us about how the process of forging new identities works (Teske 1997a, b), but what makes these organizations' work distinctive is their emphasis on bridging identities as a core part of their strategy. Although many organizations, especially progressive ones, pay lip service to this kind of work, these groups saw it as being essential to their ability to build power.

Crucially, this work did not happen only among people of color. As one ISAIAH organizer told us, "Our society tells white people it's your job to go and save brown and black people or to control them from themselves. . . . Actually what we're doing as an organization is saying [to white people], 'You need help too.'" ISAIAH's base is predominantly white, yet the organization has been explicitly working on racial justice and bringing attention to racial inequality since 2010. Multiracial teams of organizers and leaders have been thinking together for years about how to bring white people into racial-justice work. The main way ISAIAH leaders have done this is by getting white people to understand how they too are impacted by societal structures that lead to racial inequality. ISAIAH argues that when people are able to connect their personal struggles to others' stories and to social systems, they are able to build an identity around striving for social change that transcends any one issue or campaign.

This made ISAIAH's weeklong training a space where multiracial bridges could be built. One of the Somali Muslim immigrants who attended ISAIAH's weeklong right after his mosque had been bombed had experienced layers of personal trauma. Prior to the bombing, he had been detained at the airport because of suspicion that he was a terrorist given his Muslim heritage. As an immigrant, he was navigating unfamiliar and often unfriendly cultural territory in Minnesota. Yet, he found a sense of solidarity and common humanity with the relatively prosperous white people with whom he trained. As quoted above, he said, "I didn't know white people had pain." But when he discovered they did, he understood that despite significant cultural and religious differences, there was a common basis from which they could work together.

The Characteristics of Prismatic Constituencies

Despite operating in distinct sociopolitical environments, on distinct issues, and with distinct constituencies, the prisms in our case studies all demonstrated a shared set of four characteristics: they were enmeshed in a deeply intertwined network of relationships; they acted as distributed strategists; they were able to be simultaneously committed and flexible; and they developed identities that bridged across difference. These characteristics, we argue, helped our case organizations enact the structures, habits, and practices of constituency building that democratic theorists have long described as being core to self-governance.

Constituencies are thus the foundation of our prism metaphor. Leaders cultivated the constituencies in our study to express a set of characteristics these leaders needed to strategically exert power in dynamic political environments. Having constituencies that leaders know are loyal yet flexible, strongly grounded in their own values but also open to bridging to others, enables leaders to sit at the negotiating table with more tools for wielding power than they otherwise might have. A constituency that is not loyal, is narrowly focused on only one outcome, or is unwilling to bridge difference to act with other kinds of people limits the strategic choices a leader has. The kind of constituency a leader builds, thus, affects the degree of power they can exercise.

Even as these characteristics in a constituency both enable and constrain leaders, the same characteristics make demands of the constituents themselves. Across all of our cases, we saw a constant push and pull between leaders and constituents. Leaders were pushing constituents to cultivate their capacity to act as agents of change, trying to shape their motivations, skills, and worldviews. But as those constituents developed their confidence and skills, they pushed back to hold leaders and fellow constituents accountable to a shared vision. Investment in the collective act of self-governance, in other words, opened horizons of power for everyone involved but also demanded that those same people participate actively and thoughtfully in the collective.

6 *Democratic Fragility*

Democracy, *demos kratia*, is rooted in the idea that people have some control over the basic conditions and laws that rule our lives. Although the rhetoric of US democracy promises government "of, by, and for" the people, the reality is that people rarely rule. In twenty-first-century America, the link between democratic participation and power seems broken. And yet, this book describes the plausibility of what is possible in twenty-first-century American democracy—specifically, the plausibility of ordinary people coming together to take powerful action that helps realize a vision of the world they want. Our study sought to show that it can and does happen.

In documenting cases of meaningful collective action in the twenty-first century, we sought to examine the possibilities that still exist for democracy. What can organizations do to engage people in public life in ways that rebuild our democratic commitments to one another? Can we do this in a way that generates power for people to realize the promise of *demos kratia*? By showcasing case studies of organizations that bucked the trend of unresponsive government, our research hopes to identify strategic choices organizational leaders can make to meet the challenge of reclaiming democracy.

The World as It Is . . .

Our analysis of prisms of people power pushes back on several common narratives that dominate the study and practice of politics in the United States. The research that underlies this book originated with three interrelated questions that kept coming up in conversations we were having with friends, family, movement leaders, philanthropists, and our academic colleagues: What should I do? In what should I invest? And, is anything else possible? Friends and family frustrated by the politics they witnessed in their communities and in our country would reach out to us and ask, "What can I do to be most helpful?" Philanthropists and movement leaders who devote their professional lives to leading and supporting social change would contact us with similar questions: Given scarce resources, the urgency of the challenges we face, and the need to make choices, where should we focus our energies? The three of us claim to be experts in movements, organizing, and social change. It was frustrating to have so little to say in response to these queries, and so few organizations to which we could point people.

In moving between groups of people who study politics (academics) and groups of people who engage in politics (organizers, philanthropists, consultants, campaigners, etc.), we were, and continue to be, struck by the extent to which many people reflexively considered the central challenge of collective action to be about generating activism at scale. Many of the strategic resources for both academics and practitioners are devoted to understanding how to amass or refine individual tactics: door knocks, votes, clicks, dollars raised, or bodies at a protest. This focus on generating action manifests in many ways.

Among political practitioners, organizations dedicated to engaging people in public life are often held accountable to a single metric: scale. How many people can they get to take action? They measure success by the number of people they can register to vote, turn out, or, get involved in different ways. Accountability to this metric takes many forms, but it is often the measure that private donors and philanthropic foundations use to assess the value of their investments. It is also the usual way that civic-engagement consultants and many organizations report their success to the public. Many researchers use scale as the measure to assess collective action.

The assumption inherent to these models is that participation is most impactful when it is multiplied. Most progressive change campaigns presume that if enough people take action, the campaign can add those actions up to demonstrate the power for change. Some strategies will take the distribution of those people into account, calculating how many of the right kinds of people in the right places have to take action. Most of the strategic effort, then, is spent on trying to figure out how to get the right people to engage. Variants on this approach tend to be about getting more money or action of some kind. Get more people to take action ("Call your member of Congress and donate here!"), get people to take more action ("Don't just sign petitions online, show up and give money!"), or get different people to take more action ("Find people in swing districts to get involved!").

However, by articulating the challenge of collective action solely as the challenge of generating action (either at scale or distributed in the right ways), we impose two major limitations on our ability to realize the promise of democracy. First, a reflexive focus on scale undermines the importance of strategic thinking, which leaders working in dynamic political environments need, and directs attention to habitual efforts to generate collective action instead. Second, it emphasizes pulling people into action, without much consideration of what they must do once they are involved.

Taking these issues in turn, the reflexive focus on aggregating action for power implicitly limits our strategic imagination by pressuring civic and political organizations to do just one thing. This lack of imagination around grassroots engagement is exemplified by electoral campaigns. Research by Brendan Nyhan and Jacob Montgomery (2015) shows that campaign spending patterns are more sensitive to which consultant the campaign hires than the conditions of the campaign—regardless of whether the campaign is in a red state or a blue state, in a competitive district, in the North or the South, consultants advise a similar pattern of spending. Although a similar study has not been done for advocacy campaigns, the patterns are likely quite similar.

This kind of strategic inflexibility is increasingly problematic given the high levels of dynamic uncertainty in twenty-first-century American politics. We are in a political moment when governmental institutions are not reliably responsive to public pressure (Gilens 2013; Bartels 2008; Gilens and Page 2014) and societal leaders of all kinds are, in many cases, fighting for legitimacy. Viral movements like #MeToo, Black Lives Matter, and the Trump #resistance have been forcing a reckoning in American society that has challenged traditional power structures (Fung and Shkabatur 2012; Margetts et al. 2015). In moments like this, the only certainty is uncertainty. Campaigns that rely solely on one strategy, no matter how good it is, often fail in this context because they have only one tool in their toolbox. They may get the millions of signatures or bodies they need to gain access to political decision makers, but if those decision makers rebuff their requests, the campaigns often lack alternative options. What can organizational leaders do when a decision maker ignores a million signatures? Lacking relational ties with the petition signers, they cannot reliably produce those million people again. This narrow approach to building political power is particularly risky in an uncertain political environment. When governmental institutions are unresponsive to people, and the campaign leaders trying to add up actions are not perceived as legitimate by the public, the chances are low that a one-trick strategy based on scale will succeed.

Second, focusing only on the question of generating action at scale unwittingly reinforces the "action" side of collective action at the expense of the "collective" side of it. Democracy does not stop after one makes the choice to get involved. Too often, collective action gets narrowly construed as being about activating individuals to participate. An enormous number of resources are dedicated to trying to get people to vote, or to trying to make it as easy as possible for people to get involved. But what happens next? The focus on action means much less attention is devoted to the question of *how* people get involved and what capacities those people need to engage strategically and in community with others. The role of intermediary organizations and their leaders disappears in this research when we focus only on how individuals act within campaigns. In the dominant approach, the challenge is about getting many individuals to choose to act. It ignores the power that can emerge when people act not only as individuals but also as part of a group of people engaged *collectively* with others over a much longer time horizon than is typical of most protest waves.

An unintended by-product of researchers' and practitioners' disproportionate focus on getting people to take action, then, is a correspondingly disproportionate focus on the rights of people to act collectively, instead of the responsibilities required to do so. Being part of a community entails both rights and responsibilities—people have the right to realize their own interests through autonomous governance, but they also have responsibilities associated with being part of a community. Building capacity for a community that can act responsibly in concert with others requires leaders who are willing to engage in the constant push and pull of being part of a collective.

Our book calls into question the notion that scale is the only pathway to power and that the central challenge of collective action is getting people to act. In contesting these notions, we are not saying that scale and action are unimportant; rather, we argue that we need to expand both our strategic imagination and our understanding of the collective aspects of collective action. Scale matters. So too does understanding how to get people involved. But democratic collective action is much more than either or both of those things. By starving collective action of these broader strategic and collective contexts, we starve democracy itself.

The World as It Could Be . . .

In this book, we sought to demonstrate how an alternate strategic logic of collective action can work. When we were first designing this study, we got advice about the project from a range of different people. Many academics told us they doubted that the organizations themselves had made much impact. Instead, they predicted that the power of the structural forces that factor into political outcomes—the weight of the status quo, rising levels of economic inequality, the hopeless gridlock of politics at every level of government, immovable biases in the mass public, and so on—would outweigh the influence of any one organization. Many activists also told us that they expected the organizations would not matter, but their reasoning was different. Instead of pointing to structural factors, they thought the outcomes depended primarily on the strength of individual leaders.

Both explanations, while plausible, were equally dissatisfying to us. While the first set of explanations focused entirely on structural factors and ignored the agency of leaders and organizations, the other set highlighted agency to the point that the outcome of any given campaign seemed entirely idiosyncratic. Our goal was to understand whether there were any patterns that made meaningful collective action more likely. And in fact we did see a pattern, but not in any one tactic or tool. Instead, we found that leaders who shifted power had built their prisms with an eye to the internal organizational conditions that would enable strategic choices and organizational flexibility in the face of dynamic political circumstances.

We sought to show that leaders who design their organizations to act as prisms that take in, transform, and refract outward the skills and capacities of their constituency base do so through a set of practices that are distinct from commonly understood methods. In describing the distinctions between dominant models of collective action and prisms of people power, our goals are not merely academic. The fight LUCHA had to wage to lead the campaign for Proposition 206 shows how these strategic debates play out in the real world. From a normative standpoint, we argue that prisms of people power contain within them the seeds of people-powered democracy that our society must recover. Below, we highlight three underlying assumptions about the way politics work that the organizations in our study challenge.

BUILDING POWER THROUGH STRATEGIC ORGANIZATIONS AND LEADERS

First, the concept of prisms challenges the idea that democratic representation can be understood as a relationship between individuals and government without considering intermediary organizations and their leadership. Our argument began with a reframing of the collective-action problem. In thinking about constituency-based organizations and their efforts to build political power, there has been undue focus on the dilemma these organizations face in overcoming individual temptations to free ride. Implicitly, much of this work assumes that if organizations can overcome the free-rider problem and get to scale, they will develop the power they need. Yet, a bevy of historical and empirical research shows that power and resources are not the same. Organizations that accrue a great deal of resources do not necessarily achieve power. If this reality is not recognized, the danger in both practice and research is that the complex relationship between individuals, organizations, and change campaigns will be reduced to its simplest or most transactional form.

Organizations and leadership matter. Meeting the challenge of democracy has always required organizations that can cultivate and channel people's passion and resources through vehicles of collective action and overcome structural segregation to generate a sense of collective belonging. Building on work by Elinor Ostrom and Albert Hirschman, we refocused the collective-action problem to concentrate not on constraints but on capacity. We asked about how organizations strengthen their capacity to govern themselves in ways that build the commitment and flexibility of a base that in turn allows them to dynamically negotiate for power. This framing of the question depended on a definition of political power that recognized its dynamic, contingent, and nuanced nature. One challenge, then, was to identify ways to make that kind of power empirically evident. Chapter 3 demonstrated contextually specific methods we could use to make visible the way power shifted in the cases we were examining. We argued that power is not just about passing policies and winning elections but also about altering relational power dynamics in a community, shaping narratives, and shifting the political agenda. The majority of the book was dedicated to showing how the outlier organizations in our study built their constituencies, exercised strategic leadership, and generated power.

STRATEGICALLY INVESTING IN PEOPLE
AS AGENTS INSTEAD OF PROPS

Second, prisms of people power challenge the notion that people are consumers of democracy, as opposed to agents of it. In her discussion of the distinction between conceptualizations of people as consumers and conceptualizations of people as agents, democratic theorist Wendy Brown argues that democracy cannot function unless we understand how people are more than consumers of politics:

> When human beings are wholly reduced to market actors, the very idea of a self-ruling people vanishes. On the one hand, the demos is literally disintegrated into bits of human capital, each preoccupied with enhancing its individual value and competitive positioning. So the idea of popular sovereignty

becomes incoherent—there's no such thing in a market. On the other hand, democratic political life reduced to a marketplace loses its distinctive value, cadences, and coordinates. It ceases to be a domain of deliberation about how we should live together, and of sharing and equalizing power to determine common values and ends. Instead, political life is figured as a domain of competing capitals, appropriately deregulated, and with no guarantees of equality among them. (Quoted in Isquit 2015)

Prisms of people power challenge the idea that our democracy can be run the same way we run markets. Markets ultimately work through individuals making choices to stay or leave, what economist Albert Hirschman (1970) calls "exit." Politics, instead, requires leaders and organizations to convince people to stay and exercise what Hirschman calls "voice." Voice necessitates loyalty. Loyalty emerges from leaders and organizations who can create it.

People-powered politics is most powerful, in other words, when people are not interchangeable props. The logic of politics is different when people are treated as interchangeable units that can be counted up versus as individuals who are uniquely valuable because of the role they play in any civic or political effort. Investing in people as agents requires cultivating the commitments and capacities they need to exercise voice. Generating the commitments needed to exercise voice, however, is not a matter of marketing or finding the right message. It is about developing people's capacity, their sense of their own agency, and their loyalties to one another. That is the essence of the prisms we describe.

Developing people as agents of democracy—investing in their ability to have their hands on the levers of change—is not just good from a normative standpoint. It is also strategic. Chapter 4 examined the logics that make investing in building a constituency a strategic choice for leaders seeking to build power. These leaders, we argued, recognized the need to build an independent source of power that they could draw on when unexpected challenges came their way. They could not always predict when their power would be challenged, or what political obstacles might emerge in their bids for power. All of the leaders in our case studies thus clearly distinguished between access to power and actual power. Although scholars often use access as a marker of power, we showed that these leaders conceptualized their constituencies as their source of power instead. Leaders could effectively negotiate with political elites only when they held a source of power that sat outside of their relationships with those elites.

Thus, leaders focused on assembling their resources in a way that would (a) give them a set of independent resources they could use to access and wield power, and (b) maximize the set of strategic tools they had to respond to any challenge to their power. This meant that, when building a constituency and an organization, leaders made choices that allowed them to think about the long-term consequences of how they engaged their constituency, and built learning loops into their work that allowed them to adapt to constantly changing circumstances. Their attention to downstream consequences meant that they were interested in not only whether someone took action but also whether people could be engaged in action in a way that develops their long-term commitment to one another and to the organization. We called that concern a focus on civic feedbacks.

The underlying strategic logic of prisms of people power thus helps us to understand how organizations deal with ambiguity in their environment. To act effectively in the face of ambiguity, leaders in organizations must be open to change and adapt their understanding of the world (and therefore how they act) to ongoing experiences (Weick 1969, 1993). Organizations that respond to ambiguity by closely examining their experiences, like our case organizations did through learning loops, increase their capacity to interpret the environment and act effectively (Weick 2015). Prior work has outlined how faith-based organizations can use the cultural tools provided by religion to make sense of ambiguous political contexts for constituents (Wood 2002). Our study contributes to this work by further specifying how organizations' learning practices can help leaders strategically interpret and respond to uncertainty in their environment.

DEVELOPING PRAGMATIC COMMITMENTS TO STAND TOGETHER

Finally, prisms of people power challenge approaches to politics that treat collective action as a set of aggregated individual choices. These approaches often mistake scale for impact or efficiency for effectiveness. Nothing in our argument refutes the importance of scale—in fact, all of the organizations in our cases were seeking to reach more people. Nor do we seek to promote inefficiency. Our point, instead, is that scale should not be mistaken as a proxy for impact, and efficiency should not supersede effectiveness. Leaders' focus on impact and effectiveness over scale and efficiency was key to building their constituencies' capacity to exercise political power, particularly for the low-income constituencies of color in our study.

Prisms of people power depend on successfully weaving the relational fabric necessary for communities to govern effectively on behalf of the whole, not a narrow few. Prism building, in other words, is not just another tactic to be optimized but rather a fundamentally different approach to rebalancing power in America. Chapter 5 described the practices that the organizations in our study used to build constituencies based on the relational commitment and flexibility needed for people's prisms. Specifically, we found that these organizations distributed strategic work instead of centralizing it, embedded people in an expanding latticework of social relationships, and created identities that opened people to bridging across difference instead of bonding them to more people like them. The relational ties between constituents, and the latitude that organizational leaders gave them to exercise voice within the organization, created constituencies that were able to hold far more tension than is the norm in our politics. Instead of being uncompromising ideologues, these constituents acted as thoughtful agents of democracy, seeking to advance their own interests while recognizing the complex dynamics of negotiating political power.

Commitment and flexibility are often thought to be at odds with each other—a constituency that is highly committed to a cause is often assumed to be ideologically inflexible. Here we draw on Hirschman's work to show how loyalty (or commitment) can generate more, not less, flexibility. In deciding to act with others, constituents in our cases chose to commit to a common good. Most research does not differentiate between activism that is animated by specific policy goals, activism animated by idiosyncratic biographical factors, and activism animated by commitments to a group of people. We find that the latter type—born out of the decision to stand with one another—animated the work of constituencies in our study and enabled them to have an unusual flexibility across policy outcomes. With little notice, these constituents showed up for actions holding power elites accountable, and they were equipped to act strategically in these meetings. We argue that, contrary to the common assumption that leaders of collective action are often ideological extremists, the leaders in these case studies were pragmatic in their approach to politics, even if they held what might be considered ideologically extreme views.

Some may rightfully point out that previous research shows that civil society organizations, especially those that have highly committed adherents and operate in weak political and institutional contexts, can become carriers of authoritarianism (Berman 1997; Armony 2004; Riley 2010). The organizations in our study, however, mitigated these risks by creating bridging ties across lines of difference, so that the commitments they were building were not narrowly focused on the interests of homogenous identity groups. Instead, as a result of these bridging ties, members were forced to identify shared interest across a range of different kinds of identity groups.

Thus, prisms of people power are not merely conduits for generating action, or repositories of activism. Instead, they are holders and generators of the dynamically updating capabilities needed to move multiple campaigns and shift structural power over time (Teece 2007). These organizations undergirded their approach to both strategic leadership and constituency building with rigorous attention to *learning*, through which leaders constantly updated their understanding of how to act in a dynamic political environment. To investigate these learning processes, we examined the ecosystem-level relationships in which these leaders were embedded. Our key informants were enmeshed in a network of local, state, and national relationships and learning communities that shaped their own learning and behaviors. Moreover, although they differed in the specific tactics and techniques they each used, these organizations had robust and intentional learning and reflection processes built into their work. Unlike other organizations that are often seduced by the perceived ease of use of static tools, tactics, or formulas, the organizations in our study were constantly—and self-consciously—in learning mode.

Our focus on the relationships underlying prisms of people power does not mean our argument is merely about the importance of social capital (for that, see Putnam 2001). The social capital that emerges from the latticework of relationships we describe matters. But building a prism is not just about building a relationally connected community. In an uncertain and constantly changing political world, constituencies need prisms and strategic leaders to turn that relational capital into actual power through the design choices they make.

Fragility

If the argument we are making about prisms is true, why are they not more prevalent? Copious amounts of research demonstrate the inherent fragility of what we are describing here. Neither we nor the leaders in our study are under any illusions about the extent or permanence of the power shifts we documented. Across our cases, incumbents and elites were loath to cede power to the organizations that contested it. In Arizona, for example, our data-collection period coincided with multiple setbacks for the movement there. On our first visit to Phoenix, interviewees reflected at length about what one called a "bittersweet" election night in 2016. Even as Trump was elected to the presidency, organizational leaders were buoyed by significant wins at the state level: the coalition had just registered 150,000 new voters, unseated Arpaio, and, with LUCHA's leadership, passed minimum wage and paid-sick-leave legislation with 60 percent of the vote.

Two months before the election, the coalition had celebrated yet another win: on August 31, 2016, the Phoenix City Council voted to approve One PHX ID, a card that would allow undocumented, homeless, disabled, and transgender people to obtain valid government identification. One leader described how she made her decision to spearhead the campaign after her house got broken into in 2012: "Police showed up and asked me for my ID. So the idea of an ID became very core to my fight. I didn't have an ID and they continued to question me. And I was scared that I would be arrested. In that time, since we elected those three people [to the city council], for me personally, my uncle got deported, my cousin got arrested, [the break-in and police questioning] happened. . . . We realized that nothing had changed [even after electing those guys]." Disappointed in the politicians she had helped elect, this leader was not Pollyannaish about power building. Yet she still hoped that a municipal ID program, backed by her constituency, might make life just a little bit better.

But just as Proposition 206 faced subsequent court and legislative challenges—which LUCHA had so far been able to defend against—opponents of the municipal ID waged a countermovement to dismantle the effort. The No One PHX ID campaign website described the ID as a "Trojan Horse" that would be used "as an avenue to legitimize the status of noncitizens (aka 'Illegal Aliens') who reside within Phoenix City boundaries. . . . Citizens from every corner of the state should be concerned because if Phoenix were to take the bait and adopt this scam . . . it will only be a matter of time before the cancer spreads to other Arizona municipalities" (No One Phx ID 2015). When we returned to Arizona for follow-up research in May 2018, we learned that the One PHX ID card had "died before it ever began," as one local news report put it (Boehm 2018). Because the leaders of the municipal ID campaign were accountable to the constituencies they had organized behind the effort, they issued the following statement via the coalition's social-media page to explain the loss: "Hello community, we are very disappointed to notify that the city decided not to invest in the municipal IDs program and therefore they will not be issued. After many years of struggle, we assure you that this is not the end. We will continue fighting so that the needs of our communities are priorities for the people who have the responsibility to represent us."[1]

Many studies have documented how civic life in America has atrophied in terms of organizations' ability to execute the most basic functions of democracy—engaging people, keeping them involved, building community, and persisting despite setbacks like the one the municipal-ID-campaign leader and her constituents faced. Other research shows how few organizations have the ability to really deliver a constituency (e.g., Lee 2015; Skocpol 2003; Blee 2012). Why does the work of building these prisms remain restricted to outlier cases?

Designing effective prisms of people power remains an underused strategy, we argue, for two main, interrelated reasons. First, the dominant models of collective action in our political system are attached to material resources that crowd out the ability of other strategies to emerge. Second, effective prisms depend on development of a core of leaders who know how to build resilient constituencies and how to exercise strategic independence in ways that are not commonly taught. To put it in market terms, these prisms require an investment in R&D (research and development) at the outset to develop the "technology," or leadership, needed to make them work. When those investments are not made, these prisms remain episodic within the political system.

The flow of resources to particular models of collective action is perhaps most visible in electoral politics. After any electoral campaign, particularly high-profile ones like presidential elections, a battle ensues to control the "narrative" about the campaign. Pundits, campaigners, and the public issue postelection analyses covering the impact of everything from presidential debates to money, from field campaigns to television ads, from candidate qualities to staff leadership, and so on. A large body of research shows that, in the end, these factors tend to have only marginal impacts (Hillygus 2005; Sides and Vavreck 2013). Yet, an enormous amount of digital and physical ink is spilled discussing them. The amount of time and resources that go into this debate implicitly demonstrates the value that people place on "winning" the narrative about what happened in a campaign. By winning the narrative, the victor can direct a set of resources to subsequent campaigns. Consultants who convince others that their digital strategy or tool won the election are likely to get a windfall of business in the next cycle (Nyhan and Montgomery 2015; Sheingate 2016; Walker 2014).

Over time, narratives about what is necessary to win in politics harden into institutional myths about what organizations in a particular field should do to be successful (Meyer and Rowan 1977). These myths come to be taken for granted as true. Neoinstitutional theory argues that adherence to institutional myths governs whether organizations are recognized as legitimate and influences their access to resources (Powell and DiMaggio 1991). Thus, organizations face isomorphic pressures to follow commonly agreed-on "best practices," and those that do not have more difficulty gaining access to resources (Powell and DiMaggio 1991).

What do institutional myths look like in practice? Today, campaigns and organizations are encouraged to (1) utilize complex data-targeting tactics and (2) demonstrate the impact of their work with such easily measurable metrics as the number of voter contacts or actions taken. Institutional myths prioritizing the use of data ensure that strategy is handled not by leaders and constituents, but by experts who direct canvassers based on large voter databases. For organizations operating under the logic of prisms, however, these kinds of metrics do not portray the full picture of a leader's ability to exercise power. For organizations devoted to the strategic logic of prisms, actions taken matter only insofar as they are linked to building a constituency and entering into negotiations for power. But these steps are harder to make visible, particularly because existing narratives and myths about how politics "should" be done render conversations about building a constituency illegible to many influential parties. This means that organizations operating under the logic of prisms have greater challenges in demonstrating the impact of their work or even being recognized by the political establishment and wealthy funders.

The logic of prisms is probably most dominant in circles related to community organizing, but those circles are in a moment of tremendous flux. Over the last few decades, the field of community-based organizing has undergone enormous change and evolution. A new generation of leaders, many of whom are now directing and guiding the most significant local and state-based organizations, have driven changes in organizing and organizational form in response to a shifting political landscape that includes challenges such as political polarization, changing demographics, a globalized economy driven by multinational corporations, surges of migration, urbanization and deindustrialization, and persistent structural racism and extreme wealth inequality. In response to these changing political conditions, practitioners have pushed their organizations and the field to adopt a stronger analysis of race, class, and gender into their work and to develop a deeper analysis of the kinds of structural changes needed to enact the goals they want. Community organizers are moving into the electoral arena to contest for power within institutional politics in ways that movement stalwarts used to avoid. At the same time, community organizers have integrated new digital technologies into their work and are figuring out how to build larger organizations, networks, coalitions, and other organizational forms that allow them to increase the scale of their work.

All of these changes have created disruption within the field of community organizing, so that a competition to explain the uncertainty exists even within that field. As Doran wrote via email in personal correspondence providing analysis of the field in late 2018, "After a decade of deconstruction and evolution . . . it is also apparent that there is a need to re-ground the field by assessing and consolidating the lessons learned, evaluating where some ground may have been lost in the fundamentals of building people-centered vehicles for democratic participation and ownership, and do the work of constructing." Putting it more informally in a side comment, she wrote, "We are at a base camp on the way to the top of the mountain. Where you look at your stuff, see where you are, consolidate your shit, ground yourself, stabilize, project a coherent point of view, advance a pedagogy, go back and gather what you may have lost in the hectic scramble up the mountain, take the risk to construct rather than deconstruct." In this moment of uncertainty in the field, many are struggling to identify the one method or practice that will win. We argue, however, that there is no one formula. The urge to create one is based on a flawed understanding of how to handle uncertainty in politics.

The other limitation on the number of organizations designing prisms is that such designs require particular kinds of leadership. At the core of our concept of prisms is an argument about the importance of strategic leadership. Leaders are the ones who develop an analysis about power, examine the places where they can exercise agency to shift power, and build their constituency in ways that give them the latitude to do this work, or not. Building constituencies that have the capacity to exercise voice in the public arena is no easy task. Leaders have to be willing to hold themselves accountable to a constituency, develop the skills within the constituency that will allow that accountability, and be willing and able to hold all the tensions of leadership. Leadership has to be simultaneously top down and bottom up, with power distributed so that constituents develop strategic independence, yet centralized enough that constituents' decentralized leadership can be brought into a negotiation for power. Strategic leaders must be able to work inside and outside the system simultaneously, developing relationships with people in positions of power while always remaining willing to challenge them. Strategic leaders create spaces where people can bring their full humanity into the public sphere, but can be ruthlessly strategic when the politics demand it. On top of all of this, relational organizing takes a level of interpersonal risk that can be emotionally challenging for leaders (Oyakawa, McKenna, and Han 2020; Battistoni 2019).

To meet the leadership challenge required to construct prisms of people power, organizations must understand a craft of constituency building and politics that cannot be easily taught or exported to a technical tool. These capacities for democratic leadership are made, not born. Decades of social science research show that this kind of democratic transformation occurs through relationships. Through relational work, people can realize their own agency and bridge across difference to exercise agency collectively with others. Teaching the craft of strategic leadership requires an investment in the kind of dynamic learning that we saw in our organizations, particularly at the executive leadership level. Without investment in that kind of leadership network, the number of organizations that can create these powerful prisms will always be limited. We can only exercise voice with leaders equipped to build, sustain, and deploy it.

Hope

So, where is the hope? More urgently than ever before, we have to sharpen our understanding of how to help the constituencies most excluded from our democracy—especially communities of color, immigrants, poor families, and young people—strengthen their capacity to act collectively to exercise power over outcomes that matter in their lives. We live in a time of extreme political inequality, in which individuals and corporations with material wealth exercise disproportionate influence over public life. This imbalance pits ordinary people against one another in a fight for increasingly scarce resources. It also fuels racial and anti-immigrant tensions that cynical actors actively stoke to divide, demoralize, and demobilize constituencies, drive people away from government, and accelerate the imbalances across the political spectrum.

The very foundations of democracy are thus fraying in the face of heated debates about who belongs, who deserves dignity, and who among us gets to make these decisions. In moments like these, civic and political institutions should be a bulwark, creating vehicles through which ordinary people can develop countervailing democratic power. In twenty-first-century America, however, the everyday practice of democracy has become emptier even as the need for it has become more urgent. A long list of seemingly insurmountable challenges confronts society, including rising inequality, deeply rooted racism, increasing social disenfranchisement, and intractable issues of sustainability. People have taken to the streets to agitate for change, but too often reformers respond with attempts to manage or narrowly fix these problems, ignoring the relationship between these social troubles and the underlying erosion of our democracy.

Hope originates from identifying alternative strategies. By describing them, we hope that we can help give scholars and practitioners alike the tools they need to understand these strategies and employ them more intentionally. We hope this book provides key insights on ways that constituencies can rebuild the link between participation and power. We sought to generate a set of propositions about how organizations acting as prisms of people power operate in order to deepen understanding of how participation translates into political influence. By making the way these metaphorical prisms work more visible, we hope to give people some of the tools needed to become more intentional about rebuilding our civic capacities. Our democracy depends on it.

Acknowledgments

We have many people to thank for making this book possible. First and foremost, we thank all the leaders, volunteers, constituents, advocates, elected officials, funders, and other actors who made time to talk with us, fill out surveys, or endure our presence at events, meetings, and other activities. We know how precious time is for anyone doing the kind of work we describe in this book, and we are grateful that so many people opened up to us with candor and generosity. We sincerely hope that our book does justice to the many different forms of data people shared with us.

We wish we could thank everyone individually here, but for purposes of both confidentiality and brevity, we cannot. Not all of the people we interviewed or observed asked for confidentiality, but to maintain consistency across our research subjects, and to anticipate the tension between the permanence of the text and the uncertainty of the kinds of challenges and political circumstances these leaders might face in the future, we opted to protect people's confidentiality whenever possible. The downside of making that choice is that sometimes we do not call out individuals who played pivotal leadership and other strategic roles in particular events, roles for which they should get credit. Our hope nonetheless is that our book can play a small part in lifting up their work, and that it does so in a way that is sensitive to the long-term needs of the people who opened themselves up to us.

We also thank the many other people who provided support to make this book possible. The Ford Foundation and the Democracy Research Fund gave crucial financial support for all the field research. We are especially grateful to Ethan Frey of the Ford Foundation and other anonymous partners in the fund who believed in the project from the very beginning. Hahrie is also grateful to Xavier de Souza Briggs, Rakesh Rajani, and Ethan at the Ford Foundation for providing a year of support for data analysis and writing. The book needed much more than just financial support to happen, however. There were a number of people who ably assisted the research, including Jeff Feng, Sami Ghanem, Maya Halthore, Geoffrey Henderson, Alice Lepissier, Joshua Meyer-Gutbrod, Ryann Schutt, and Anna Song. This project would not have been possible without their dedicated work, good cheer, insight, and support.

As with any academic book, we owe a large debt to a broad intellectual community. Academic scholarship is a funny thing, because people give and take credit in individualistic ways. Yet, in our experience, the process of developing, articulating, and refining a set of ideas is a collective endeavor. Our book is no exception. In particular, we thank people—academics, organizers, friends—who kindly provided feedback on our ideas and the manuscript at different stages: Andy Andrews, Andrea Campbell, Ethan Frey, Marshall Ganz, David Karpf, Peter Levine, Kiki Lundberg, John McCarthy, Jenny Oser, Woody Powell, Paul Speer, Scott Reed, Daniel Schlozman, Ed Walker, Richard Wood, and anonymous reviewers. We also thank another set of people who were constant interlocutors as we were developing the ideas, including core leaders in each of the case studies profiled throughout the book, as well as Joy Cushman and Arisha Hatch. Finally, we are grateful to people who provided feedback in places where we presented versions of this work, including those at seminars at Brigham Young University; Cornell University; the Harvard Kennedy School; Johns Hopkins University; Northwestern University; Princeton University; Stanford University; the University of California, Los Angeles; the University of Minnesota; the University of Portsmouth Digital Advocacy Pioneers Conference; the University of Southern California; Vanderbilt University; and the Social Science Research Council's Democratic Anxiety, Democratic Resilience conference in Germany. We also appreciate the opportunities we received for feedback from a wide range of practitioner-oriented audiences at meetings hosted by the Australian Council for Trade Unions, the Chan-Zuckerberg Initiative, Facebook, the Funders Committee on Civic Participation, the Ford Foundation, the Hewlett Foundation, and the Organizing Learning Meetings (in December 2018 and June 2019).

We could not be more delighted to be working with the University of Chicago Press and Chuck Myers in particular. He understood the project from the outset and has been a kind and steady guide throughout the process. We are also especially grateful to Larry Jacobs from the University of Minnesota, who offered early support for the project, provided enormously useful feedback along the way, and helped us sharpen the work a great deal. And, where would we be without Audra Wolfe, of The Outside Reader? We cannot imagine having found a better developmental editor for our book. We thoroughly enjoyed working with her, and hope to continue what we now think of as a friendship!

Last but certainly not least, we each have people to thank in our personal lives.

For Hahrie, gratitude begins and ends with Hunter, Kaya, Jaemin, and, in our hearts, Kaeson. Kaya and Jaemin had debates over dinner about how they would feel if the book was (or was not) dedicated to them. I watched with bemusement because it is hard to imagine writing a book that is not implicitly for them. Being a family with Hunter, Kaya, and Jaemin has taught me how to act in community with others from a place of love, compassion, and dignity. Our experience of loving and losing Kaeson taught us all something about how to navigate the myriad complexities that are at the core of who we are as humans. I know those lessons are in this book, and I hope that in writing the book we can play a small part in helping to articulate how the lessons so many of us learn in our families can be instantiated in the institutions we build in our democracy. Our world desperately needs it.

For Liz, this book project was a source of solace in an otherwise pessimistic political moment. For the opportunity to collaborate on it, I owe a debt of gratitude to wedding officiant extraordinaire Marshall for introducing me to both the craft of organizing and Hahrie, and to Hahrie for introducing me to Michelle. I am lucky to have the collective support of the hilarious and wonderful families of which I am a part, especially my nuclear and extended McKenna clan. The Spitz and Fishenfeld families made Brazil my second home, and I am especially grateful to Vovô Laizer for the always incisive perspective he brings to life and work. Last but not least, my understanding that relationships are the glue of collective action would be empty and academic without Alexandre, whose integrity, insight, and capacity to love still surprise me every day.

For Michelle, working on this book would not have been possible without the unwavering love and support of family. This includes my husband Todd Callais and my stepdaughter Riley, who sustained and encouraged me throughout the year I traveled around the country collecting the ethnographic data for this book. Also, in everything I do I must acknowledge my parents, Steve and Cindy Oyakawa. They have constantly supported me in more ways than I can possibly account for or repay.

Appendix A: Previous Research

Our core research question asks how vehicles of collective action—like AMOS, New Virginia Majority, ISAIAH, PLAN, Kentuckians for the Commonwealth, and the network of immigrant rights organizations in Arizona—build and exercise political power under conditions of uncertainty. How do we make sense of the contrast between the initial failure of Greg Landsman's petition campaign and the success of AMOS's organizing drive around universal preschool in Cincinnati? Naturally, we are far from the first people to ask questions about how collective action becomes powerful. Many scholars have come before us, and we recognize our indebtedness to the large body of findings they have developed. Our hope is to build on and extend their work by integrating existing research in new ways, recasting their insights in new light, and adding our own data and findings to the mix. In this appendix, we dive more deeply into some of the literatures that we seek to bridge, and show how they connect to the research design and methods that we used.

Regarding previous research, we particularly seek to bridge three main literatures from political science, sociology, and management studies. First, what do we learn from research on the sources of participation, and civic and political engagement? Second, what does the literature on collective action—including the literature on social movements, civic associations, and interest groups—teach us? A large portion of that work examines whether and how these organizations achieve their goals. Third and finally, what can we learn from the management literature, which looks mostly at the structure of for-profit organizations? This research has a greater focus on questions of transformative strategy and the organizational roots of particular outcomes—how can these findings translate to the kind of constituency-based civic and political organizations that we examine?

For our purposes, the key question is how insights from these divergent literatures can be put together to understand how the leaders in our cases cultivated the political power their constituencies sought. Findings from the participation and collective-action literatures help us see why an organizationally grounded approach to understanding the sources of political power can help. It builds on existing insights about the key social bases of participation and the role of agentic strategy in shaping the outcomes of collective action. The management literature, in contrast, points to the importance of dynamic processes in understanding the organizational sources of political effectiveness. Unlike traditional approaches to examining the link between participation and power, this approach directly accounts for the inherent uncertainty of the political process and the need for constituency-based organizations to make uncertain—and sometimes risky—bids for power. The management literature thus shifts our focus to the unique resources these organizations build and how strategic leadership deploys those resources.

The Sources of Collective Action and Civic and Political Participation

In his seminal book *The Logic of Collective Action,* Mancur Olson (1965) threw down a gauntlet that generations of scholars of collective action have since taken up. Why is it, he asks, that so many people participate in collective action given the improbability that their action will be pivotal in making a difference? He points to the irrationality of things like people signing Greg Landsman's pledge cards or attending AMOS's public meetings. From a purely instrumental standpoint, none of these actions is likely to make a difference in the ultimate outcome. So, why participate? Why sacrifice precious time? Or, to put it another way, how can advocacy leaders like Greg and Troy get people to participate, given the seeming irrationality of action?

Economist Albert Hirschman's 1970 book *Exit, Voice, and Loyalty* deepened this analysis. His book starts with the question of how managers should respond when firms are not performing up to par (in slack economies). While his analysis begins with firms that "produce saleable outputs for customers," he argues that it extends to "organizations (such as voluntary associations, trade unions, or political parties) that provide services to their members without direct monetary counterpart" (Hirschman 1970, 3). He argues that customers (or members) have two choices in response to underperforming organizations: exit, the choice to leave; or voice, the choice to express their dissatisfaction to management. Voice, and the willingness to choose it over exit, becomes the resource that leaders of collective action have to manage. Organizations that want to diminish exit and encourage voice need leadership. The challenge for management (or leaders) is to develop enough loyalty in their members that members choose to stay and exercise voice instead of exiting.[1] How do leaders cultivate constituents who have the willingness and capacity to exercise voice, constituents who are willing to stick with them even when the going gets tough?

Other scholars extended this work to bring in questions of leadership. Elinor Ostrom's (1990) Nobel Prize–winning research on the management of common-pool resources highlights questions of self-governance. Her analysis starts with the free-rider problem famously posed by Olson. Unlike Olson, however, she rejects the idea that external authority (whether created by pure privatization or governmental control) is the only way to solve the problem. Such solutions, she argues, focus on constraint instead of possibility, assuming the need for outside forces to alter the inherent incentives to free ride. "What makes these models so dangerous—when they are used metaphorically as the foundation for policy—is that the constraints that are assumed to be fixed for the purpose of analysis are taken on faith as being fixed in empirical settings, unless external authorities change them" (Ostrom 1990, 6). By examining the way communities around the world have solved collective-action problems, Ostrom identifies an alternative approach that focuses instead on strengthening the capacities of people to self-manage the collective resources they share.[2]

Similarly, John Ahlquist and Margaret Levi (2014) argue that leadership choices about governance practices explain why some organizations can mobilize around causes that fall outside of their members' narrow self-interest. They start by asking why some organizations are better able than others to move their constituencies to engage in activism beyond the "particularized grievances that are the raison d'être of the organization" (Ahlquist and Levi 2014, 1). Ahlquist and Levi develop the idea of "contingent consent," or the idea that members will go along with (or "consent" to) their leaders when members feel that those leaders have, over time, been accountable to their needs. Leadership practices grounded in accountability thus make it more likely that leaders will generate the kind of loyalty they need to mobilize their members.

Other research on collective action examines the question of overcoming free riding. Taking Olson's framework as a starting point, a large body of research emerged on the question of who participates. What can we learn from looking at who actually gets involved in a movement? This work has examined the individual traits and characteristics that have conditioned people's involvement (e.g., Wolfinger and Rosenstone 1980). Recent iterations of this research demonstrate the importance of the way people's resources—their free time, education, knowledge, civic skills, and the like—shape the likelihood of their participation (Verba, Schlozman, and Brady 1995). Much of this work, however, would not predict high rates of participation among the kind of people who are AMOS constituents. AMOS's constituency lacks the demographic and socioeconomic traits commonly associated with high rates of participation, as do those constituencies associated with most of the cases discussed in this book (Han 2009).

Other related work examines the incentives that motivate participation. Olson (1965) answers his own question by arguing that leaders of collective action make participation possible by offering what he calls "selective incentives." Groups like AMOS, in this framework, would need to offer additional motivations for people to participate, things that emerge as a by-product of their action regardless of whether the group achieves a win on a particular policy outcome. J. Q. Wilson (1973) famously identifies three types of incentives that shape participation: purposive (goals I want to achieve through participation), solidaristic (social), and material (concrete material gains I might get). In most cases, scholars in this tradition would explain the participation of AMOS constituents as fulfilling solidaristic or abstract purposive goals. Even though these constituents lack the resources commonly associated with participation, they derive social benefits from acting with others and fulfill such abstract goals as a sense of civic duty or commitment to their community.

Related research has examined the way people's social interactions, relationships, and contexts shape their choices to get involved (Rosenstone and Hansen 1993; Rolfe 2012; Sinclair 2012; Han 2016; Green and Gerber 2015; Leighley 2001). Research on the social bases of participation has led to a burgeoning area of study examining the sociopolitical contexts within which participation is generated and the strategies organizations can use to engage people. A large body of field experiments on tactical interventions have helped identify ways to activate participation in voting (see Green and Gerber 2015 for a summary of get-out-the-vote studies) and other forms of activism (e.g., Han 2016). This work includes studies on things like messaging and deep canvassing, and other research on how best to talk to people about different issues (Levine 2015; Stokes and Warshaw 2017; Broockman and Kalla 2016). Given the importance of digital strategies in twenty-first-century organizations, other work has begun exploring patterns in how organizations shift online participants to off-line involvement (Hestres 2015; Bimber, Flanagin, and Stohl 2012). Much of this research has drawn on theory from social psychology, using psychological principles to understand ways to spur different attitudes and behaviors among people (Rogers, Fox, and Gerber 2013; Cialdini and Goldstein 2004).

Most of the literature on political participation focuses implicitly on activation, or how strong messaging or well-executed canvassing campaigns can move people with preexisting proclivities to action. The research, in other words, focuses less on how to cultivate people's motivational capacities and more on how to activate those that already exist. This leads to significant gaps in our understanding of the nature of political participation, particularly as related to the kinds of organizations that are the subject of this study. For instance, because existing research focuses mainly on activation, we have less knowledge about groups of people who are less likely to have those preexisting proclivities for participation. Meta-analyses of some of this research show that activation programs like GOTV actually increase existing structural inequalities because they optimize our understanding of how to reach out to the white, middle-class people who are most likely to engage anyway (Enos and Fowler 2016; Arceneaux and Nickerson 2009). This bias emerges from the fact that proclivities toward engagement are not distributed evenly in the general population. Instead, people with greater structural privilege are more likely to have had the early life experiences that would make those proclivities more likely to be present (Jennings and Niemi 1981; Jennings 2004).

Important exceptions exist. Some research focuses particularly on activating constituencies of color (García Bedolla and Michelson 2012) or on engaging people for the longer term (Rothenberg 1992), but most research does not. Additional work is needed to understand how to effectively engage low-income people, constituencies of color, and others who do not self-select into particular movements and campaigns.

Other bodies of work in existing scholarship show that movements and organizations can engage people through not only selection (transaction) but also socialization (transformation). There is a wide range of studies that show people's propensities to participate are surprisingly malleable when they are embedded in collective, organizational contexts (Warren 2001; Munson 2009). We know that particular organizational interventions—certain kinds of actions, use of particular social networks, and so on—can build persistent participation at a broader scale (Speer and Christens 2011; Christens and Speer 2015; Andrews et al. 2010; Baggetta, Han, and Andrews 2013; Han 2014; McKenna and Han 2014). In addition, other research discusses the role of movements and organizations in shaping identities and values that provide an overarching framework for understanding persistent engagement (Snow, Soule, and Kriesi 2007; Klandermans 1997; Teske 1997b; Munson 2009; Polletta and Jasper 2001). These studies thus lay the foundation for a series of questions that better help us understand the processes through which prisms of people power might emerge.

A focus on internal democracy as practiced through self-governance has a long tradition in both research and practice. Historically, this is particularly the case with membership-based civic associations in the United States (Skocpol, Ganz, and Munson 2000; Skocpol 2003; Ober 2017). These associations were often defined by the fact that they had leaders elected from the membership who had to develop collective practices of self-governance. These collective-governance practices were a critical part of how these organizations developed people's capacities for citizenship and acted as Tocquevillian "schools of democracy" (Verba, Schlozman, and Brady 1995; Fung 2003). In the latter half of the twentieth century, however, the ecosystem of these civic associations became more professionalized and the prevalence of such practices of self-governance within the organizations declined (Walker 2014; Blee 2012; Lee 2015).

Political Power in Studies of Interest Groups, Social Movements, and Civic Associations

What are the sources of power for interest groups, social movements, and civic associations? Organizations like the ones in our case studies have been the subject of study from a wide range of different perspectives. Existing research on social-movement and interest-group outcomes provides a robust sense of the structural factors that affect an organization's ability to achieve its goals.

We argue that understanding the arc of the campaigns in our cases requires a look at not only the structural factors but also the agentic ones. While all of the external factors outlined above matter, an additional set of agentic practices operates at a meso-organizational level. These factors may be particularly important for organizations like the ones we study that do not have the structural characteristics that we know are associated with success (Ganz 2009). To understand a politics of voice, and the success of our cases, we need to understand these factors.

Some insights can be drawn from existing research. Social-movement scholars have examined the way resources, organizational repertoires, strategy, strategic capacities, tactical diffusion, and interorganizational relations shape organizational effectiveness (Clemens 1997; Clemens and Minkoff 2004; Clemens 1993; Wang and Soule 2012; King, Felin, and Whetten 2010; King 2017; Soule 2013; King and Walker 2014). Perhaps the most well-developed set of studies on the organizational and movement-level factors that shape political outcomes is the resource mobilization tradition (e.g., Jenkins 1983; McCarthy and Zald 2001). The core finding in this literature is that movement success depends on the extent to which a movement accrues and deploys resources, such as money, skills, time, energy, or new participants.

While resources clearly matter—all of the leaders in our cases recognized the importance of the range of financial, human, and other resources they needed to garner—so do choices about how to deploy those resources. Much of the resource-mobilization literature conceives of organizational factors as relatively static traits.[3] There are some notable exceptions that examine the strategic choices actors make within movements (Clemens 1997; Ganz 2000; McCammon 2012) and that treat organizational factors as competencies that can be learned and adapted to strengthen movements over time (Polletta 2002). From that work, we can begin to develop an understanding of how strategic choices matter in making choices about how to deploy resources.

Only in this way can we account for the uncertainty that movement organizations inevitably face. Throughout the campaigns in our study, the organizations were interacting with shifting configurations of targets, allies, and competitors, always amid changing political conditions. Although some existing theories account for the extent to which meso-level factors affect movement success *holding all else constant*, they are not able to explain how constituency-based organizations constantly adapt to sustain their resource advantage in the face of an unstable and changing world. What are the internal practices that enable organizational leaders and participants to strategically respond to an uncertain environment?

The Management Literature

To understand the transformative potential of organizations for building and exercising political power, we have to understand how organizations work. Although classic studies of political organizations were common in the mid-twentieth century, more recent work has not examined the organizational sources of power or participation (see Ahlquist and Levi 2014; Clemens 1997; Ganz 2009; and King 2017 for examples of exceptions). We thus turn to the management literature. This work examines not only the extent to which organizations possess a certain set of resources or characteristics, but also the dynamic practices and processes through which those resources are constantly created, renewed, and strategically deployed.

Much research on strategy looks at the internal capacities of organizations. Early work recognized the importance of strategic capacities in explaining the sustained competitive advantage of some firms over others (e.g., Porter 1996).[4] The resource-based view emphasizes internal efficiency rather than industry structure and market power (Teece, Pisano, and Shuen 1997). The resource-based view holds that resources that are valuable, rare, inimitable, and non-substitutable—so-called VRIN resources—are the source of sustained competitive advantage (Barney 1991). Two key assumptions underpin this view: strategic resources are heterogeneously distributed across firms, and these differences persist over time (Barney 1991). The kernel of competitive advantage is that strategies based on VRIN resources cannot be duplicated by competing firms (Eisenhardt and Martin 2000). In a political context, the idea is that groups like AMOS want to develop resources that depend on AMOS alone and cannot be easily generated by other leaders or organizations; only then will it be able to advocate for its views.

Time adds another dimension to this analysis that necessitates an additional set of considerations. Some scholars argue that resource-based views are too static and that more dynamic accounts of firm outcomes and competitive advantage are needed (Teece 2012). The level of resources a firm has tends to be pretty stable over time, and thus cannot explain all of the variation in firm success (Ambrosini and Bowman 2009; Teece, Pisano, and Shuen 1997; Eisenhardt and Martin 2000). We need explanations that can better account for heterogeneity across firms to explain how firms *sustain* their competitive advantage in dynamic markets (Ambrosini and Bowman 2009; Eisenhardt and Martin 2000; Teece 2012; Teece, Pisano, and Shuen 1997).

A part of management literature focuses on questions of risk and uncertainty. Leih and Teece (2016) distinguish between the two, arguing that resource-based approaches address risk but ignore uncertainty. Risk can be quantified with (conditional) probabilities; uncertainty cannot. Since there is a probability distribution associated with risky outcomes, risk can be managed through insurance or hedging (e.g., futures contracts). This approach does not work with uncertainty, however, because uncertainty refers to the "unknown unknowns," or "Black Swan" events (Leih and Teece 2016). In fact, managers can be lulled into a sense of false security by conflating good risk management with good management under uncertainty. Therefore, deep uncertainty calls for strong dynamic capabilities.

Putting these pieces together, this literature would argue that leaders like Troy need to take into consideration the fact that AMOS is playing a long game of power-building, and that it will undoubtedly face challenges that the organization cannot anticipate. The long time horizon and likelihood of uncertainty thus necessitate investments in long-term capabilities that renew themselves over time. Management scholars call these dynamic capabilities.

A dynamic capability is not a resource as conceptualized in the resource-based views. Rather, it is a process that impacts VRIN resources and is embedded in the firm. The dynamic-capabilities framework finds its legs in a Schumpeterian world subject to increasing returns (and thus path dependency) and uncertainty, where rents can be competed away, knowledge can be copied, and employees can be poached. The approach gives considerable latitude to managerial actions to impact on organizational outcomes. The dynamic-capabilities framework extends the resource-based view to explain how the stock of VRIN resources can be refreshed in volatile environments (Ambrosini and Bowman 2009; Helfat and Peteraf 2003).

The "dynamic" aspect of the dynamic capabilities approach relates to how the resource base is changed by the use of dynamic capabilities (Ambrosini and Bowman 2009). It is not just about how many resources a firm has, in other words, but how it uses, deploys, and regenerates those resources. These scholars defined dynamic capabilities as "the firm's ability to integrate, build, and reconfigure internal and external competencies to address rapidly changing environments" (Teece, Pisano, and Shuen 1997, 516). The key analytical parameter here, as with civic feedbacks, is the changing environment.

To understand dynamic capabilities, it is useful to understand what they are not. Scholars distinguish between ordinary capability, also called "zero-level capabilities" (Winter 2003) or "lower-order capabilities" (Lessard, Teece, and Leih 2016), and dynamic capabilities. Ordinary capabilities are operational in nature and allow a firm to pursue a given organizational program (Lessard, Teece, and Leih 2016). They are how a firm makes its living (Winter 2003) and typically include administration, operations, and governance (Teece 2012, 2014). Dynamic capabilities, in contrast, might include new product development, expansion into new geographic markets, and assigning product mandates across regions (Lessard, Teece, and Leih 2016). They are how a firm ensures its survival and relevance into the future.

Ordinary capabilities are about "doing things right" (or technical fitness), whereas dynamic capabilities are about "doing the right thing at the right time" (evolutionary fitness) (Helfat and Peteraf 2003; Leih and Teece 2016; Teece 2012, 2014). Ordinary capabilities can be measured and benchmarked, and they can be bought and imitated. Strong ordinary capabilities are called "best practices" (Lessard, Teece, and Leih 2016). Best practices tend to diffuse quickly, as exemplified by the implementation of the M-form (multidivisional) organizational structure that proliferated in the twentieth century (Teece 2014), but managers can also risk falling into a "best practice" trap where sclerosis and inertia become the rules of the game. Given the fact that they can be easily emulated, ordinary capabilities, even strong ones, are unlikely to provide the basis for durable competitive advantage (Teece

2012). Teece (2014) argues that firms which are "d-ineffective"—that is, have weak dynamic capabilities—are unlikely to survive long, even if they are "x-efficient." In other words, they are very good at doing what they do now.

By contrast, dynamic capabilities cannot be bought. They are "firm-specific, complex, interdependent, and slow to develop" (Lessard, Teece, and Leih 2016, 214) and therefore must be built from within. The development of dynamic capabilities is highly contingent on the firm having prescient and entrepreneurial management (Leih and Teece 2016; Teece 2012; Zahra, Sapienza, and Davidsson 2006).[5] Grounding our study in this literature points to a need to examine questions of leadership, and the strategic choices they make about how to build and deploy the constituency and leadership resources they need.

Appendix B: Research Methods

The bulk of our discussion of research methods can be found in chapter 2, where we describe the overall logic we used to select our cases and gather the data. In this appendix, we provide further details for readers more interested in the nitty-gritty of case selection, data collection, and data analysis. This discussion is designed to complement, rather than replace, the discussion in chapter 2; points made there are not repeated.

Case Selection Data

In considering our four core cases, a key question to ask is whether we can rule out the possibility that all of the outcomes are explained by existing research. We argue, however, that even as we saw progressive power being built across the four core cases, each organization faced distinct social, economic, and political conditions. Table B.1 offers a snapshot of some of the structural criteria on which we maximized variation in our selection process. For instance, our case states varied considerably in terms of GDP, job, and economic inequality over the past three census periods (1990–2010) and were skewed even more in terms of demographic shifts. While Arizona ranked second in the nation in terms of population growth in the past decade, for instance, Ohio ranked forty-sixth. Likewise, Virginia was fourteenth in the nation in terms of GDP growth over the past generation, but Ohio was forty-ninth.

In terms of political and civic indicators (table B.1), we also see a good mix. Some of the states in this study are often considered battleground (or swing) states in presidential elections. Others are more stable. We also wanted states that varied in terms of their state-level political makeup, measured by control of the state legislature and governor's mansion in previous cycles. We did not want an organization's success (or failure) to achieve a progressive political outcome to be a foregone conclusion. Thus, the Democratic presidential-vote

Table B.1. State-Level Variation in Case Selection Indicators

Census Region—Division	Population Growth (1990–2010)	Rank	POC Population Growth (1990–2010)	Rank	Foreign-Born Population Growth (1990–2013)	Rank
AZ West—Mountain	0.7440	2	1.5951	12	2.1838	16
MN Midwest—West North Central	0.2123	23	2.2822	5	2.4149	12
OH Midwest—East North Central	0.0636	46	0.5524	43	0.7418	39
VA South—South Atlantic	0.2931	16	0.8944	30	1.8921	21

	Economic Context					
	GDP Growth (1990–2010)	Rank	Job Growth (1990–2010)	Rank	Gini Coefficient Average (2009–2013)	Rank
AZ West—Mountain	1.1194	3	0.69	3	0.4585	27
MN Midwest—West North Central	0.5939	22	0.26	24	0.4423	13
OH Midwest—East North Central	0.2244	49	0.09	47	0.4577	25
VA South—South Atlantic	0.7429	14	0.28	19	0.4624	30

Sources: Data on population growth, the economic context, and union membership all come from the US Census Bureau. Data on Democratic presidential vote in the states comes from the US Presidency Project at the University of California, Santa Barbara. Data on partisan control of governorships comes from the National Governors Association. Data on partisan control of state legislatures comes from Ballotpedia. Data on the density of civic organizations comes from the National Center for Charitable Statistics.

share in the past five general elections hovered around 50 percent in three of the four cases; in the most recent election, two of our core states voted for Clinton (Minnesota, Virginia) and two for Trump (Arizona, Ohio). Finally, we chose cases that varied in terms of their changes in union membership rates over time and the number of civic organizations (charities, nonprofits, nongovernmental entities) per capita, based on data from the National Center for Charitable Statistics (NCCS).

The fact that these organizations were able to achieve progressive power in all of these states, despite working in such varied structural settings, raises the question of whether there are any commonalities across cases. Each case represents a set of constituency-based organizations that sought to advance an agenda that was uncertain at best at time 1. By time 2, the organizations we studied had made significant progress on their political agenda. Were there

# of Years of Dem. Governor, 2000–2016	# of Years of Republican Legislature, 2000–2013	Avg. % Dem. Pres. Vote, 2000–2016	Rank
6	12	44.78	31
6	2	50.44	20
4	12	48.18	28
11	10	48.70	26

Civic Context			

Change in Union Member Rates (1990– 2010) %	Rank	Civic Orgs. per 1000 Inhabitants, 2010	Rank
–0.18	16	3.4	49
–0.23	19	6.6	14
–0.35	34	5.9	20
–0.45	45	5.2	32

common practices and processes they and their allies used that enabled them to strategically navigate the changing economic, political, demographic, and civic environments in which they were embedded? Drawing on the conceptual tools outlined above, we hypothesized that there could be some practices, capabilities, or strategies that equipped the organizations under study to shift the balance of political power in their states.

Data Collection

In all of our cases, we began by interviewing key leaders from an anchor organization identified by expert respondents (One Arizona, Kentuckians for the Commonwealth, ISAIAH, Progressive Leadership Alliance of Nevada, the AMOS Project, and New Virginia Majority). In the interview, we asked the leader to begin by describing their victories and their story of how those un-folded. Using that as a starting point, we asked them to describe the organiza-tional history, structure, decision-making processes, leadership-development processes, base-building practices, and strategic challenges they faced along the way. In gathering the organizational story, we also asked them to identify coalition partners, community allies, and political targets. Simultaneously, we researched any publicly available information we could find about the case. This included searching organization websites, media mentions, and, in some cases, previously published research.

Based on our initial observations of and interviews with the anchor or-ganization, we then used information gathered from that investigation to identify a list of other state-level political actors to conduct further in-depth interviews. This list included allies, competitors, partners, targets, funders, and other relevant parties. We sought to interview as many people as possible to gather historical depth and breadth on our case until we reached satu-ration. We also conducted multiple interviews over the phone or through videoconferencing technology. Each interview lasted an average of seventy minutes and was professionally transcribed.

In addition to taking the snowball approach to identifying people of inter-est and conducting interviews, we also conducted fieldwork whenever we could. Although most of the cases we were examining were retrospective campaigns, we wanted to use fieldwork to generate a more textured sense of the constituency and community within which these organizations were working, as well as a sense of how the organization operated. Instead of just asking people how the organization made decisions, developed strategy, or interacted with constituents and leaders, we wanted to observe the processes ourselves. Thus, we traveled to the case states to sit in on leadership meetings and constituency events, and even shadowed leaders from some of our cases when they were lobbying in legislatures. From this fieldwork and these inter-views, we generated a set of organizational documents that included meeting minutes, emails, weekly leader reports, communications, and other forms of documentation of the organization's work.

Data Analysis

The analyses presented in this book examine patterns across all four of our core cases and two extension cases. Our challenge in analyzing the data was in figuring out how to make sense of the large volume of information we had gathered over the eighteen-month duration of our research. Because our study was an inductive one, we analyzed the data as we were gathering it, constantly cycling between immersing ourselves in particular cases, stepping back to look at similarities and differences emerging across the cases, generating propositions about the patterns we saw emerging, and then diving back into the cases to refine, deepen, and clarify our initial ideas.

We began by cataloging all of our data in a large database. We hired a research assistant, our "data czar," to perform an initial intake on all data that we received. This enabled us to sort through the different types of data—audio recordings, interview transcripts, copies of emails, pictures of particular locations, survey and network data, and so on. Our data czar would do an initial assessment of all the data we gathered and catalog the data's source, its date, the type of data, the case for which it was relevant, and, where relevant, the topic on which this data provided information (for instance, each interview was coded as being with organizational leaders, allies, targets, or media, etc.). This catalog enabled us to keep track of where we had data and what we were missing, to ensure that we were capturing the breadth of what we needed.

We then went through an iterative data-reduction process in which we sorted the data into different categories depending on what ideas and questions it spoke to. To do so, we used a qualitative-data-analysis software called NVivo. All of our data was uploaded into NVivo and the three of us, along with a team of research assistants, sorted all the data into substantive categories. In sorting the data, we began with a set of overarching codes (such as "power") that we wanted to use, but then worked with the research team to develop emergent codes based on what we were seeing. We used a shared spreadsheet to keep track of our codebook and had regular discussions among the research team to discuss, clarify, debate, and refine the codes and the underlying ideas they represented. The main goal of this initial data-reduction process was to sort the data into thematic nodes that each represented a broad topic we learned about from examining this data.

After sorting the data, we went into each node to do a more targeted coding. This allowed us to dive into all the information we had gathered about the way these organizations understood power, for instance, and analyze it in a more tractable way. What shared patterns did we see? What contradictions emerged? What did not make sense? We had at least two different coders go through each node to ensure that we had multiple perspectives on the data. In many cases, more than two coders analyzed the key nodes.

Throughout this process, we also tacked back and forth between developing a specific analysis of each specific case and comparing findings across all the cases. What did we see as commonalities across the six cases? As we identified propositions about what those patterns were, we would dive back into the data to test the ideas against the data. For instance, as we identified propositions about how these organizations understood power, we would develop a set of codes that would exemplify those propositions and then try going back to code the data along those lines. That allowed us to refine and clarify the ideas.

Appendix C: Additional Data from the Arizona Case

Table C.1. Restrictive Immigration-Related Laws and Resolutions Passed in Arizona before Pearce Recall, 2005–2011

Year	Bill or Resolution Number	NCSL Description
2005	HB 2259	Allows immigration status to factor into sentencing.
2005	HB 2592	Prevents cities from constructing day labor centers if the centers assist unauthorized immigrants.
2005	SB 1372	Gives local law enforcement the ability to arrest smugglers and to penalize human trafficking.
2006	HB 2448	Requires US citizenship or legal immigrant status to receive health benefits. An unauthorized immigrant can receive emergency medical services only.
2006	HJR 2001	Requests the US Congress and the US Department of Homeland Security to supplement ICE with state auxiliary reserve units under the Coast Guard.
2006	SB 1137	Limits eligibility for the Comprehensive Care for the Elderly program to citizens and those with legal alien status (section 1).
2007	SM 1004	Requests that Congress continue funding and completion of SBInet, a program that assists in the apprehending and processing of people who cross Arizona's border illegally; facilitates legitimate cross-border travel and commerce by the target date of December 31, 2008.
2007	HB 2181	Provides funds for immigration law enforcement in the state of Arizona.
2007	HB 2467	Requires a person to have citizenship, permanent residency, or lawful presence in the United States in order to receive state public benefits. It also requires a person who applies for public benefits to submit documentation proving his or her lawful presence in the United States.

Table C.1. Continued

Year	Bill or Resolution Number	NCSL Description
2007	SB 1265	Relates to the determination of an individual's country of citizenship after that person has been brought to the agency for incarceration; requires the agency to transmit any information regarding the individual's country of origin and criminal record to the court and the prosecuting agency for the purpose of determining whether that person is lawfully present in the United States and whether that person should be given the option of bail.
2007	HCM 2012	Requests that the rules of engagement for National Guard troops on the Mexican border be changed to allow soldiers to defend against, engage, pursue, and apprehend illegal entrants and that the National Guard should be placed in a primary enforcement role until the Border Patrol receives its full complement of officers as approved by Congress.
2007	HB 2779	Prohibits employers from knowingly or intentionally hiring undocumented workers and requires all employers to use the Basic Pilot Program to determine employees' legal status.
2007	HB 2016	Provides for the detention of a material witness if testimony of a person is material in a criminal proceeding and if it is shown that it may become impracticable to secure the presence of the person by subpoena because of the immigration status of the person.
2007	SB 1291	Specifies that a member of the Arizona Board of Appraisals must be a US citizen or "qualified alien" as defined by federal law (8 USC 1641).
2007	HB 2391	Requires spirituous liquor licensees to be a citizen of the United States and a bona fide resident of Arizona or a legal resident alien who is a bona fide resident of this state.
2007	HB 2202	Establishes a division of adult education within the Arizona Department of Education. In relation to immigrants, the department must adopt rules for the establishment and conduct of classes for immigrant and adult education, including the teaching of English to foreigners. The department is also tasked to stimulate and correlate the Americanization work of various agencies.
2007	HB 2787 – Act 261	Amends Arizona law to deny release on bail for a felony if there is probable cause that the individual is an illegal alien.
2008	SB 1096	This law appropriates $40.7 million for English language immersion programs (*and was supported by 87 and 12 percent of Senate Republicans and Senate Democrats, respectively*).

Table C.1. Continued

Year	Bill or Resolution Number	NCSL Description
2008	HB 2745	Adjusts the prohibitions against knowingly or intentionally employing an unauthorized alien and eliminates independent contractors from the definition of employee.
2008	HB 2842	Expands the existing definition of smuggling of human beings to include the use of property ("drop houses") by a person or an entity that knows that the person or persons transported or to be transported are not US citizens, permanent resident aliens, or persons otherwise lawfully in this state.
2008	HB 2486	States that an undocumented alien or a nonimmigrant traveling with or without documentation is a prohibited possessor of a deadly weapon.
2009	SB 1001	Appropriates $10 million for the multi-jurisdictional task force known as the Gang and Immigration Intelligence Team Enforcement Mission (GIITEM).
2009	HB 2569	Increases the penalty for the offense of human smuggling across state and national borders involving the use of a deadly weapon or dangerous instrument.
2009	SB 1281	Expands the classification of sex trafficking by including a sexually explicit performance and knowingly trafficking a minor with the knowledge that they will engage in any prostitution or sexually explicit performance; relates to destruction of a person's identification, passport, government document or immigration document; relates to extortion and financial harm (*supported by 100 percent of Senate Republicans and 0 Senate Democrats*).
2009	HB 2426	Prohibits participation by the state in any enhanced driver's license program established for the purpose of satisfying the requirements of the Federal Western Hemisphere Travel Initiative or the Real ID Act.
2009	SB 1282	Extends the definition of human smuggling to include those who have attempted to enter, entered, or remained in the United States in violation of law.
2009	HB 2306	Requires that an applicant for a business license in the state provide documentation of citizenship or alien status prior to the issuance of such license; provides that documentation of citizenship or status is not required upon renewal or reinstatement of a license in certain circumstances.

Table C.1. Continued

Year	Bill or Resolution Number	NCSL Description
2010	SB 1070	Key provisions include a requirement that law enforcement reasonably attempt to determine the immigration status of a person involved in a lawful stop, detention, or arrest in the enforcement of any other local or state law or ordinance where reasonable suspicion exists that the person is an alien and is unlawfully present, except if it may hinder or obstruct an investigation; allows an officer to make a warrantless arrest if the person to be arrested has committed any offense that makes the person removable from the United States; allows state residents to sue state and local agencies for noncompliance; establishes a state violation for failure to carry an alien registration document; and makes it unlawful for an unauthorized alien to knowingly apply for or perform work in Arizona.
2011	SB 1117	Allows the Speaker of the House and the Senate President to direct counsel to initiate a legal proceeding or appear on chambers' behalf regarding any challenge in a state or federal court to the immigration law SB 1070.
2011	SB 1612	Appropriates $9 million to Gang and Immigrant Enforcement for the enforcement of federal immigration law and implementing Arizona's immigration law.
2011	SB 1621	Establishes a Gang and Immigration Intelligence Team Enforcement Mission Fund. The bill stipulates access to the fund by county sheriffs, other county officials, and law enforcement agencies.
2011	HB 2191	Stipulates that a person unlawfully present in the United States shall not be awarded punitive damages in any court action.
2011	SB 1398	Helps fund Arizona's Gang and Immigration Intelligence Team by levying a penalty assessment on every fine collected for a civil traffic or motor vehicle violation, and violations of other local ordinances.
2011	SB 1046	Mandates that a youth held in state custody may be discharged if ICE enforces a detainer demanding custody of the youth for immigration proceedings.

Sources: Bill data and descriptions come from the Arizona State Legislature (www.azleg.gov) and the National Conference of State Legislatures (www.ncsl.org). Legislation abbreviations include HB (House Bill), SB (Senate Bill), HJR (House Joint Resolution), SM (Senate Memorial), SCM (Senate Concurrent Memorial), and HCM (House Concurrent Memorial).

Table C.2. Restrictive Immigration-Related Bills in Arizona Passed after Pearce Recall, 2012–2018

Year	Bill or Resolution Number	NCSL Description
2012	SB 1523	Appropriates $1,213,200 to the county attorney immigration enforcement fund and $2,390,000 to the Gang and Immigration Intelligence Team Enforcement Mission border security and law enforcement subaccount.
2012	SB 1531	Funds the Gang and Immigration Intelligence Team Enforcement Mission fund and the county jail reimbursement costs relating to illegal immigration.
2012	HB 2639	Defines a nonresident to mean both citizens and aliens not permanently residing in Arizona. This distinction applies to game and fish licenses, permits, tags and stamps.
2012	HB 2286	Allows a police officer to immobilize or impound a car that is being used to transport, harbor, or conceal illegal aliens.
2012	SB 1149	Makes it illegal for unauthorized aliens to be in possession of a firearm.
2014	SB 1001a	Makes it unlawful for a person who is in violation of a criminal offense to do any of the following: (1) Transport or move or attempt to transport or move an alien in this state, in furtherance of the illegal presence of the alien in the United States, in a means of transportation if the person knows or recklessly disregards the fact that the alien has come to, has entered or remains in the United States in violation of law. (2) Conceal, harbor or shield or attempt to conceal, harbor or shield an alien from detection in any place in this state, including any building or any means of transportation, if the person knows or recklessly disregards the fact that the alien has come to, has entered, or remains in the United States in violation of law. (3) Encourage or induce an alien to come to or reside in this state if the person knows or recklessly disregards the fact that such coming to, entering, or residing in this state is or will be in violation of law.
2014	HB 2703	Sets aside funds for county attorney immigration enforcement for the purpose of enforcing title 23, chapter 2, article 2 or Arizona Revised Statutes. It also budgets for a Gang and Immigration Intelligence Team Enforcement Mission border security and law enforcement subaccount. It mandates the enforcement of Arizona's "Legal Arizona Workers Act" and SB 1070, "Support Our Law Enforcement and Safe Neighborhoods Act."
2014	HB 2639	Classifies knowingly accepting the identity of another person and using it to verify their work eligibility as a class three felony.

Table C.2. Continued

Year	Bill or Resolution Number	NCSL Description
2014	SB 1397	Eliminates border crossing identification cards and voter cards issued by the government of Mexico as acceptable forms of age verification when purchasing liquor.
2014	HB 2667	Prohibits any undocumented alien or a nonimmigrant alien from possessing a firearm, excluding nonimmigrant aliens who possess a hunting license from any state or those who are attending a competitive or sporting firearms event. This law also requires employers to verify that prospective employees qualify for employment under Federal "alienage" standards.
2014	HB 2050	Makes persons who are nonresident aliens temporarily residing in the United States, who hold an F-1, J-1, M-1, or Q-1 visa when services are performed, ineligible for membership in the Arizona State Retirement System.
2015	SB 1271	Amends existing law permitting construction and maintenance of a secure fence as close as practical to the Arizona-Mexico border, instead of within one mile of the border.
2016	SCM 1012	Urges the US Congress to direct appropriations to appropriate federal agencies to secure the border of the United States.
2016	SB 1247	Allows inmates to take part in the Community Reentry Work Program if the inmate meets certain conditions, including no detainers from the US Immigration and Customs Enforcement.
2016	SCM 1006	Urges the US Congress to act to increase the number of US customs and border protection personnel at the ports of entry in Arizona.
2017	HB 2515	Requires that prospective candidates for appointment by the Arizona governor provide a full set of fingerprints in order to obtain state and federal criminal records prior to their appointment. This criteria applies to members of the administrative review board since they are appointed by the governor. Members of the board are responsible for ensuring that no investment contracts contribute to illegal immigration in the United States.

Sources: Bill data and descriptions come from the Arizona State Legislature (www.azleg.gov) and the National Conference of State Legislatures (www.ncsl.org). Legislation abbreviations include HB (House Bill), SB (Senate Bill), HJR (House Joint Resolution), SM (Senate Memorial), SCM (Senate Concurrent Memorial), and HCM (House Concurrent Memorial).

Table C.3. List of Organizations in Arizona's Progressive Alignment Coalition, 2018

Table	Organization	Full Name (if applicable)
Arizona Wins 501(c)(4) table	AFSCME	Locals 2384, 2960, 3282, 449 (part of the American Federation of State, County, and Municipal Employees)
	AAN	Arizona Advocacy Network
	AEA	Arizona Education Association (part of the National Education Association)
	AZLIST	Arizona List
	ASA	Arizona Students Association
	CWA	Communications Workers of America
	Equality AZ	Equality Arizona
	PAFCO	Protecting Arizona's Family Coalition
	La Machine	
	Sierra Club	Sierra Club Grand Canyon Chapter
	FASB	Friends of Arizona School Boards Association
	UFCW	United Food and Commercial Workers Local 99
One Arizona 501(c)(3) table	AZ C4C	Arizona Coalition for Change
	ADAC	Arizona Dream Act Coalition
	CNL	Center for Neighborhood Leadership (now Poder in Action)
	CAIR	Council on American-Islamic Relations
	FAS	Foundation for Arizona Students
	CHISPA	League of Conservation Voters Latino Organizing Program
	MPHC	Mountain Park Health Center
	NMinistries	Neighborhood Ministries (part of Faith in Action, formerly PICO)
	OCA	Organization of Chinese Americans Greater Phoenix (part of Asian Pacific American Advocates)
	PAZ	Promise Arizona
	Puente	Puente Human Rights Movement (part of the National Day Laborer Organizing Network)
	YEA	Young Engaged Arizona (part of the Bus Federation)
	AAF	Arizona Advocacy Foundation
	ITCA	Inter-Tribal Council of Arizona
Both tables	LUCHA-ACE	Living United for Change in Arizona/Arizona Center for Empowerment
	MFV-MFVEF	Mi Familia Vota (Education Fund)
	PPFA AZ	Planned Parenthood Federation of America
	CASE	Central Arizonans for a Sustainable Economy (part of UNITE HERE! C4)

Notes

1   To protect our respondents from unpredictable political consequences,
    the quotes and stories from the community organizers and activists will be
    anonymous. The only exceptions are the executive directors of the organi-
    zations under study and the first names of the individuals in this opening
    vignette, all of whom gave us permission to use their real names.

2   The term DREAMer refers to the primarily undocumented young people
    who make up the movement to demand political, social, and civic recogni-
    tion for immigrants, and emerged in the mid-2000s. The name derives from
    the Development, Relief, and Education for Alien Minors Act, which was
    first introduced in 2001 and would have provided permanent legal residency
    status to DREAMers. The act has so far failed to pass in Congress, though the
    movement has achieved other significant wins, such as Deferred Action for
    Childhood Arrivals (DACA), along the way.

3   Our account of this conversation between Michele and Jeff came from inter-
    views we did with each of them in October 2017 and December 2018, respec-
    tively.

4   In fact, there were several high-profile petitions that circulated in response
    to SB 1070. Rage Against the Machine singer Zack de la Rocha promoted the
    petition and a "sound strike"—which garnered support from celebrities like
    Kanye West and Los Tigres del Norte—that called on musicians to boycott
    all performances in the state. We learned of these petitions through review
    of contemporaneous media reports rather than our research on the state's
    immigrant rights movement eight years after the fact. This was not the
    chosen strategy of the leaders in our study.

5   By historical standards, the SB 1070 vigil-protest was significant in itself.
    According to the Dynamics of Collective Action (DOCA) protest database,
    which includes 346 vigils that took place across the United States between
    1960 and 1995 (McAdam et al. 2009), only 2 percent (n = 7) lasted longer
    than two weeks. Three-quarters, or 257 of them, are coded as having lasted
    only one day. The two vigils in the DOCA database that outlasted the SB
    1070 vigil were (1) a 1978 yearlong lunchtime vigil to protest Soviet treat-

ment of Jewish dissidents, with an estimated size of between ten and forty-nine participants in 1978, and (2) a nuclear arms–freeze vigil that had lasted for 259 Saturdays by 1988, with an estimated size of hundreds of participants. Only two vigils in the thirty-five-year period are reported to have lasted longer than 100 days. Meanwhile, just 7 percent (n = 17) of vigils in the DOCA database had estimated head counts of more than a thousand people, whereas on May Day 2010, the *New York Times* reported that "hundreds of thousands" of people demonstrated across the country in protest of the Arizona law (Preston 2010).

6   Although we do not adjudicate between competing schools of thought on community organizing, we build on important research in that area, including but not limited to Alinsky 1971; Piven 2006; Warren 2001; Warren and Mapp 2011; Smock 2004; McAlevey 2016; Wood and Fulton 2015.

7   Note that we discuss the generalizability of our findings to organizations across the political spectrum in both chapter 2 and chapter 6.

CHAPTER TWO

1   This quotation, as well as the quotation about the "presidential press gaggle" in June 2013, is also used in Han, Campbell, and McKenna 2019.

2   The dashed lines depict the complex interrelationships among all of the factors represented in the diagram. A social-movement organization's dynamic capabilities both are shaped by and shape the context within which it works. Similarly, if an organization achieves the power it wants, that newfound power feeds back to shape the context and the dynamic capabilities of the field in which the organization is operating.

3   We describe our process of data collection and analysis in greater depth in appendix B.

4   This training happened to take place during the same month that SB 1070 was drafted at an ALEC meeting. Emails released through a records request show that then–Arizona state senate president Russell Pearce was a member of ALEC's Public Safety and Elections Task Force and was joined in this December 2009 meeting by officials from for-profit prison and bail companies like the Corrections Corporation of America (CCA) (Steigerwald 2012). The American Civil Liberties Union also drew on Pearce's email history to argue that SB 1070 was not only economically motivated but also racially motivated. In one email, written in 2007 with the subject line "INVASION USA [*sic*]," Pearce wrote that "nasty illegals and their advocates grow in such numbers that law and order will not subdue them. . . . We are much like the Titanic as we inbreed millions of Mexico's poor, the world's poor and we watch our country sink" (Steigerwald 2012).

5   Multiple scholars (Skocpol, Williamson, and Hertel-Fernandez 2015; Hertel-Fernandez and Skocpol 2016; Skocpol and Hertel-Fernandez 2016) have shown that, in contrast to the Democrats' nationally focused strategy,

Republicans built powerful state-level policy networks through ALEC to help pass "model" legislation like SB 1070.

6   Tenants and Workers United still exists and is now one of NVM's organizing "hubs."

CHAPTER THREE

1   According to the Department of Corrections, African Americans made up 58.5 percent of Virginia's prison population as of 2014 (Nolan 2016)—but only 19.4 percent of the state population as of the 2010 Census.

2   McAuliffe's case-by-case reinstatement of rights was a response to a Virginia Supreme Court decision made months before, which had overturned the governor's blanket restoration of political rights for more than two hundred thousand returning citizens. Acting on behalf of the state's GOP, House Speaker Bill Howell and Senate Majority Leader Thomas K. Norment Jr. then cited him for contempt for defying the courts. By April of the following year, McAuliffe had individually restored the rights of 156,000 Virginians, "my proudest achievement during my time as Governor," he said in a press release (McAuliffe 2017).

3   Voter-registration figures and quotes are taken from New Virginia Majority Education Fund's 2016 *Voter Registration Report*, shared with us by Jon Liss, the organization's coexecutive director, on January 18, 2017.

4   Some of the scholars cited here note that the lack of focus on uncertainty also leads to a lack of focus on the importance of leadership and organizational strategy, a critique we agree with and expand on.

5   Some research in this tradition examines other dimensions of activism that can be scaled to build power, including things like the intensity of support or how that support is distributed. These approaches argue that what matters is not necessarily the number of actions but the intensity of the adherents or how those adherents are distributed across the political terrain. As we discuss further below, we do not dispute the importance of numbers, intensity, or distribution. Rather, we argue that treating any of these resources in static ways without theorizing strategic choice assumes a linear relationship that does not exist.

6   In documenting outcomes that are potentially worse than failure (or could be indicators of incumbents responding to power shifts), scholars have also examined the conditions under which movements provoke backlash—stimulating repression or inspiring countermovements (Earl et al. 2004; McAdam and Su 2002; Meyer and Staggenborg 1996).

7   Note that the debate is about not only what and how to measure power but also how to assess the causal impacts on power shifts that may occur. The foregoing account of the case study in Virginia could be used to set up an argument about how a movement organization influenced an important state-level policy outcome. When a sequence of events leads to a visible

win like this, it is tempting to stipulate that the case qualifies as a success and turn to analyses of the dynamics that help explain the observed outcome. Such research, often classified as "movement-centric," tends to rely on process-based accounts of how grassroots groups like NVM interact with and extract concessions from the state (Walder 2009; McAdam and Boudet 2012; Fligstein and McAdam 2012). These studies have been criticized for being underdetermined because they fail to account for spurious factors and ultimately come up short on questions of whether the movement was dispositive in achieving some outcome of interest (Amenta 2014, 21). Unable to control for the many known determinants of complex political outcomes, social-movement scholars make "the most of what they have" (Amenta, 17) to help explain the relatively rare phenomenon of an under-resourced challenger obtaining some degree of influence over a more powerful actor.

8   We used Bonacich (2007)'s eigenvalue measure to calculate the nodes' relative influence score for each point in time.

9   As noted, specifically, the People's Platform called for a minimum wage of $15 per hour, paid sick leave, and affordable health insurance for private preschool providers (who were likely to be drawn from the poorer, black constituencies in Cincinnati). The platform additionally specified that any universal preschool program should funnel resources toward Cincinnati's poorest children and families to address racial disparities in the city, and that parents should be allowed to exercise voice in the design of the preschool program.

10   NVM's eigenvalue was similarly high on the "exchanged information" measure (sixth-most influential, with a score of .68) and the "received electoral support" measure (seventh-most influential in the network, with a score of .764).

11   In addition to her involvement in the Pearce recall, Raquel has held leadership positions in numerous Arizona-based movement organizations, including Reform Immigration for America, Promise AZ, Mi Familia Vota, and Planned Parenthood. Raquel told us that Worsley, who retired in 2018, became one of the few Republicans, along with state senator Kate Brophy McGee, whom the movement "really count[s] on in the Senate to stop anti-immigrant legislation."

12   Disaggregating by party and chamber, the trends show that polarization has also increased. Two years after SB 1070's passage, Arizona Senate Democrats reached their lowest (most liberal) score on the index (–1.507); House Democrats did so in 2016 (–1.589). Conversely, all of the Arizona House and Senate Republicans' highest scores came after SB 1070. In addition to reaching its most conservative levels, the state GOP also held clear majorities. Since 1979, Arizona Republicans have controlled both chambers of the state legislature, with the exception of a brief Democratic takeover of the state senate in 1991–1992 and a tied session in 2001–2002.

13   We excluded thirty-four bills or resolutions in the fourteen-year time series

because they fell outside the scope of our study. For instance, we excluded bills like a visa waiver program for Polish immigrants (HCR [House Concurrent Resolution] 2007), a resolution recognizing Scottish Americans' contributions to Arizona (HCR 2020), a law prohibiting female genital mutilation (SB 1342), support for a strategic partnership with Azerbaijan (HR 2006), and other pieces of legislation not germane to the immigrant communities we observed in our case study.

14 Note that the analysis in this paragraph does not include voter-approved ballot initiatives and legislatively referred state statues like Proposition 300, which passed in 2006 and made public services like child care, adult education, in-state tuition, and financial aid for college students contingent on immigration status.

15 Because the NCSL's immigration research arm started reporting only bills enacted (rather than both introduced and enacted) after 2009, we evaluated legislative productivity by conducting a keyword search using the Arizona legislature's bill-tracking database (available at www.azleg.gov). We restricted the analysis to house and senate bills introduced and coded as immigration-related by the Arizona legislature, regardless of their eventual passage (there were ninety-one total; we removed 2010 and 2011 from the analysis, the discontinuity years when twenty immigration-related bills were introduced, and compared 2004–2009 to 2012–2017). As with the NCSL data, this represents only a partial analysis of legislative productivity because it does not take into account the substance of the bills passed, only the number.

CHAPTER FOUR

1 This quote also appears in Oyakawa 2017.
2 For a history of the evolution of community organizing, see Warren 2001; Smock 2004; and Wood and Fulton 2015.
3 Note that throughout our discussion of this campaign, we use ISAIAH to refer to both the 501(c)(3) and 501(c)(4) work that ISAIAH and FiMN did. The organizations strictly followed federal law in separating partisan and nonpartisan work in the campaign. We refer to that work using ISAIAH's name for the purposes of clarity and consistency in how we tell their story in the book.
4 To calculate how long the seventy-eight delegates listed in ISAIAH's database had been involved with the organization, we measured the time between the date of their first event tag and the date of the November 2018 election.

CHAPTER FIVE

1 This quote also appears in Oyakawa, McKenna, and Han 2020.
2 This quote also appears in Oyakawa, McKenna, and Han 2020.

CHAPTER SIX

1   One PHX ID, Facebook, February 12, 2018, accessed June 18, 2019, https://
www.facebook.com/508602899275366/posts/hola-comunidad-estamos
-muy-decepcionados-de-notificarles-que-la-ciudad-decidio-n/115162214
1640102/. This message was posted on the One PHX ID Facebook page first
in Spanish and then in English. Expressing her disappointment, one constituent responded to the update, writing, "Now the elections are coming up
and they're going to want our support. But when we seek out their support
when they have the power to do something they don't want to support us."

APPENDIX A

1   Hirschman argues that this problem of generating loyalty is particularly
acute for historically disadvantaged constituencies. Leaders interested in
developing collective empowerment for their constituencies, Hirschman
contends, need to generate loyalty among their constituents so that they
exercise voice instead of choosing to exit. In applying this logic of exit and
voice to the public sphere, Hirschman argues that the upward mobility portion of the American dream is, in many ways, synonymous with a culture of
exit. When Americans are dissatisfied with the Old World or present conditions, whatever they may be, they often seek avenues for exit. Modern-day
examples of this include the market logic that governs health insurance in
the United States, the only country in the developed world without universal
health care, or the rapid growth of charter schools as an alternative to fix-
ing the nation's underfunded public-school system. Exit is thus embedded in
notions of social mobility, where individuals can leave behind poor-quality
goods like the failing district school and move on up to a privately managed
charter. Hirschman argues, however, that "in the case of a minority that has
been [historically] discriminated against," solely relying on exit "is bound
to be unsatisfactory and unsuccessful even from the point of view of the
individuals who practice it" (1970, 110). Drawing a link to the black power
movement, he engages with arguments from black power leaders that social
mobility for some (that is, exit) is not liberatory because it does not allow for
the collective community to move up as well. To achieve collective empowerment, constituencies, especially those that are historically marginalized,
need to generate loyalty, which means they have to stay invested in the collective to exercise voice.

2   Ostrom and extensions of her work develop the idea of what has been called
a "poly-centric political system" in which multiple "centers of decision-
making which are formally independent of each other . . . take each other
into account in competitive relationships, enter into various contractual and
cooperative undertakings or have recourse to central mechanisms to resolve
conflicts" (Ostrom, Tiebout, and Warren 1961, 831). Poly-centricity focuses

on collaborative governance arrangements that identify ways to share power across multiple actors in a political system.

3   In fact, some research on social-movement industries suggests that competition for limited resources leads to highly specialized (and increasingly rote) organizational repertoires, which in turn decrease movement survival (Soule and King 2008).

4   In much of this work, the unit of analysis is the industry, and the goal of firms is to extract monopoly rents. Therefore, firms' competitive strategies are aimed at altering their strategic position vis-à-vis other players.

5   Scholars continue to debate exactly what processes and practices constitute a firm's dynamic capabilities. Teece (2007, 2012, 2014) offers a tripartite system of competencies. The first micro-foundation of dynamic capabilities is *sensing*, the ability to identify opportunities and threats. Entrepreneurial management with vision is a crucial ingredient for this competency. The second micro-foundation is *seizing*, which refers to the mobilization of resources to capture the (previously sensed) opportunity. To be effective at seizing, firms must have motivated employees, good incentive design, and relationships with external stakeholders. The third core competency is *transforming*, where the goal is continued renewal and flexibility. Other scholars have developed alternate understandings of dynamic capabilities.

References

Achen, Christopher H., and Larry Bartels. 2016. *Democracy for Realists: Why Elections Do Not Produce Responsive Government*. Princeton, NJ: Princeton University Press.

Ahlquist, John, and Margaret Levi. 2014. *In the Interest of Others: Organizations and Social Activism*. Princeton, NJ: Princeton University Press.

Alinsky, Saul. 1971. *Rules for Radicals: A Pragmatic Primer for Realistic Radicals*. New York: Vintage Books.

Ambrosini, Veronique, and Cliff Bowman. 2009. "What Are Dynamic Capabilities and Are They a Useful Construct in Strategic Management?" *International Journal of Management Reviews* 11, no. 1: 29–49.

Amenta, Edwin. 2006. *When Movements Matter*. Princeton, NJ: Princeton University Press.

Amenta, Edwin. 2014. "How to Analyze the Influence of Movements." *Contemporary Sociology* 43: 16–29.

Amenta, Edwin, and Neal Caren. 2004. "The Legislative, Organizational, and Beneficiary Consequences of State-Oriented Challengers." In *The Blackwell Companion to Social Movements*, edited by David Snow, Sarah Soule, and Hanspeter Kriesi, 461–88. Malden, MA: Blackwell.

Amenta, Edwin, Neal Caren, Elizabeth Chiarello, and Yang Su. 2010. "The Political Consequences of Social Movements." *Annual Review of Sociology* 36: 287–307.

Amenta, Edwin, Neal Caren, and Sheera Olasky. 2005. "Just the Facts: Newspaper Coverage of Social Movement Organizations in the 20th Century." *Contexts* 4: 48–49.

Anderson, Elizabeth. 2017. *Private Government: How Employers Rule Our Lives (and Why We Don't Talk About It)*. Princeton, NJ: Princeton University Press.

Andrews, Kenneth T. 2001. "Social Movements and Policy Implementation: The Mississippi Civil Rights Movement and the War on Poverty, 1965 to 1971." *American Sociological Review* 66: 71–95.

Andrews, Kenneth T. 2004. *Freedom Is a Constant Struggle: The Mississippi Civil Rights Movement and Its Legacy*. Chicago: University of Chicago Press.

Andrews, Kenneth T., Neal Caren, and Alyssa Browne. 2018. "Protesting Trump." *Mobilization: An International Quarterly* 23, no. 4: 393–400.

Andrews, Kenneth T., and Bob Edwards. 2004. "Advocacy Organizations in the U.S. Political Process." *Annual Review of Sociology* 30: 479–506.

Andrews, Kenneth T., Marshall Ganz, Matthew Baggetta, Hahrie Han, and Chaeyoon Lim. 2010. "Leadership, Membership, and Voice: Civic Associations That Work." *American Journal of Sociology* 115: 1191–242.

Anselm, Hager, Lukas Hensel, Johannes Hermle, and Christopher Roth. 2019. "Does Political Activism Increase Trust in Democracy?" Paper presented at the Annual Meeting of the Midwest Political Science Association, Chicago, IL.

Anzia, Sarah. 2019. "Looking for Influence in All the Wrong Places: How Studying Subnational Policy Can Revive Research on Interest Groups." *Journal of Politics* 81: 343–51.

Anzia, Sarah, and Terry Moe. 2016. "Do Politicians Use Policy to Make Politics? The Case of Public-Sector Labor Laws." *American Political Science Review* 110: 763–77.

Arceneaux, Kevin, and David Nickerson. 2009. "Who Is Mobilized to Vote? A Re-Analysis of 11 Field Experiments." *American Journal of Political Science* 53: 1–16.

Armony, Ariel. 2004. *The Dubious Link: Civic Engagement and Democratization*. Stanford, CA: Stanford University Press.

Ashby, Steven. 2017. "Assessing the Fight for Fifteen Movement from Chicago." *Labor Studies Journal* 42, no. 4: 366–86.

Baggetta, Matthew, Hahrie Han, and Kenneth Andrews. 2013. "Leading Associations: How Individual Characteristics and Team Dynamics Generate Committed Leaders." *American Sociological Review* 78: 544–73.

Barney, Jay B. 1991. "Firm Resources and Sustained Competitive Advantage." *Journal of Management* 17: 99–120.

Bartels, Larry. 2008. *Unequal Democracy: The Political Economy of the New Gilded Age*. Princeton, NJ: Princeton University Press and the Russell Sage Foundation.

Battistoni, Alyssa. 2019. "Spadework: On Political Organizing." *n+1* 34. https://nplusonemag.com/issue-34/politics/spadework/.

Baumgartner, Frank, Jeffrey M. Berry, Marie Hojnacki, David C. Kimball, and Beth L. Leech. 2009. *Lobbying and Policy Change: Who Wins, Who Loses, and Why*. Chicago: University of Chicago Press.

Baumgartner, Frank, and Beth Leech. 1998. *Basic Interests*. Princeton, NJ: Princeton University Press.

Baumgartner, Frank, and Christine Mahoney. 2005. "Social Movements, the Rise of New Issues, and the Public Agenda." In *Routing the Opposition: Social Movements, Public Policy, and Democracy*, edited by David S. Meyer, Valerie Jenness, and Helen Ingram, 65–86. Minneapolis: University of Minnesota Press.

Benford, Robert D., and David Snow. 2000. "Framing Processes and Social Movements: An Overview and Assessment." *Annual Review of Sociology* 26: 611–39.

Berman, Shari. 1997. "Civil Society and the Collapse of the Weimar Republic." *World Politics* 49, no. 3: 401–29.

Bimber, Bruce, Andrew Flanagin, and Cynthia Stohl. 2012. *Collective Action in Orga-*

nizations: *Interaction and Engagement in an Era of Technological Change*. New York: Cambridge University Press.

Birkland, Thomas A., and Regina A. Lawrence. 2009. "Media Framing and Policy Change after Columbine." *American Behavioral Scientist* 52: 1405–25.

Blee, Katherine. 2012. *Democracy in the Making: How Activists Form Groups*. New York: Oxford University Press.

Bobo, Kim, Jackie Kendall, and Steve Max. 2010. *Organizing for Social Change: Midwest Academy Manual for Activists*. Santa Ana, CA: Forum Press.

Boehm, Jessica. 2018. "Controversial Phoenix ID Cards for Immigrants Dies before It Ever Began." *AZ Central*, February 12, 2018. https://www.azcentral.com/story /news/local/phoenix/2018/02/12/controversial-phoenix-id-cards-immigrants -dies/308987002/.

Bonacich, Phillip. 2007. "Some Unique Properties of Eigenvector Centrality." *Social Networks* 29: 555–64.

Braunstein, Ruth. 2012. "Storytelling in Liberal Religious Advocacy." *Journal for the Scientific Study of Religion* 51: 110–27.

Braunstein, Ruth, Brad Fulton, and Richard Wood. 2014. "The Role of Bridging Cultural Practices in Racially and Socioeconomically Diverse Civic Organizations." *American Sociological Review* 79: 705–25.

Brennan Center. 2018. "Voting Rights Restoration Efforts in Virginia." Brennan Center for Justice at New York University School of Law. April 20, 2018. https:// www.brennancenter.org/our-work/research-reports/voting-rights-restoration -efforts-virginia.

Broockman, David, and Joshua Kalla. 2016. "Durably Reducing Transphobia: A Field Experiment on Door-to-Door Canvassing." *Science* 352: 220–24.

Buechler, Steven. 2000. *Social Movements in Advanced Capitalism: The Political Economy and Cultural Construction of Social Activism*. New York: Oxford University Press.

Burawoy, Michael. 2005. "2004 Presidential Address: For Public Sociology." *American Sociological Review* 70: 4–28.

Burstein, Paul. 2003. "The Impact of Public Opinion on Public Policy: A Review and an Agenda." *Political Research Quarterly* 56: 29–40.

Burstein, Paul, and William Freudenburg. 1978. "Changing Public Policy: The Impact of Public Opinion, Antiwar Demonstrations, and War Costs on Senate Voting on Vietnam War Motions." *American Journal of Sociology* 84: 99–122.

Burstein, Paul, and Sarah Sausner. 2005. "The Incidence and Impact of Policy-Oriented Collective Action: Competing Views." *Sociological Forum* 20: 403–19.

Carmines, Edward G., and James A. Stimson. 1981. "Issue Evolution, Population Replacement, and Normal Partisan Change." *American Political Science Review* 75: 107–18.

Chereb, Sandra, and Sean Whaley. 2015. "Nevada Legislature OKs Record Budget, Adjourns." *Las Vegas Review-Journal*, June 2, 2015. https://www.reviewjournal .com/news/politics-and-government/nevada/nevada-legislature-oks-record -budget-adjourns/.

Christens, Brian, and Paul Speer. 2015. "Community Organizing: Practice, Research, and Policy Implications." *Social Issues and Policy Review* 9: 193–222.

Chua, Amy. 2018. *Political Tribes: Group Instinct and the Fate of Nations*. New York: Penguin Press.

Cialdini, Robert B., and Noah J. Goldstein. 2004. "Social Influence: Compliance and Conformity." *Annual Review of Psychology* 55: 591–621.

Clemens, Elisabeth. 1993. "Organizational Repertoires and Institutional Change: Women's Groups and the Transformation of U.S. Politics, 1890–1920." *American Journal of Sociology* 98: 755–98.

Clemens, Elisabeth. 1997. *The People's Lobby: Organizational Innovation and the Rise of Interest Group Politics in the United States, 1890–1925*. Chicago: University of Chicago Press.

Clemens, Elisabeth, and Debra Minkoff. 2004. "Beyond the Iron Law: Rethinking the Place of Organizations in Social Movement Research." In *The Blackwell Companion to Social Movements*, edited by David Snow, Sarah Anne Soule, and Hanspeter Kriesi, 155–70. Malden, MA: Blackwell Publishing.

Cossyleon, Jennifer E. 2018. "'Coming Out of My Shell': Motherleaders Contesting Fear, Vulnerability, and Despair through Family-focused Community Organizing." *Socius* 4: 1–13.

Cress, Daniel M., and David A. Snow. 2000. "The Outcomes of Homeless Mobilization: The Influence of Organization, Disruption, Political Mediation, and Framing." *American Journal of Sociology* 105: 1063–104.

Cushman, Joy. 2011. "What We Can't Teach: Courage and Commitment in Campaigns." New Organizing Institute blog. February 24, 2011.

Dahl, Robert. 2005. *Who Governs? Democracy and Power in an American City*. New Haven, CT: Yale University Press. First published 1961.

Delehanty, Jack, and Michelle Oyakawa. 2018. "Building a Collective Moral Imaginary: Personalist Culture and Social Performance in Faith-Based Community Organizing." *American Journal of Cultural Sociology* 6, no. 2: 266–95.

DiMaggio, P. J., and W. W. Powell. 1983. "The Iron Cage Revisited: Institutional Isomorphism and Collective Rationality in Organizational Fields." *American Sociological Review* 48: 147–60.

Downs, Anthony. 1957. *An Economic Theory of Democracy*. New York: Harper and Row.

Drutman, Lee. 2015. *The Business of America Is Lobbying*. New York: Oxford University Press.

Earl, Jennifer, Andrew Martin, John McCarthy, and Sarah Soule. 2004. "The Use of Newspaper Data in the Study of Collective Action." *Annual Review of Sociology* 30: 65–80.

Eisenhardt, Kathleen, and Jeffrey Martin. 2000. "Dynamic Capabilities: What Are They?" *Strategic Management Journal* 21: 1105–21.

Eliasoph, Nina. 1998. *Avoiding Politics: How Americans Have Produced Apathy in Everyday Life*. Cambridge: Cambridge University Press.

Eliasoph, Nina. 2011. *Making Volunteers: Civic Life after Welfare's End*. Princeton, NJ: Princeton University Press.

Emirbayer, Mustafa, and Ann Mische. 1998. "What Is Agency?" *American Journal of Sociology* 103: 962–1023.

Enos, Ryan D. 2017. *The Space between Us: Social Geography and Politics*. New York: Cambridge University Press.

Enos, Ryan D., and Anthony Fowler. 2016. "Aggregate Effects of Large-Scale Campaigns on Voter Turnout." *Political Science Research and Methods* 6, no. 4: 733–51.

Ferree, Myra Marx. 2003. "Resonance and Radicalism: Feminist Framing of the Abortion Debates of the United States and Germany." *American Journal of Sociology* 109: 304–44.

Ferree, Myra Marx, William Gamson, Jürgen Gerhards, and Dieter Rucht. 2002. *Shaping Abortion Discourse: Democracy and the Public Sphere in Germany and the United States*. New York: Cambridge University Press.

Fiske, Warren. 2016. "McAuliffe Held Va. Record for Restoring Felon Voting Rights before His Blanket Action." Politifact Virginia. May 9, 2016. https://www .politifact.com/factchecks/2016/may/09/terry-mcauliffe/mcauliffe-held-va -record-retoring-felon-voting-rig/.

Fligstein, Neil, and Doug McAdam. 2012. *A Theory of Fields*. New York: Oxford University Press.

Flores, Edward Orozco, and Jennifer Cossyleon. 2016. "'I Went through It so You Don't Have To': Faith-Based Community Organizing for the Formerly Incarcerated." *Journal for the Scientific Study of Religion* 55, no. 4: 662–76.

Ford, Matt. 2016. "The Racist Roots of Virginia's Felon Disenfranchisement." *The Atlantic*. April 27, 2016. https://www.theatlantic.com/politics/archive/2016 /04/virginia-felon-disenfranchisement/480072/.

Fung, Archon. 2003. "Associations and Democracy: Between Theories, Hopes, and Realities." *Annual Review of Sociology* 29: 515–39.

Fung, Archon, and Jennifer Shkabatur. 2012. "Viral Engagement: Fast, Cheap, and Broad, but Good for Democracy?" In *From Voice to Influence: Understanding Citizenship in a Digital Age*, edited by Danielle Allen and Jennifer S. Light, 155–77. Chicago: University of Chicago Press.

Gamson, William. 1995. "Constructing Social Protest." In *Social Movements and Culture*, edited by Hank Johnston and Bert Klandermans, 85–106. Vol. 4 of *Social Movements, Protest, and Contention*, edited by Bert Klandermans and David S. Meyer. Minneapolis: University of Minnesota Press.

Ganz, Marshall. 2000. "Resources and Resourcefulness: Strategic Capacity in the Unionization of California Agriculture, 1959–1966." *American Journal of Sociology* 105: 1003–62.

Ganz, Marshall. 2009. *Why David Sometimes Wins: Leadership, Organization, and Strategy in the California Farm Worker Movement*. New York: Oxford University Press.

Ganz, Marshall. 2018a. "How to Organize to Win." *The Nation*, March 16, 2018. https://www.thenation.com/article/archive/how-to-organize-to-win/.

Ganz, Marshall. 2018b. "Organizing: People, Power, and Change." Course reader for

Spring 2018 Management, Leadership, and Decision Science 377 (MLD 377), 1–115. Cambridge, MA: Harvard Kennedy School.

Ganz, Marshall, Tamara Kay, and Jason Spicer. 2018. "Social Enterprise Is Not Social Change." *Stanford Social Innovation Review* (Spring 2018): 59–60. https://ssir.org/articles/entry/social_enterprise_is_not_social_change.

Garcia, Ellie. 2010. "Arizona Protests Hit Anti-Immigrant Law." *The Militant*, May 10, 2010.

García Bedolla, Lisa, and Melissa Michelson. 2012. *Mobilizing Inclusion: Transforming the Electorate through Get-out-the-Vote Campaigns*. New Haven, CT: Yale University Press.

Gaventa, John. 1982. *Power and Powerlessness: Quiescence & Rebellion in an Appalachian Valley*. Champaign: University of Illinois Press. First published 1980.

Gecan, Michael. 2002. *Going Public: An Organizer's Guide to Citizen Action*. Boston: Beacon Press.

Gerring, John. 2007. *Case Study Research: Principles and Practices*. New York: Cambridge University Press.

Gibson, Helen. 2015. "Felons and the Right to Vote in Virginia: A Historical Overview." *The Virginia News Letter* 91 (January 2015): 1–9. Weldon Cooper Center for Public Service. https://vig.coopercenter.org/sites/vig/files/VirginiaNewsLetter_2015_V91-N1.pdf.

Gilens, Martin. 2013. *Affluence and Influence: Economic Inequality and Political Power in America*. Princeton, NJ: Princeton University Press.

Gilens, Martin, and Benjamin Page. 2014. "Testing Theories of American Politics: Elites, Interest Groups, and Average Citizens." *Perspectives on Politics* 12: 564–81.

Gillion, Daniel Q. 2013. *The Political Power of Protest: Minority Activism and Shifts in Public Policy*. Cambridge: Cambridge University Press.

Giugni, Marco. 1998. "Was It Worth the Effort? The Outcomes and Consequences of Social Movements." *American Sociological Review* 24: 371–93.

Giugni, Marco, and Maria Grasso. 2019. "Mechanisms of Responsiveness: What MPs Think of Interest Organizations and How They Deal with Them." *Political Studies* 63, no. 3: 557–75.

Giugni, Marco, Doug McAdam, and Charles Tilly, eds. 1999. *How Social Movements Matter*. Vol. 10 of *Social Movements, Protest, and Contention*, edited by Bert Klandermans and David S. Meyer. Minneapolis: University of Minnesota Press.

Gottlieb, Julian. 2015. "Protest News Framing Cycle: How *The New York Times* Covered Occupy Wall Street." *International Journal of Communication* 9: 231–53.

Green, Donald, and Alan Gerber. 2015. *Get out the Vote: How to Increase Voter Turnout*. 3rd ed. Washington, DC: Brookings Institution Press.

Greenhouse, Steven, and Jana Kasperkevic. 2015. "Fight for $15 Swells into Largest Protest by Low-Wage Workers in US History." *The Guardian*, April 15, 2015.

Gupta, Arun. 2013. "Fight for 15 Confidential." *In These Times*, November 11, 2013. http://inthesetimes.com/article/15826/fight_for_15_confidential.

Hacker, Jacob S., and Paul Pierson. 2010. *Winner-Take-All Politics: How Washington Made the Rich Richer*. New York: Simon and Schuster.

Hacker, Jacob S., and Paul Pierson. 2020. *Let Them Eat Tweets: How the Right Rules in an Age of Extreme Inequality*. New York: Liveright.

Han, Hahrie. 2009. *Moved to Action: Motivation, Participation, and Inequality in American Politics*. Palo Alto, CA: Stanford University Press.

Han, Hahrie. 2014. *How Organizations Develop Activists: Civic Associations and Leadership in the 21st Century*. New York: Oxford University Press.

Han, Hahrie. 2016. "The Organizational Roots of Political Activism: Field Experiments on Creating a Relational Context." *American Political Science Review* 110: 296–307.

Han, Hahrie, Kenneth T. Andrews, Marshall Ganz, Chaeyoon Lim, and Matthew Baggetta. 2011. "The Relationship of Leadership Quality to the Political Presence of Civic Associations." *Perspectives on Politics* 9: 45–59.

Han, Hahrie, Andrea Campbell, and Elizabeth McKenna. 2019. "Civic Feedbacks: Organizing Strategy and Groups' Influence over Public Policy." Paper presented at the American Political Science Association Annual Meeting, Washington, DC, August 30, 2019.

Haney Lopez, Ian. 2013. *Dog Whistle Politics: How Coded Racial Appeals Have Reinvented Racism and Wrecked the Middle Class*. New York: Oxford University Press.

Hansen, John Mark. 1991. *Gaining Access: Congress and the Farm Lobby, 1919–1981*. Chicago: University of Chicago Press.

Heinemann, Ronald, John G. Kolp, Anthony Parent, and William Shade. 2007. *Old Dominion, New Commonwealth: A History of Virginia 1607–2007*. Charlottesville: University of Virginia Press.

Helfat, Constance E., and Margaret A. Peteraf. 2003. "The Dynamic Resource-Based View: Capability Lifecycles." *Strategic Management Journal* 24: 997–1010.

Hertel-Fernandez, Alexander, and Theda Skocpol. 2016. "How the Right Trounced Liberals in the States." *Democracy: A Journal of Ideas* 39 (Winter 2016). https://democracyjournal.org/magazine/39/how-the-right-trounced-liberals-in-the-states/.

Hestres, Luis E. 2015. "Climate Change Advocacy Online: Theories of Change, Target Audiences, and Online Strategy." *Environmental Politics* 24: 193–211.

Hicks, William D., Seth C. McKee, and Daniel A. Smith. 2016. "The Determinants of State Legislator Support for Restrictive Voter ID Laws." *State Politics & Policy Quarterly* 16: 411–31.

Hillygus, Sunshine. 2005. "Campaign Effects and the Dynamics of Turnout Intention in Election 2000." *Journal of Politics* 67: 50–68.

Hirschman, Albert. 1970. *Exit, Voice, and Loyalty: Responses to Decline in Firms, Organizations, and States*. Cambridge, MA: Harvard University Press.

Hojnacki, Marie, David C. Kimball, Frank Baumgartner, Jeffrey M. Berry, and Beth L. Leech. 2012. "Studying Organizational Advocacy and Influence: Reexamining Interest Group Research." *Annual Review of Political Science* 15: 379–99.

Isaac, Larry. 2008. "Movement of Movements: Culture Moves in the Long Civil Rights Struggle." *Social Forces* 87: 33–63.

Isquit, Elias. 2015. "Neoliberalism Poisons Everything: How Free Market Mania

Threatens Education—and Democracy." Salon, June 15, 2015. https://www.salon .com/2015/06/15/democracy_cannot_survive_why_the_neoliberal_revolution _has_freedom_on_the_ropes/.

Jasper, James. 1997. *The Art of Moral Protest: Culture, Biography, and Creativity in Social Movements*. Chicago: University of Chicago Press.

Jenkins, J. Craig. 1983. "Resource Mobilization Theory and the Study of Social Movements." *Annual Review of Sociology* 9: 527–53.

Jenkins, J. Craig, and Craig M. Eckert. 1986. "Channeling Black Insurgency: Elite Patronage and Professional Social Movement Organizations in the Development of the Black Movement." *American Sociological Review* 51: 812–29.

Jennings, M. Kent. 2004. "American Political Participation Viewed through the Lens of the Political Socialization Project." In *Advances in Political Psychology*, edited by Margaret G. Hermann, 1–18. Oxford: Elsevier.

Jennings, M. Kent, and Richard Niemi. 1981. *Generations and Politics*. Princeton, NJ: Princeton University Press.

Kalla, Joshua, and David Broockman. 2017. "The Minimal Persuasive Effects of Campaign Contact in General Elections: Evidence from 49 Field Experiments." *American Political Science Review* 112: 148–66.

Kallick, David Dyssegaard. 2014. "AZ Business Leaders: An Anti-Immigrant Reputation Hurts Our Economy." Huffington Post, April 16, 2014. https://www.huffpost .com/entry/az-business-leaders_b_5155368.

Key, Valdimer O. 1956. *Politics, Parties, and Pressure Groups*. 3rd ed. New York: Thomas Crowell.

King, Brayden G. 2017. "The Relevance of Organizational Sociology." *Contemporary Sociology: A Journal of Reviews* 46: 131–37.

King, Brayden G., Teppo Felin, and David A. Whetten. 2010. "Finding the Organization in Organizational Theory: A Meta-Theory of the Organization as a Social Actor." *Organization Science* 21: 290–305.

King, Brayden G., and Edward T. Walker. 2014. "Winning Hearts and Minds: Field Theory and the Three Dimensions of Strategy." *Strategic Organization* 12: 134–41.

Klandermans, Bert. 1997. *The Social Psychology of Protest*. Cambridge, MA: Blackwell.

Kriesi, Hanspeter. 1996. "The Organizational Structure of New Social Movements in a Political Context." In *Comparative Perspectives on Social Movements*, edited by John D. McCarthy, Doug McAdam, and Mayer J. Zald, 152–83. Cambridge: Cambridge University Press.

Lacey, Marc, and Katharine Seelye. 2011. "Recall Election Claims Arizona Anti-Immigration Champion." *New York Times*, November 10, 2011. https://www .nytimes.com/2011/11/10/us/politics/russell-pearce-arizonas-anti-immgration -champion-is-recalled.html.

LaCombe, Matthew. Forthcoming. "The Political Weaponization of Gun Owners: The NRA's Cultivation, Dissemination, and Use of a Group Social Identity." *Journal of Politics*.

Lee, Caroline. 2015. *Do-It-Yourself Democracy: The Rise of the Public Engagement Industry*. New York: Oxford University Press.

Lee, Frances. 2016. *Insecure Majorities: Congress and the Perpetual Campaign*. Chicago: University of Chicago Press.

Lee, Taeku. 2002. *Mobilizing Public Opinion: Black Insurgency and Racial Attitudes in the Civil Rights Era*. Chicago: University of Chicago Press.

Lee, Taeku. 2008. "Race, Immigration, and the Identity-to-Politics Link." *Annual Review of Political Science* 11: 457–78.

Leighley, Jan. 2001. *Strength in Numbers? The Political Mobilization of Racial and Ethnic Minorities*. Princeton, NJ: Princeton University Press.

Leih, Sohvi, and David Teece. 2016. "Campus Leadership and the Entrepreneurial University: A Dynamic Capabilities Perspective." *Academy of Management Perspectives* 30: 182–210.

Lemons, Stephen. 2011. "Activist Randy Parraz Led an Army of Non-Partisan Warriors to Take Down Russell Pearce." *Phoenix New Times*, November 17, 2011. https://www.phoenixnewtimes.com/news/activist-randy-parraz-led-an-army-of-non-partisan-warriors-to-take-down-russell-pearce-6451803.

Lessard, Donald, David J. Teece, and Sohvi Leih. 2016. "The Dynamic Capabilities of Meta-Multinationals." *Global Strategy Journal* 6: 211–24.

Levine, Adam. 2015. *American Insecurity: Why Our Economic Fears Lead to Political Inaction*. Princeton, NJ: Princeton University Press.

Lipset, Seymour M. 1956. *Union Democracy: The Internal Politics of the International Typographical Union*. Glencoe, IL: Free Press.

Luders, Joseph. 2010. *The Civil Rights Movement and the Logic of Social Change*. New York: Cambridge University Press.

Lukes, Steven. 2005. *Power: A Radical View*. New York: Palgrave Macmillan. First published 1974.

Mackin, Anna. 2016. "Executive Constraints and Repression in Democratic Contexts: The Case of Land Protests in Brazil." *Political Research Quarterly* 69: 175–88.

Madestam, Andreas, Daniel Shoag, Stan Veuger, and David Yanagizawa-Drott. 2013. "Do Political Protests Matter? Evidence from the Tea Party Movement." *Quarterly Journal of Economics* 128: 1633–85.

Madison, James. 1788. "The Structure of the Government Must Furnish the Proper Checks and Balances between the Different Departments." *Federalist*, no. 51. *New York Packet*, February 8, 1788.

Manville, Brooke, and Josiah Ober. 2003a. "Beyond Empowerment: Building a Company of Citizens." *Harvard Business Review*, January 2003. https://hbr.org/2003/01/beyond-empowerment-building-a-company-of-citizens.

Manville, Brooke, and Josiah Ober. 2003b. *A Company of Citizens: What the World's First Democracy Teaches Leaders about Creating Great Organizations*. Cambridge, MA: Harvard Business Review Press.

Margetts, Helen, Peter John, Scott Hale, and Taha Yasseri. 2015. *Political Turbulence: How Social Media Shape Collective Action*. Princeton, NJ: Princeton University Press.

Mason, Liliana. 2018. *Uncivil Agreement: How Politics Became Our Identity*. Chicago: University of Chicago Press.

McAdam, Doug. 1982. *Political Process and the Development of Black Insurgency: 1930–1970*. Chicago: University of Chicago Press.

McAdam, Doug, and Hilary Schaffer Boudet. 2012. *Putting Social Movements in Their Place: Explaining Opposition to Energy Projects in the United States, 2000–2005*. Stanford, CA: Stanford University Press.

McAdam, Doug, John McCarthy, Susan Olzak, and Sarah Soule. 2009. Dynamics of Collective Action Database. Stanford, CA: Stanford University. https://web .stanford.edu/group/collectiveaction/cgi-bin/drupal/.

McAdam, Doug, and Yang Su. 2002. "The War at Home: Anti-War Protests and Congressional Voting, 1965–73." *American Sociological Review* 67: 696–721.

McAdam, Doug, Sidney Tarrow, and Charles Tilly. 2001. *Dynamics of Contention*. New York: Cambridge University Press.

McAlevey, Jane. 2016. *No Shortcuts: Organizing for Power in the New Gilded Age*. New York: Oxford University Press.

McAuliffe, Terry. 2017. "Governor McAuliffe Restores More Voting Rights than Any Governor in American History." Vote Smart. April 27, 2017. https://votesmart .org/public-statement/1159695/governor-mcauliffe-restores-more-voting -rights-than-any-governor-in-american-history#.Xmv9tpNKhTY.

McCammon, Holly J. 2012. *The U.S. Women's Jury Movements and Strategic Adaptation: A More Just Verdict*. Cambridge: Cambridge University Press.

McCarthy, John D., and Mayer N. Zald. 1977. "Resource Mobilization and Social Movements: A Partial Theory." *American Journal of Sociology* 82: 1212–41.

McCarthy, John D., and Mayer N. Zald. 2001. "The Enduring Vitality of the Resource Mobilization Theory of Social Movements." In *Handbook of Sociological Theory*, edited by Jonathan H. Turner, 533–65. Handbooks of Sociology and Social Research. Boston, MA: Springer.

McGirr, Lisa. 2002. *Suburban Warriors: The Origins of the New American Right*. Princeton, NJ: Princeton University Press.

McKenna, Elizabeth. Forthcoming. "Taxes and Tithes: The Organizational Foundations of Bolsonarismo." *International Sociology* 1-21. DOI: 10.1177/0268580920949466.

McKenna, Elizabeth, and Hahrie Han. 2014. *Groundbreakers: How Obama's 2.2 Million Volunteers Transformed Campaigning in America*. New York: Oxford University Press.

McVeigh, Rory. 2009. *The Rise of the Ku Klux Klan: Right-Wing Movements and National Politics*. Minneapolis: University of Minnesota Press.

Meyer, David S. 2004. "Protest and Political Opportunities." *Annual Review of Sociology* 30: 125–45.

Meyer, David S., and Suzanne Staggenborg. 1996. "Movements, Countermovements, and the Structure of Political Opportunity." *American Journal of Sociology* 101: 1628–60.

Meyer, David S., and Sidney Tarrow, eds. 1998. *The Social Movement Society: Contentious Politics for a New Century*. Lanham, MD: Rowman & Littlefield Publishers, Inc.

Meyer, J. W., and B. Rowan. 1977. "Institutionalized Organizations: Formal-Structure as Myth and Ceremony." *American Journal of Sociology* 83: 340–63.

Mintzberg, Henry. 1987. "Crafting Strategy." *Harvard Business Review* 65: 66–76.

Morris, Aldon. 2003. "The Anatomy of a Limited Perspective." *Ethnicities* 3: 263–69.

Morris, Aldon D. 1986. *The Origins of the Civil Rights Movement.* New York: Simon and Schuster.

Morris, Aldon D. 2000. "Reflections on Social Movement Theory: Criticisms and Proposals." *Contemporary Sociology* 29: 445–54.

Morris, Aldon D., and Suzanne Staggenborg. 2004. "Leadership in Social Movements." In *The Blackwell Companion to Social Movements*, edited by David A. Snow, Sarah A. Soule, and Hanspeter Kriesi, 171–96. Malden, MA: Blackwell Publishing.

Munson, Ziad. 2009. *The Making of Pro-Life Activists: How Social Movement Mobilization Works.* Chicago: University of Chicago Press.

Mydans, Scott. 1995. "Taking No Prisoners, in Manner of Speaking." *New York Times*, March 4, 1995. https://www.nytimes.com/1995/03/04/us/taking-no-prisoners -in-manner-of-speaking.html.

Nepstad, Sharon. 2008. *Religion and War Resistance in the Plowshares Movement.* New York: Cambridge University Press.

Nepstad, Sharon, and Bob Clifford. 2006. "When Do Leaders Matter? Hypotheses on Leadership Dynamics in Social Movements." *Mobilization* 11: 1–22.

New York Times. 2017. "Here's the Democracy Alliance's 'Resistance Map.'" *New York Times*, October 7, 2017.

Nolan, Jim. 2016. "McAuliffe Says Felons Whose Rights Are Restored Will Get 'Thorough Review' by State Agencies." *Richmond Times-Dispatch*, August 22, 2016. https://www.richmond.com/news/mcauliffe-says-felons-whose-rights -are-restored-will-get-thorough/article_ba5642fa-b3b8-5849-9e00-1219191 e9b5a.html.

No One Phx ID. 2015. Facebook, April 22, 2015. https://www.latest.facebook.com /pg/No-One-Phx-ID-1632824720270378/about/.

Nyhan, Brendan, and Jacob Montgomery. 2015. "Connecting the Candidates: Consultant Networks and the Diffusion of Campaign Strategy in American Congressional Elections." *American Journal of Political Science* 59: 292–308.

Obama, Barack. 2018. "Author Dave Eggers in Conversation with President Barack Obama." Filmed November 2018 during the Obama Foundation summit in Chicago. YouTube video, 57:43. https://www.youtube.com/watch?v=N7ZHDoNhScY.

Ober, Josiah. 2017. *Demopolis: Democracy before Liberalism in Theory and Practice.* New York: Cambridge University Press.

Olson, Mancur. 1965. *The Logic of Collective Action.* Cambridge, MA: Harvard University Press.

Olzak, Susan, and Emily Ryo. 2007. "Organizational Diversity, Vitality, and Outcomes in the Civil Rights Movement." *Social Forces* 85: 1561–91.

Ostrom, Elinor. 1990. *Governing the Commons: The Evolution of Institutions for Collective Action.* New York: Cambridge University Press.

Ostrom, Elinor, Charles Tiebout, and Robert Warren. 1961. "The Organization of Government in Metropolitan Areas: A Theoretical Inquiry." *American Political Science Review* 55: 831–42.

Oyakawa, Michelle. 2015. "Turning Private Pain into Public Action': The Cultivation of Identity Narratives by a Faith-Based Organization." *Qualitative Sociology* 38: 395–415.

Oyakawa, Michelle. 2017. "Building a Movement in the Non-Profit Industrial Complex." PhD diss., Department of Sociology, Ohio State University.

Oyakawa, Michelle, Elizabeth McKenna, and Hahrie Han. 2020. "Habits of Courage: Reconceptualizing Risk in Social Movement Organizing." *Journal of Community Psychology*.

Padgett, John, and Christopher K. Ansell. 1993. "Robust Action and the Rise of the Medici, 1400–1434." *American Journal of Sociology* 98: 1259–319.

Phillips, Steve. 2016. *Brown Is the New White: How a Demographic Revolution Has Created a New American Majority*. New York: New Press.

Pierson, Paul. 2015. "Goodbye to Pluralism? Studying Power in Contemporary American Politics." Paper presented at the Wildavsky Forum for Public Policy, Goldman School of Public Policy, Berkeley, CA, April 2015.

Pierson, Paul, and Eric Schickler. 2020. "Madison's Constitution under Stress: A Developmental Analysis of Political Polarization." *Annual Review of Political Science* 23: 3.1–3.22.

Piven, Frances Fox. 2006. *Challenging Authority: How Ordinary People Change America*. Lanham, MD: Rowman & Littlefield Publishers.

Piven, Frances Fox, and Richard A. Cloward. 1977. *Poor People's Movements: Why They Succeed, How They Fail*. New York: Vintage.

Piven, Frances Fox, and Richard A. Cloward. 1995. "Collective Protest: A Critique of Resource-Mobilization Theory." In *Social Movements*, edited by S. M. Lyman, 137–67. London: Palgrave Macmillan.

Polletta, Francesca. 2002. *Freedom Is an Endless Meeting*. Chicago: University of Chicago Press.

Polletta, Francesca, and M. Kai Ho. 2006. "Frames and Their Consequences." In *The Oxford Handbook of Contextual Political Analysis*, edited by Robert Goodin and Charles Tilly, 187–209. New York: Oxford University Press.

Polletta, Francesca, and James Jasper. 2001. "Collective Identity and Social Movements." *Annual Review of Sociology* 27: 283–305.

Porter, Michael. 1996. "What Is Strategy?" *Harvard Business Review* 74, no. 6: 61–78.

Powell, Walter W., and Paul J. DiMaggio, eds. 1991. *The New Institutionalism in Organizational Analysis*. Chicago: University of Chicago Press.

Preston, Julia. 2010. "Immigration Advocates Rally for Change." *New York Times*, May 1, 2010.

Putnam, Robert. 1993. *Making Democracy Work: Civic Traditions in Modern Italy*. Princeton, NJ: Princeton University Press.

Putnam, Robert. 2001. *Bowling Alone: The Collapse and Revival of American Democracy*. New York: Simon and Schuster.

Rasmussen, Anne, and Stefanie Reher. 2019. "Civil Society Engagement and Policy Representation in Europe." *Comparative Political Studies* 52, no. 11: 1648–76.

Rasmussen, Anne, Stefanie Reher, and Dimiter Toshkov. 2019. "The Opinion-Policy Nexus in Europe and the Role of Political Institutions." *European Journal of Political Research* 58: 412–34.

Reich, Rob. 2018. *Just Giving: Why Philanthropy Is Failing Democracy and How It Can Do Better*. Princeton, NJ: Princeton University Press.

Riccardi, Nicholas. 2010. "Arizona Passes Strict Illegal Immigration Act." *Los Angeles Times*, April 13, 2010.

Riley, Dylan. 2010. *The Civic Foundations of Fascism in Europe: Italy, Spain, and Romania, 1870–1945*. Baltimore, MD: Johns Hopkins University Press.

Rogers, Todd, Craig Fox, and Alan Gerber. 2013. "Rethinking Why People Vote: Voting as Dynamic Social Expression." In *The Behavioral Foundations of Public Policy*, edited by Eldar Shafir, 91–107. Princeton, NJ: Princeton University Press.

Rolfe, Meredith. 2012. *Voter Turnout: A Social Theory of Political Participation*. Cambridge: Cambridge University Press.

Rosenstone, Steven J., and John Mark Hansen. 1993. *Mobilization, Participation, and Democracy in America*. New York: Macmillan Publishing Company.

Rothenberg, Lawrence S. 1992. *Linking Citizens to Government: Interest Group Politics at Common Cause*. New York: Cambridge University Press.

Santos, Fernanda. 2019. "Joe Arpaio's Surprising Legacy in Arizona." *Politico*, November 10, 2019. https://www.politico.com/magazine/story/2019/11/10/joe-arpaio-arizona-latino-activists-elected-office-229906.

Schattschneider, Elmer Eric. 1960. *The Semisovereign People: A Realist's View of Democracy in America*. New York: Rinehart & Winston.

Seawright, Jason, and John Gerring. 2008. "Case Selection Techniques in Case Study Research." *Political Research Quarterly* 61: 294–308.

Sheingate, Adam. 2016. *Building a Business of Politics: The Rise of Political Consulting and the Transformation of American Democracy*. New York: Oxford University Press.

Shor, Boris. 2018. "Aggregate State Legislator Shor-McCarty Ideology Data, May 2018 Update." V2. Harvard Dataverse. https://dataverse.harvard.edu/dataset.xhtml?persistentId=doi:10.7910/DVN/BSLEFD.

Shor, Boris, and Nolan McCarty. 2011. "The Ideological Mapping of American Legislatures." *American Political Science Review* 105: 530–51.

Sides, John, and Daniel Hopkins. 2015. *Political Polarization in American Politics*. New York: Bloomberg Press.

Sides, John, and Lynn Vavreck. 2013. *The Gamble: Choice and Chance in the 2012 Presidential Election*. Princeton, NJ: Princeton University Press.

Sinclair, Betsy. 2012. *The Social Citizen: Peer Networks and Political Behavior*. Chicago: University of Chicago Press.

Skocpol, Theda. 2003. *Diminished Democracy: From Membership to Management in American Civic Life*. Norman: University of Oklahoma Press.

Skocpol, Theda. 2013. *Naming the Problem: What It Will Take to Counter Extremism and*

Engage Americans in the Fight against Global Warming. Cambridge, MA: Harvard University.

Skocpol, Theda, and Morris Paul Fiorina. 1999. *Civic Engagement in American Democracy*. Washington, DC: Brookings Institution Press.

Skocpol, Theda, Marshall Ganz, and Ziad Munson. 2000. "A Nation of Organizers: The Institutional Origins of Civic Voluntarism in the United States." *American Political Science Review* 94: 527–46.

Skocpol, Theda, and Alexander Hertel-Fernandez. 2016. "The Koch Effect: The . Impact of a Cadre-Led Network on American Politics." Paper presented at the Inequality Mini-Conference, Southern Political Science Association, San Juan, PR, January 8, 2016.

Skocpol, Theda, and Vanessa Williamson. 2012. *The Tea Party and the Remaking of Republican Conservatism*. New York: Oxford University Press.

Skocpol, Theda, Vanessa Williamson, and Alexander Hertel-Fernandez. 2015. Research on the Shifting U.S. Political Terrain. Harvard University, Cambridge, MA. https://terrain.gov.harvard.edu/.

Smock, Kristina. 2004. *Democracy in Action: Community Organizing and Urban Change*. New York: Columbia University Press.

Snow, David A., Sarah A. Soule, and Hanspeter Kriesi. 2007. *The Blackwell Companion to Social Movements*. New York: Wiley-Blackwell.

Soule, Sarah. 2013. "Bringing Organizational Studies Back in to Social Movement Research." In *The Future of Social Movement Research: Dynamics, Mechanisms, and Processes*, edited by Jacquelien Van Stekelenburg, Conny Roggeband, and Bert Klandermans, 107–24. Minneapolis: University of Minnesota Press.

Soule, Sarah, and Brayden King. 2008. "Competition and Resource Partitioning in Three Social Movement Industries." *American Journal of Sociology* 113: 1568–610.

Speer, Paul, and Brian Christens. 2011. "Contextual Influences on Participation in Community Organizing." *American Journal of Community Psychology* 47: 253–63.

Staggenborg, Suzanne. 2016. *Social Movements*. New York: Oxford University Press.

Steigerwald, Laura. 2012. "Emails from ALEC Member Russell Pearce Show Anti-Immigrant Law May Have Been Racially Motivated." *PR Watch*, July 27, 2012. The Center for Media and Democracy. https://www.prwatch.org/news/2012 /07/11676/emails-alec-member-russell-pearce-show-anti-immigrant-law-may -have-been-racially-.

Stokes, Leah, and Christopher Warshaw. 2017. "Drivers of Public Support for Renewable Energy in the United States: Evidence from Surveys and an Experiment." *Nature Energy* 2, no. 8. https://dx.doi.org/10.1038/nenergy.2017.107.

Stone, Walter J., and Alan I. Abramovitz. 1983. "Winning May Not Be Everything, but It's More Than We Thought: Presidential Party Activists in 1980." *American Political Science Review* 77: 945–56.

Stone, Walter J., and Ronald B. Rapoport. 1994. "Candidate Perception among Nomination Activists: A New Look at the Moderation Hypothesis." *Journal of Politics* 56: 1034–52.

Strolovitch, Dara. 2007. *Affirmative Advocacy: Race, Class, and Gender in Interest Group Politics*. Chicago: University of Chicago Press.

Tarrow, Sidney. 1998. *Power in Movement: Social Movements, Collective Action and Mass Politics in the Modern State*. New York: Cambridge University Press.

Teece, David J. 2007. "Explicating Dynamic Capabilities: The Nature and Micro-foundations of (Sustainable) Enterprise Performance." *Strategic Management Journal* 28: 1319–50.

Teece, David J. 2012. "Dynamic Capabilities: Routines versus Entrepreneurial Action." *Journal of Management Studies* 49: 1395–401.

Teece, David J. 2014. "The Foundations of Enterprise Performance: Dynamic and Ordinary Capabilities in an (Economic) Theory of Firms." *Academy of Management Perspectives* 28: 328–52.

Teece, David J., Gary Pisano, and Amy Shuen. 1997. "Dynamic Capabilities and Strategic Management." *Strategic Management Journal* 18: 509–33.

Teles, Steven. 2010. *The Rise of the Conservative Legal Movement: The Battle for Control of the Law*. Princeton, NJ: Princeton University Press.

Teske, Nathan. 1997a. "Beyond Altruism: Identity-Construction as Moral Motive in Political Explanation." *Political Psychology* 18: 71–91.

Teske, Nathan. 1997b. *Political Activists in America: The Identity Construction Model of Political Participation*. New York: Cambridge University Press.

Tilly, Charles. 2000. "Processes and Mechanisms of Democratization." *Sociological Theory* 18: 1–16.

Tilly, Charles, and Sidney Tarrow. 2007. *Contentious Politics*. Boulder, CO: Paradigm Publishers.

Truman, David B. 1951. *The Governmental Process: Political Interests and Public Opinion*. New York: Alfred A. Knopf.

Tufekci, Zeynep. 2015. "Algorithmic Harms beyond Facebook and Google: Emergent Challenges of Computational Agency." *Journal on Telecommunications and High Tech* 13: 203–18.

Tufekci, Zeynep. 2017. *Twitter and Tear Gas: The Power and Fragility of Networked Protest*. New Haven, CT: Yale University Press.

Uba, Katrin. 2009. "The Contextual Dependence of Movement Outcomes: A Simplified Meta-Analysis." *Mobilization* 14: 433–48.

Uggen, Christopher, Ryan Larson, and Sarah Shannon. 2016. "6 Million Lost Voters: State-Level Estimates of Felony Disenfranchisement." The Sentencing Project. October 6, 2016. https://www.sentencingproject.org/publications/6-million-lost-voters-state-level-estimates-felony-disenfranchisement-2016/.

Vasi, Ion Bogdan, Edward T. Walker, John S. Johnson, and Hui Fen Tan. 2015. "'No Fracking Way!' Documentary Film, Discursive Opportunity, and Local Opposition against Hydraulic Fracturing in the United States." *American Sociological Review* 80: 934–59.

Verba, Sidney, Kay Lehman Schlozman, and Henry Brady. 1995. *Voice and Equality: Civic Voluntarism in American Politics*. Cambridge, MA: Harvard University Press.

Voss, Kim. 1998. "Claim Making and the Framing of Defeats: The Interpretation of Losses by American and British Labor Activists, 1886–1895." In *Challenging Authority: The Historical Study of Contentious Politics*, edited by Michael Hanagan, Leslie Page Moch, and Wayne Brake, 136–48. Minneapolis: University of Minnesota Press.

Walder, Andrew. 2009. "Political Sociology and Social Movements." *Annual Review of Sociology* 35: 393–412.

Walker, Edward. 2014. *Grassroots for Hire: Public Affairs Consultants in American Democracy*. New York: Cambridge University Press.

Walker, Edward, Andrew Martin, and John McCarthy. 2008. "Confronting the State, the Corporation, and the Academy: The Influence of Institutional Targets on Social Movement Repertoires." *American Journal of Sociology* 114: 35–76.

Walker, Jack L., Jr. 1991. *Mobilizing Interest Groups in America: Patrons, Professions, and Social Movements*. Ann Arbor: University of Michigan Press.

Wang, Dan, and Sarah Anne Soule. 2012. "Social Movement Organizational Collaboration: Networks of Learning and the Diffusion of Protest Tactics, 1960–1995." *American Journal of Sociology* 17: 1674–722.

Warren, Mark. 2001. *Dry Bones Rattling: Community Building to Revitalize American Democracy*. Princeton Studies in American Politics. Princeton, NJ: Princeton University Press.

Warren, Mark R., and Karen L. Mapp. 2011. *A Match on Dry Grass: Community Organizing as a Catalyst for School Reform*. New York: Oxford University Press.

Weick, Karl E. 1969. *The Social Psychology of Organizing*. Reading, MA: Addison-Wesley.

Weick, Karl E. 1993. "Sensemaking in Organizations: Small Structures with Large Consequences." In *Social Psychology in Organizations*, edited by J. K. Murnighan, 10–37. Englewood Cliffs, NJ: Prentice Hall.

Weick, Karl E. 2015. "Ambiguity as Grasp: The Reworking of Sense." *Journal of Contingencies & Crisis Management* 23: 117–23.

Wilson, James Q. 1973. *Political Organizations*. New York: Basic Books.

Winter, Sidney G. 2003. "Understanding Dynamic Capabilities." *Strategic Management Journal* 24: 991–95.

Wolfinger, Raymond E., and Steven J. Rosenstone. 1980. *Who Votes?* New Haven, CT: Yale University Press.

Wood, Richard. 2002. *Faith in Action: Religion, Race, and Democratic Organizing in America*. Chicago: University of Chicago Press.

Wood, Richard, and Brad Fulton. 2015. *A Shared Future: Faith-Based Organizing for Racial Equity and Ethical Democracy*. Chicago: University of Chicago Press.

Woolcock, Michael. 1998. "Social Capital and Economic Development: Toward a Theoretical Synthesis and Policy Framework." *Theory and Society* 27: 151–208.

Zahra, Shaker, Harry Sapienza, and Per Davidsson. 2006. "Entrepreneurship and Dynamic Capabilities: A Review, Model and Research Agenda." *Journal of Management Studies* 43: 917–55.

Zullow, Robert, and Graham Moomaw. 2016. "Voting Activists Were Prepped for Felons Order That Surprised Election Officials." *Richmond Times-Dispatch*, June 25, 2016.

Index

The letter *f* following a page number denotes a figure, and the letter *t* a table.